Black Inventors in the Age of Segregation

Johns Hopkins Studies in the History of Technology
Merritt Roe Smith, *Series Editor*

Black Inventors in the Age of Segregation

Granville T. Woods, Lewis H. Latimer & Shelby J. Davidson

Rayvon Fouché

The Johns Hopkins University Press
Baltimore & London

Printed in the United States of America on acid-free paper
9 8 7 6 5 4 3 2

The Johns Hopkins University Press
2715 North Charles Street
Baltimore, Maryland 21218-4363
www.press.jhu.edu

Library of Congress Cataloging-in-Publication Data

Fouché, Rayvon, 1969–
Black inventors in the age of segregation : Granville T. Woods, Lewis H. Latimer, and Shelby J. Davidson / Rayvon Fouché.
p. cm. — (Johns Hopkins studies in the history of technology)
ISBN 0-8018-7319-3 (hardcover : alk. paper)
1. Woods, Granville, 1856–1910. 2. Latimer, Lewis Howard, 1848–1928. 3. Davidson, Shelby J. (Shelby Jeames), b. 1868. 4. African American inventors—Biography. 5. Inventions—United States—History—19th century. 6. Inventions—United States—History—20th century. I. Title. II. Series.
T39 .F68 2003
609.2′273—dc21

2002015860

A catalog record for this book is available from the British Library.

For Sharra and Eads

Contents

Figures

Acknowledgments

This book began as a basic question about how African American inventors of the late nineteenth and early twentieth centuries negotiated the difficult American racial terrain. Through the guidance of Ron Kline, Robert Harris, and Pearce Williams, an answer to part of this simple question became a dissertation. I have learned much from their examples. Pearce Williams taught me how to be a passionate researcher and separate the wheat from the chaff. Robert Harris directed me to a more nuanced understanding of African-American history. I owe much gratitude to Ron Kline, whom I can only hope to emulate as a mentor and scholar. This project would not have reached completion without his support and productive criticism.

I wish to thank the friends, colleagues, and teachers who through their comments, words, and ideas have provided support and inspiration throughout the completion of this project: Howard Brick, Susan Curtis, Larry Davis, Garrett Duncan, Gerald Early, Ron Eglash, Robert Friedel, Leonard Harris, David Hess, Paul Israel, Carolyn Johnson, Bill McIver, Art Molella, Tim Parsons, Tracy Sharpley-Whiting, Siobhan Somerville, Charis Thompson, Vernon Williams, and Langdon Winner.

I am grateful to the following institutions for their financial support: Cornell University, the Lemelson Center for the Study of Invention and Innovation, Washington University in St. Louis, Purdue University, and Rensselaer Polytechnic Institute.

I want to thank those at the Johns Hopkins University Press who guided the manuscript to print. I especially would like to thank my editor Bob Brugger for his belief in the project, and Melody Herr for helping me manage the last details.

I also thank my family for their endless support: Marilynn Fouché,

DeVonne Fouché, Chris Watkins, Sierra Watkins, Francesca Watkins, Lois Vostral, and Henry Vostral.

Finally, I thank Sharra Vostral for her friendship, understanding, and unwavering optimism, but most of all I thank her for being in the right place at the right time to reveal the beauty of three.

Black Inventors in the Age of Segregation

Introduction

In the current historical moment, information—no matter how trivial or how important—circulates more rapidly than ever. American society is bombarded with an ever increasing volume of digitized information that has become exponentially harder to process. For me, this torrent of informational bits and bytes is seen most clearly in my overflowing e-mail in-box. Usually a rivulet of information flows in my direction, but at certain times of the year, like Black History Month, the steady current turns into a deluge. A portion of these transmissions are lists: lists containing the overlooked contributions that Americans of African heritage have made to every facet of American society and culture. Internet-based forms of communication enable these lists to be distributed quickly and easily and redeployed to do their most basic work of informing people about the unknown achievements of African Americans. Of course there are many types of lists, but some of the most popular are those referring to late nineteenth- and early twentieth-century inventions by African Americans, proudly pronouncing that African Americans have invented everything from the lightbulb to the ice-cream scoop.

Black inventor lists, at a most basic level, function as a means to reform the versions of American history as well as American technological history that have written black people out of the narratives. Yet, the lists do not always support such noble causes. They also represent and promote the widespread historical reduction of black inventors. For the most part, all that we know and think we need to know about black inventors can be summarized in names, inventions, and patent numbers. These three pieces of information dominate the historical understanding about black inventors' lived experiences. We know very little, or nothing at all, about what it means to be a black inventor historically and contemporarily. The historical reduction of their lives is the major problem in the already problematic consumption and appropriation of black inventors. This historical reduction conceals the complex and contradictory human identities of black inventors as well as the difficulties they endured to gain the patent protection that would, in the best situations, enable them to profit from their work. This historical reduction robs black inventors of their humanity—their frailties and strengths—and produces disembodied icons celebrated merely for their patented material production. By reinscribing a narrow understanding about black inventors into our collective knowledge of African American people, this reduction mutes, and at worst silences, deeper discussions about the historical and contemporary meanings of black inventors within American society and culture.

In American society, a society obsessed with every minute detail of its historical past, it is strange and unfortunate that popular and scholarly American history disregards the ways black people produce, shape, and affect technological change. Historians have ignored technology as an institutionalized force that marginalizes black people within American society and culture. Many scholars have overlooked technology because of the perception that it is just "stuff" and therefore value-neutral, nongendered, and nonracist. This perception allows the unproblematic acceptance of technology as a simple black box, which, in turn, supports the assumption that technology can be fully understood by its most simple material form and function.[1] The belief in the uncomplicated meanings of technology promotes the misperception that technologies have one real meaning. Yet, this is far from true. In American society, the automobile's dominant meaning is most closely understood as a device that transports people from one location to another. But automobiles have many more complicated meanings within our culture, from a status symbol to a weapon that can kill. When human actors interact with technology, they reinforce, redefine, or subvert the technology's dominant meaning or function. Since technologies traditionally do not design and build themselves, they usually do not exhibit biases on their own. Thus, in a built technological world, human agents must not ignore their place in the construction of the forms and the production of the meanings of technology.[2] Technology in American society is one of the most efficient systems for transmitting a set of ideological beliefs. We must come to realize that all technologies are information technologies that transmit ideologies, beliefs, sentiments, and desires. Herein resides the power that is played out through the invention, design, construction, implementation, and use of technology. Those doing the programming—the meaning building, fixing, and stabilizing—are the ones imposing their values, beliefs, and sensibilities on the world through technology. Not surprisingly, this control is localized within certain capitalist institutional structures that do not strongly support racial, gender, and economic equality.[3]

Often technologies have such cultural currency that even those people suppressed by the ideological agendas embedded within technologies unproblematically accept these objects into their everyday lives. For instance, African Americans have consumed and watched televisions for decades, even when a great deal of the existing programming negatively represented black people.[4] Technologies are, of course, far from value-neutral objects. This lack of neutrality produces a situation in which choices involving technological use and implementation, as well as the technologies themselves, regularly elevate a version of human experience by devaluing others.[5] Unfortunately for African Americans, their experiences tend to be those that are undervalued technologically. By probing the connections between African Americans and technology, we can understand a great deal about the ways in which African Americans have negotiated an adversarial American society that has been strongly influenced by ideological agendas mediated through technology. By looking more closely at the relationships between communities of black people and technology, we can observe how technology can subjugate African Americans. But at the same time, we can identify how African Americans consume and use technology and produce meanings for technological artifacts, practices, and knowledge that regularly subvert the constructed meanings of these technological products.[6] It is in this counterhegemonic way that the relationships between African Americans and technology are sites where African Americans have gathered resources during their struggle for racial equality in past centuries.

Black inventors play many roles in the American race game. The main role for black inventors in black communities is that of race champion or hero. Heroes, of course, are very important for an oppressed people. In time of distress, communities often rely on and construct heroes that meet their needs. They create positive images around which communities can unite. Moreover, these heroes represent fairly well the needs, hopes, and desires of a people at a specific moment.[7] In the early twentieth century black people needed heroes with myth-making qualities, like being equal to or beating the "white man." Black inventors, as early twentieth-century techno-heroes, filled this need by merely existing. If black people could invent—an ability believed to be God-given at the turn-of-the-century—and receive patents, the arguments about black intellectual inferiority certainly could be called into question. Thus, African American people had heroes that were not only celebrated as great African Americans, but heroes that were useful in the struggle for racial equality. In a sense, black inventors became political objects to battle against American racial discrimination.

By the late twentieth century, the situation for black people within American society had changed, and black communities desired mythical figures with hero-making qualities, namely, possessing the ability to succeed in a racist, segregatory society. Black inventors also fulfilled this need. As many Americans living in the late twentieth century began to perceive the United States as less racist—promoted by the overrepresentation of integration within mass media—black Americans still considered themselves to be inhabiting a racially hostile society.[8] As racism became less overt, black inventors became long-suffering historical celebrities to remind black people that they shall overcome someday. This evolution in the representation of black inventors has produced conveniently packaged mythical heroes for public consumption during moments such as Black History Month. As a result, the realities of their lives—their achievements, accomplishments, and failures—are twisted and stretched to no longer correlate to their actual existences. What is most interesting about the representational transformation of black inventors is that at this current historical moment, their mythic qualities have the most cultural value. Black inventors have been shoe-horned into the molds of the heroes and mythical figures to address racial issues of the twentieth century and have transcended the reality of their daily lives.

The time has come to bring some of the reality back into the lives of black inventors and to revitalize them for this century. New visions for black inventors should not valorize or condemn them, but explore how they exist within black cultural experiences and understand the multiple social and cultural meanings and uses of black inventors. A deeper and more thoughtful examination of black inventors and their lives engages the more substantive issues of race, technology, and American identity that historically have been ignored. To achieve this, it is necessary to question the veracity of the claims about black inventors and to investigate what these claims conceal, maintain, and advocate. We need to ask: why are flawless representations of black inventors regularly reproduced, and what specific cultural and social purposes do they serve? Are these representations the cumulative result of both historical and contemporary appropriations of black inventors by various communities to support multiple ideological agendas? Can histories inform, enlighten, and reform American society's understanding of black inventors? Asking questions that move beyond two-dimensional representations of black inventors destabilizes the black inventor myth and disrupts the often overly heroic representations of black inventors that is currently exhibited within American society and culture. Reassessing black inventors will not deconstruct, minimize, or devalue their lives or their inventions. A reexamination will, however, strip away some of the myths and mythology and recover the human existences of complex individuals who succeeded in environments where racial prejudice prevailed. A new type of black inventive hero—a hero with human qualities—is needed.

This new black inventive "hero" can accept the multiple meanings of black inventors before and after the turn of the twentieth century. Tracing the historical roots of the inventor mythology and its relation to African American inventors is a crucial starting point. Moreover, exploring how the ideology of the American dream and the cultural appropriation of black inventors problematically informs our contemporary understanding of black inventors sheds new light on black inventors. In assessing black inventors from this new vantage point, I will examine three different black inventor experiences: Granville T. Woods, an independent inventor, Lewis H. Latimer, a corporate consultant, and Shelby J. Davidson, a federal employee. Their lives do not exhaustively represent the relationships among African Americans, technology, race, identity, and invention, but they do uncover the deep contours of an individual black inventor's life in a racially stratified world. The lives of these three men demonstrate how African Americans shaped, subverted, and challenged, as well as conformed to and accommodated, a variety of American cultural communities through technological work. The story about each man's inventive life illustrates how invention could be used to reap financial rewards, to enter adversarial technical environments, and to maintain status within a racially constrictive institutional setting. But more important, each man's life exemplifies the irony of the black inventor myth. The irony is that none of these men can live up to the expectations of that myth. The black inventor myth contains many of the same elements traditionally associated with great white inventors, but it has confined black inventors in a distinctly different manner. To further understand the black inventor myth it is important to examine its four main tenets.

The first tenet is that patents equal financial success. The popular understanding is that if an inventor receives a patent he or she is automatically guaranteed wealth, but this is far from the truth. A patent is finite legal monopoly granted by a government. In order to benefit from this exclusive right to ownership, the patentee needs to have access to the resources that can produce and distribute the intellectual property protected by the patent. In most cases, African American inventors did not possess these resources and often sold their patents to whoever would purchase them. More often than not, little or no money was made by African American inventors from their patents. For Granville Woods, one of the only black men during this period that supported himself primarily by his inventive production, substantial financial success eluded his grasp. Moreover, Woods—known by some as the "black Edison" and described as the greatest inventor in the history of his race—did not consider himself to be an American Negro. As a man born in Australia, he did not carry the legacy of American slavery nor did he possess the same trepidation of whites as a Negro born in the United States. Woods, a true inventive opportunist, used anything and everything available to promote his inventive ideas. His lack of white racial fear contributed to his limited patenting success, but his dark-brown skin did not allow him to escape the racial persecution most black Americans experienced after Emancipation. Unable to avoid being treated as a Negro, Woods often had to work with individuals who did not have his best interest in mind. His physical appearance was the major factor that prevented him from experiencing the monetary rewards of white inventors of his caliber.

The second tenet is that black inventors invented purely to uplift the race. The assumption is that black inventors, in their desire to contribute to the race, intended for their patents to be seen as material artifacts of the race's progress. But some black inventors had no interest in the racial issues of the day and did not have much, if any, contact with the larger African American community. For Lewis Latimer—one of the best-known black inventors—inventing was not a vocation; it was a tool to acquire the proper credentials to assimilate into white American society. As he became more respected within the corporate electrical community, he abandoned inventing and became a legal expert for the Edison Companies and later General Electric. His career successfully showed that a black man had the intellectual capacity to become a respected member of civilization. His assimilation also paid social dividends in the elitist black community of New York City. Latimer did not grapple with a type of Du Boisian double-consciousness; there was only one consciousness—white civilization.

The third tenet is that an object or process patented by a black inventor is the first of its kind. The underlying assumption is that if a black person had not invented this object, device, or process our society would be perpetually without it. Shelby Davidson invented adding machine devices, but adding machines existed before and after he received his patents. If Davidson had not patented these devices, computation still would have taken place. Davidson, however, did attempt to invent himself into a position where his technical knowledge would become essential to the operation of the Post Office Division of the Treasury Department. As his value rose within the Treasury Department, so did his social standing within the African American community. He became a member of the most elite black clubs and associations in Washington, D.C. His inventive success had a reciprocal effect on his professional and social standing. But his inventing and technical knowledge did not save him from the growing institutionalized racism within his government agency.

These first three tenets heavily contribute to the limited understanding of black inventors. The final tenet is racial oppression. Black inventors experienced and reacted to the realities of their racial identification differently. All three had to overcome American society's virulent racism to receive a patent, but it is naïve to assume that racism affected their lives in the same way. Nevertheless, the effects of racism defined the roles that invention played in black inventors' lives. The experiences of Woods, Latimer, and Davidson present three different perspectives of how black inventors lived with American racial discrimination in the late nineteenth and early twentieth centuries.

In its current form, the black inventor myth is very difficult to disrupt because of its ideological power and content. To further unravel the black inventor myth and reconceptualize our understandings of black inventors, this book illustrates the ways in which the inventor mythology, the American dream, upper-class black uplift ideology, and technology all met in intriguing ways in the lives of black inventors during the late nineteenth and early twentieth centuries. By examining these issues together, we can reclaim the three-dimensionality of black inventors' lives obliterated by their reduction to celebrated patents or shrouded by their elevation to heroic icons. In working against the essentialism that confines African American inventors, we must no longer see African American inventors as simple race champions in a long-suffering way, but as contradictory men of their times. In part, I want to reconstruct the activities of black inventors during the late nineteenth and early twentieth centuries that have been glossed over and oversimplified and restore some of their humanity as they negotiated racially valenced technological, cultural, and social worlds. I want to pull back a bit from their inventions and describe the symbiotic relationships between their inventions, the process of inventing, and their everyday existences as black men in America.

Black inventors need to be examined on their own terms and within their own technical environments. We must understand black inventors as they are, rather than as we would want them to be. By terminating our dependence on the overinflated and heroic contemporary understandings of black inventors and refocusing our analyses on their everyday experiences, we will allow black inventors' lives to speak. By embracing their lived experiences, we can more clearly discern what black inventors considered themselves to be doing and comprehend the multiple ways in which inventing also influenced their everyday lives. As we dig deeper into their inventive lives, revealing the difficulties associated with their technological accomplishments as well as their human failings, the work of black inventors becomes all the more impressive. Black inventors do not have to be flawless race champions for us to appreciate, sympathize with, and accept them. We must rescue the complexity—the greatness and imperfection—of black inventors to understand more fully their relevance in America today. As we begin the twenty-first century, a century in which technology will dominate as never before, it is time to look back to past centuries' technological evolution and reassess the lived experiences of African Americans who participated in the evolution of technology in twentieth-century America.

Chapter One

Inventing the Myth of Racial Equality

It is quite within the mark to say that no class of men of modern times has made so distinct a contribution to what is popularly called "modern civilization" as have the inventors of the world, and it is equally within bounds to say that the American inventor has led all the rest in practical utility as well as scientific perfection of his inventive skills.

—Henry E. Baker (the first African American patent examiner), 1902

The dawn of the twentieth century began one of the most unprecedented periods of technological development in world history. In large part, the creative, inventive, and technical work that laid the foundation for this technological era took place in the late nineteenth century. Noted historian of technology Thomas P. Hughes indicates that the United States began to develop into a modern technological nation at the end of the nineteenth century.[1] This shift from what Lewis Mumford terms a paleotechnic to a neotechnic era drastically influenced the shape of American society and culture.[2] The creation of a neotechnic or modern technological nation was not only about the creation of technological infrastructure, but also about the rise of the inventor as a cultural hero, icon, and, ultimately, myth.[3] By the early part of the twentieth century, the triumphs of inventors and entrepreneurs like Thomas Edison and Henry Ford seemed to herald the imminent submission of the natural and manufactured worlds to those men possessing the desire and intellect to harness the power of science and technology. Their heroic celebrity took on mythic proportions.[4] This mythology supported the understanding that through an inventor's command and control of the scientific and technological, he (the myth is strongly masculine) could design, construct, and, most important, invent modern America, and consequently the modern world. To most Americans, inventors were natural heroes.

The creation of heroes has been tremendously important for American society. By helping define what it means to be an American and creating a positive and progressive metanarrative about our collective historical past, heroes fulfill many needs within American society and culture. The iconic great inventor is one of many cultural images that enable Americans to communicate about a common American origin, identity, and purpose. Historical icons, from George Washington to Helen Keller to John F. Kennedy, and all that our society has built around these figures stabilize our understandings of our cultural surroundings and a collective past. The mythology of such historical icons can represent the best of what we want our culture to be. As a result, these myths are tremendously ideologically loaded. Inventors of the late nineteenth and early twentieth centuries exemplified an ideological Americanness. Wyn Wachhorst indicates that inventors represented "the gospel of technological progress, the rural Protestant virtues (hard work, initiative, perseverance, prudence, honesty, frugality, etc.), the success mythology of the self-made man, individualism, optimism, practicality, anti-intellectualism, the American Adam and the New World Eden (America as a new beginning for mankind), the sense of world mission, democracy, egalitarianism, the idealization of youth, and others."[5] The ability of inventors to embody so many idealized qualities made them powerful and authoritative ambassadors of American success.

Some of the most important aspects of the mythology are its Horatio Alger qualities. Inventors, men of difficult if not disadvantaged situations, were able to learn from their mistakes and carry on to eventual success by clearly displaying Yankee ingenuity and spirit.[6] Moreover, the inventor myth implied that all inventors possessed the God-given gift of inventive ability. It was this innate intellectual acumen that enabled inventors to bring forth the technological ideas that would propel the United States to world leadership. The myth controls what we know about these inventors. We know infinitely more about their inventions than their lives. We know more about their final triumphs than about what enabled them to reach that point. It is the techno-heroic image that the inventor myth produces that intimately links together some of American society's most valorized nonstatesmen, such as Alexander Graham Bell, Thomas

Edison, Henry Ford, Samuel Morse, Elmer Sperry, Charles Steinmetz, and the Wright brothers.

But where are black inventors located within this myth? It is very hard to find black people that the myth would elevate to a techno-icon at the beginning of the twentieth century. A significant reason for the absence of black inventors is the historical reality of the American society that constructed the myth—in specific, the deeply held belief in the wholesale inferiority of African Americans. It is this perception that has helped keep the inventor myth very white.

The constructed belief of black inferiority can be traced to the founding of this nation and is clearly represented by the racist tradition of chattel slavery. Yet after Emancipation, black people proved that they were capable of being productive members of American society.[7] Nevertheless, at the beginning of Reconstruction, most white citizens believed that black freedmen were incapable of handling their newly granted liberty. Many white Southerners thought black people would not know how to care for themselves without the structured environment of the plantation. Northern abolitionists did not base their emancipatory efforts upon the belief that the black population possessed similar intellectual capabilities, but on a religious ideology that supported the equal treatment of all human beings. The perceived failure of Reconstruction, the racial apartheid of Jim Crow, the racism masked by religious authorities, and the racialized scientific truths of eugenics and social Darwinism further reinforced the misperception of black inferiority into the twentieth century.[8] At Harvard in 1929, Theodore Lothrop Stoddard spoke for a large portion of white America when he debated the eminent black scholar W. E. B. Du Bois on the question "Should the Negro Be Encouraged to Cultural Equality?" Stoddard argued that "as never before, we possess a clear appreciation of racial realities . . . We know that *our* America is a *White* America . . . And the overwhelming weight of both historical and scientific evidence show that only so long as the American people remain white will its institutions, ideals and culture continue to fit the temperament of its inhabitants—and hence continue to endure."[9] For Stoddard and many others, America was a white America and should remain that way.

The racial discrimination inflicted upon African Americans directly affected black inventors. Prior to Emancipation, the United States Patent Office would only grant white men patents.[10] In 1858, when plantation owner Oscar J. E. Stuart attempted to patent the double cotton scraper that his slave Ned invented, Attorney General Jeremiah S. Black firmly determined that "a machine invented by a slave, though it be new and useful, cannot, in the present state of the law, be patented. I may add that if such a patent was issued to the master, it would not protect him in the courts against persons who might infringe it."[11] The Patent Office made it abundantly clear that an invention by a slave was not worthy of patent protection. The implication was that slaves were not human beings and definitely not citizens. With this reasoning, it was inconceivable for the Patent Office to grant a Negro a patent. Even when American society began to accept the fact that African Americans did invent, black inventors were framed in a negative context. Some even went to the extent of denying that black people possessed American ingenuity. A white attorney expressed this perception by making the following comment in a patent rights battle involving a black inventor: "It is a well-known fact that the horse hay rake was first invented by a *lazy negro* [*sic*] who had a big hay field to rake and didn't want to do it by hand" (emphasis added).[12] The stereotype of black inferiority promoted the belief that African American people invented to sustain poor work habits rather than to create efficient solutions to existing problems. Black inventors had to overcome the racist perception of black inferiority before their inventive talents might be recognized, let alone be appropriated into the inventor myth.

This larger belief in black inferiority was one of a number of obstacles to invention for African Americans. Black people who wanted to invent had to deal not only with the racial boundaries built into the fabric of America society, but also with the existing obstacles within inventing and engineering cultures. Since invention is not and was not a solitary project as the myth would have one believe, this racism had a significant impact on black people's inventing opportunities. Unfortunately for aspiring black inventors of the late nineteenth and early twentieth centuries, two main cultural communities—the "shop" culture and the "school" culture—existed from which an inventor-to-be could acquire the requisite technical skills and knowledge.[13] Machine shops and other similar trade-based organizations, normally run by men informally trained in science or engineering, were useful places for aspiring inventors to acquire technical training. The shop culture of independent inventors and inventor-entrepreneurs was a difficult environment for black people to enter. The necessary apprenticeships, like apprenticeships in other fields, were primarily reserved for white men. This closed-door policy for African Americans was not for a lack of training. Quickly following Emancipation, black people, in many cases, received better basic educational training than their white counterparts.[14] The new educational opportunities available after Emancipation would have generated more technical creativity by black Americans if the racial climate had permitted, but the machine shop subculture did not readily accept African Americans.

Similarly, the school culture of research scientists and engineers did not admit many people who were nonwhite or nonmale until after the Second World War. At the close of the nineteenth century, as Jim Crow began to take root and as legally mandated racial segregation began to reemerge, the location of invention began to migrate from the shop culture to the school culture. The change in the location of invention related directly to the rise of corporate America and the desire to mass produce technological innovation through a corps of similarly trained men graduating from newly founded technical and engineering institutions.[15] This would have been a great opportunity for black men if they had been able regularly to gain admittance into white institutions of higher learning. Of course, there were exceptions. The Massachusetts Institute of Technology graduated a black engineering student every few years from 1892 onward, but finding employment commensurate with their level of education was nearly impossible.[16] Beginning in 1898, black institutions like Tuskegee taught the basics of electricity, but this program mainly focused on teaching students how to run the school's electric power plant.[17] These skills should not be taken lightly. They were extremely useful and would have put any graduate on a par with most electrical workmen of the time. Nevertheless, the inability of black people to receive training within the shop or the school culture restricted the opportunities of black inventors. The fabricated legacy of black intellectual inferiority, fortified by the tradition of racism, hindered African American admission to shop and school cultures and prevented them from receiving the necessary technical training of an inventor.

African Americans who acquired the necessary technical knowledge, training, and skills did not have the same inventive opportunities as nonblack inventors. Many aspiring inventors were unable to build the contacts that could assist them in developing their ideas. Professional organizations and societies that were vitally important in making business connections systematically excluded black people. Consequently, professionalization became another way to prevent people of African heritage from entering technical and inventive communities. Furthermore, African Americans had a greater difficulty in surmounting the functional barriers of invention. Inventing required capital. The vast majority of African Americans did not have the financial resources to initiate patent applications, let alone the wherewithal to support inventive research. Inventing took time. Many African Americans had to spend much of their time supporting themselves and family members. This responsibility ordinarily did not leave much time for inventive creativity. African Americans also did not have connections to people conversant in the legal aspects of invention. The paucity of black patent lawyers increased their patenting difficulties. Some black inventors initiated patent applications themselves because dealing with white patent attorneys or solicitors was usually far from amicable. There were only a few solutions to these problems: learn the legal and/or technical skills from a friend or colleague; hire or collaborate with someone who had the technical or legal expertise; find someone who would financially support the development of the inventive idea; or quit. As one proceeded to develop an inventive idea, these difficulties magnified. The financial gains traditionally associated with transmitting an invention into a marketable product eluded most black inventors. For even the best trained, the opportunities to move beyond the idea stage usually did not materialize.

The inventor myth proclaims that the best of American technology is actualized by those men who exemplified Euro-American superiority, and by the early decades of the twentieth century invention became synonymous with American progress and advancement through technological ingenuity. Technology as a panacea for social and cultural ills became a key element in American society's progression toward prosperity. But these men, and more recently women, and their technological creations should not always be seen as favorable. Technologies have a darker side. They can perpetuate capitalist modes of production and oppression, social and cultural fragmentation, as well as human destruction. Thus, inventions and technologies profoundly affect larger social and cultural relationships and not always in a positive manner as the inventor myth would have us believe. The same cultural environment that produced the inventor myth supports the American dream. Technology is a constitutive element of the accoutrements of the American dream. Yet, African Americans' access to the American dream was as limited as their access to inventive opportunities.

African American Inventors and American Identity

At the Democratic Leadership Council in 1993, former President Clinton clearly expressed what is understood to be the American dream.[18] "The American dream that we were all raised on is a simple but powerful one—

if you work hard and play by the rules you should be given a chance to go as far as your God-given ability will take you."[19] As we well know, the American dream is an incredibly powerful concept providing the hope that tomorrow can bring a brighter day. From the perspective of many African Americans, the American dream is something infrequently seen and even more rarely experienced.[20] To access the American dream, one initially has to have a fair chance at succeeding. Early in the last century most black people had a difficult time being considered American citizens, let alone gaining an opportunity to pursue success freely and equally. Yet there was hope, perhaps not in the American dream, but at least in a belief that the future could be better. Black cultural icons embodied this optimism. Hope came from Booker T. Washington asking Negroes to "cast down their buckets," take their proper place in relation to white American society, and wait for the Negroes' day eventually to come.[21] W. E. B. Du Bois represented the hope that if the best of both races would come together amicably, the race problem could be solved.[22] Unfortunately, there was a substantial obstacle: black people were still perceived as incapable, incompetent, and genetically inferior. At a less lofty level than that of Washington and Du Bois, many African Americans campaigned to undo the historically rooted concept of black inferiority. Several African Americans compiled biographical texts to supply factual evidence about the contributions African Americans made to American society and culture.[23] Their mission was to inform white, as well as black Americans, that the best of the black community contained intelligent, hard-working, and accomplished men and women. Supporters of this reformative work were cautiously optimistic that once American society recognized the achievements of black Americans, as well as their loyalty to America, the walls of racial prejudice would begin to crumble. But these biographical sketches most often played only a "protective ideological function" that thinly insulated African Americans from the most malevolent racial attacks.[24]

One of the first of these volumes, William J. Simmons's *Men of Mark,* appeared in 1887. The title clearly indicated what type of men Simmons would chronicle in his tome of nearly 1200 pages. Simmons displayed a version of the American dream when he questioned: "If the persons herein mentioned could rise to the exalted stations which they have and do now hold, what is there to prevent any young man or woman from achieving greatness?"[25] The individual character sketches in *Men of Mark* mimicked narratives of white heroes in American history. Both American historical icons and Negro intellectual heroes played similar roles: to indoctrinate a youthful audience with the proper plan for future success as devoted Americans. Yet Simmons's volume was not just for black youth to discover great Negro figures to emulate; it was also to be used by white Americans to reevaluate the progress of American Negroes. To this end, Simmons wrote "I wish the book to show to the world—to our oppressors and even our friends—that the Negro race is still alive, and must possess more intellectual vigor than any other section of the human family, or else how could they be crushed as slaves in all these years since 1620, and yet to-day stand side by side with the best blood in America, in white institutions, grappling with abstruse problems in Euclid and difficult classics, and master them? Was ever such a thing seen in another people . . . in one quarter of a century?"[26]

This and similar texts endeavored not only to display African American contributions to American society, but also to show white Americans that Negroes were capable of being civilized. By civilized, they meant being part of and contributing to civilization. At the beginning of the twentieth century, civilization meant more than just the technological artifacts of modern society; the term also referred to the moment in human history when people with the proper intellect, will, and desire pulled themselves up from the depths of savagery and barbarism.[27] The underlying implication of civilization was that only the white race had risen to the point of being civilized. Every other racial group—mired in various states of primitivism—was striving to reach the pinnacle of civilization. To refute this racialized version of civilization, African Americans needed to illustrate that black people, like white people, had risen above the barbarity of their ancestors. This proof alone, however, would not enable black people to claim that they had reached civilization. African Americans had to tap into the newly emerging collective American identity. This Americanness would soon be understood to exemplify civilization. If black people could prove they were good, loyal, productive, and intelligent Americans, their claim to civilization could not be denied. Of course, this was not an easy maneuver because in the early twentieth century Americanness frequently meant whiteness.

Physician D. W. Culp brought forth the issue of civilization in his edited volume of 1902, *Twentieth Century Negro Literature*. Its subtitle—*A Cyclopedia of Thought on the Vital Topics Relating to the American Negro by One Hundred of America's Greatest Negroes*—is more appropriate. Culp indicated that great efforts were being made to display and celebrate the nineteenth-century accomplishments of other races and nationalities, and it was time for someone to do the same for Negroes. The essays in Culp's volume endeavored to inform black and white people about the important contributions they made to the development of American civilization. He insisted that his volume reflect the views and opinions of the most erudite, and therefore most valuable, voices of black America. Culp believed that these leaders would elevate the black population "to that plane of civilization occupied by the other enlightened peoples of the world."[28] It is evident from Culp's writings that not all black people had risen to that all important place of civilization. His discussion of civilization was inherently elitist. Social class had always played an important part in the notion of civilization, and the authors of these texts clearly understood this reality. They, as well as those they wrote about, were firmly ensconced in the black middle and upper classes. Nevertheless, these types of works aspired to produce change, and to a small degree they did.

The multiple issues that shaped the experiences of African American people also impacted the lives of African American inventors. Black inventors were an important component of the empirical evidence proving black people were civilized. Whether they acknowledged it or not, black inventors were members of African American communities, and their inventions and their public images influenced the lives of black people. Understanding the connection between invention and the various programs of black uplift and progress—exemplified in the works by Simmons and Culp—is vital in placing black inventors and their inventions in a late nineteenth- and early twentieth-century African American cultural context. Prior to Emancipation, black uplift ideology focused upon attaining freedom. But after Emancipation, this ideology changed in form and function, and its metamorphosis was complex at best. The new forms of black uplift revolved around various plans to diminish the historical and cultural gulf between black and white by showing that black Americans were developing and becoming more like white Americans. Moreover, uplift was meant to demonstrate to the white population that black citizens possessed, had acquired, or were striving to obtain the intellectual, social, and cultural requirements to progress toward the always elusive civilization.

The act of invention (and more specifically patenting) was an instrument used to provide evidence that African Americans could and would eventually achieve civilization. It played on the mythology of the solitary genius inventor—a person who had a special creative gift with which only few individuals were born. If black people could invent, the race could claim intellectual equality since certain African Americans possessed this inherited ability. If black inventors could patent objects that would eventually be incorporated into American material culture, black citizens would have irrefutable evidence that African Americans contributed to American civilization through highly regarded technological means. African Americans could use black inventive genius as an instrument to transcend societal barriers held in place by the racial discrimination embedded within American culture. Moreover, inventions and patents demonstrated hard work, self-sufficiency, business acumen, and, most important, success in the white world. Inventions symbolized the technical, creative, and intellectual capability of Americans of African descent. The most prominent black leaders of the period did not disregard invention and its political implications. In an article from 1903 entitled "Possibilities of the Negro: The Advance Guard of the Race," Du Bois wrote of invention as an example of the tangible contributions Afro-Americans made to American civilization.[29] In 1895, when Booker T. Washington gave his controversial speech at the Atlanta Cotton States and International Exposition, the building that housed the Negro exhibit displayed inventions by black men.[30]

Black inventors were important to the growing black middle and upper classes that arose after Emancipation. Several black inventors came from these social classes, and many of those who did not, became part of the black upper classes as a result of their patenting. This group of "new people" considered themselves the bridge between white civilization and the black masses.[31] They considered guiding the black masses toward American civilization as their fundamental task. To this end, the black upper classes effectively used black inventors, and other men of intellectual achievement, such as black elected government officials, college professors, and ministers as examples of successes that the black masses should strive to reach. However, they also used these examples of success to distinguish themselves from the black masses. Several black intellectuals began to claim that there was a distinction between the Negro masses and themselves, thereby redefining racial uplift ideology. Instead of working from the bottom-up, they inverted racial uplift to work from the top down. W. E. B. Du Bois exemplified this sentiment in his essay "The Talented Tenth" when he argued that American society willingly ignored the fact that millions of Negro men and women had achieved a level of sophistication comparable to that of the highest European civilizations. He and others felt that the best of civilized society would be responsible for saving the race. In this essay, Du Bois asked "Can the masses of the Negro people be in any possible way more quickly raised than by effort and example of this aristocracy of talent and character? Was there ever a nation on God's fair earth civilized from the bottom upward?" Du Bois appropriately responded to his rhetorical question by stating that "it is, ever was and ever will be from the top downward that culture filters. The Talented Tenth rises and pulls all that are worth the saving up to their vantage ground."[32]

In their efforts to achieve racial equality, many black elites used the same racial analogies, metaphors, and representations to separate themselves from the black masses that white Americans used to differentiate white people from black people.[33] Some African American intellectuals began to assert that Africa was the "home of the primitive races," as did black scholar and vice-president of Wilberforce University William Scarborough during a meeting of the exclusive Bethel Literary and Historical Association in Washington, D.C., in 1905.[34] Others commented that the Negro masses were not responsible enough for full franchise and implied further that there were cultural, social, and intellectual differences between the black masses and the black upper classes. Yet, one should not make a presentist mistake and condemn these individuals. Western society and culture produced some of the most historically valued black voices, like W. E. B. Du Bois, Booker T. Washington, William Monroe Trotter, and Marcus Garvey. They all possessed the cultural sensibilities of their time, just as most well-to-do white Americans of the period did, and in regard to race, each displayed many of the dominant American culture's social characteristics and ideologies.[35] In varying degrees, the dominant American culture had colonized the minds of the black upper classes. As a result, the black elite assisted in the reformulation of African American representations on white American culture's ideologies and phenotypic aesthetics.

The black upper classes, who had shown that they had the ability to participate in the white world, considered it their duty to present themselves as examples of what the Negro masses should emulate if they intended to reach civilization. This was a way for the black elite to impose social and cultural control over the masses, to illustrate the definable differences between the black elite and the Negro masses to the white society, and to support their own social-climbing aspirations. The nuances of these cultural distinctions were lost upon the white population. White people, for the most part, saw the black population as a homogeneous unit and did not discern the class boundaries the black elite created and enforced. While reinforcing class distinctions, the black upper classes simultaneously promoted the ascription of racial homogeneity onto themselves by appropriating white racial rhetoric's singular meaning of blackness. By simplistically speaking of *the* race question, black elites assisted in removing the complexities and nuances of the post-Reconstruction white racial warfare waged against African Americans. Moreover, as the black elite constantly maneuvered to distance themselves from the black masses, they continued to speak publicly and write of *the* Negro despite the diversity in the black community. These rhetorical actions may have been in part to solidify the black community as a unified force struggling against American racism, but the assertion that black people are all "in the same boat" was "subject to White supremacist abuse."[36] The result was that a large section of white American society interpreted the black elite's vocalization of "oneness" as a reaffirmation of wholesale black inferiority and a reification of white supremacy. Through the emerging mass media, including advertising, film, and music, the sentiments of black inferiority were manifested in tangible form. These outlets created new and very authoritative ways of rearticulating blackness as deviant, pathological, and in general, undesirable.[37] This state of affairs has not drastically changed.

African American Inventors and Contemporary American Culture

The historical legacy of upper-class African Americans deploying black inventors as human evidence of Negro intellectual achievement has important consequences for contemporary America. For a great white inventor such as an Edison or a Ford the image of the individual—the icon—is of greatest importance in understanding their meanings for American culture. The heroic icon provided human proof that certain men possessed the inventor gift and that the American dream could be achieved. The icon became more important than the human being. In many ways, American society disembodied the human inventor and made him an artificial ideal for future generations to revere and emulate.[38] African American people, who were trying to prove intellectual and racial equality, gladly linked black inventors with the mythology of their white counterparts. By coupling black inventors with valorized captains of American industry, black people could gain respect and equality by association.

Black inventors of this period, however, were not fashioned into icons. Indeed, they inspired Negro youth to believe that even in a racist society great things were possible. But early in the twentieth century, the human icon was much less important than the material invented artifact. To show that Negroes had contributed something concrete to American progress, a human being was important, but an artifact was essential. The artifact clearly illustrated that African Americans had achieved civilization. Inventions that received the federal stamp of approval with a patent confirmed that black people could achieve civilization. Furthermore, inventions could be counted and displayed, and, as a result, inventions and patents became powerful tools to destabilize concepts of black inferiority. Thus, at the turn of the century, as American society elevated white inventors to icons, African American society reduced black inventors to their inventions.

In contemporary American society, new meanings and uses for black inventors have emerged. Currently black inventors no longer fundamentally serve as human evidence substantiating black intellectual acuity. They still do perform this role in a historical context by continuing to instill racial pride and inspiring African American youth to succeed. This, of course, is very important in a world that is increasingly becoming noted for the growing race/class technological divide. Yet, the early twentieth-century use of black inventors as physical evidence of African Americans' progress has been reframed significantly in the recent past. Currently, black inventors represent the deliberate omission of black people from American history. Black inventors are exemplars of black people who battled against an oppressive racialized system and won. This redefinition stabilized during the civil rights movement when black leaders like Martin Luther King, Jr., openly spoke about the meaning of the historical erasure of African American people. King argued that we must challenge the violence done to their identity when African Americans are written out of American history.[39] In referencing this missing history and identity, King called upon black inventors like Granville T. Woods and Jan Matzeliger to help make his point. King, however, situated his comments about black inventors within early twentieth-century contributionism. King linked Woods's patent production with success and American progress when he wrote of Woods as "an expert in electric motors, whose many patents speeded the growth and improvement of the railroads at the beginning of this century."[40] Thus, as African American communities renegotiated the cultural meanings of black inventors, older meanings continued to persist.

As the dominant popular representation of black inventors embodied the heroic ideals of inspiration and racial uplift, it also incorporated a new role of the flawless race champion. In historical hindsight, a black inventor's successful transgression into a traditionally white intellectual domain was interpreted as revolutionary. At one level, an African American "first" in a racially hostile society should be interpreted as revolutionary. This revolutionary interpretation, however, assumes that all black inventors had strong racially located agendas and intended to be race freedom fighters. Not all African American inventors consciously worked to improve the everyday lives of African American people by disturbing American society's racial structure. It is within this context that African American history has recovered black inventors and fabricated them into flawless race-championing icons. In some instances, the reclamation process, because of limited historical research, has licensed contemporary myth making. This present-day reappropriation of black inventors is most poignantly represented in the proliferation of black inventor lists during Black History Month. These comforting and pacifying representations help maintain the limited understanding of black inventors' lives. Consequently, it is no accident that these heroic representations have become quite popular.

The post–civil-rights-movement iconic black inventor taps into and supports the fallacy of the American dream for all racial audiences. Contemporary American society can find comfort in plugging black inventors into clarified, overcome-the-odds narratives. They also can enable black people to forget the depressing past of racial exploitation in exchange for stories about those who by dint of their undeniable skills, talents, and efforts overcame the disadvantages of racism. This current black inventor mythology enables the dominant American culture to assuage its racial guilt and use black inventors to prove that not all black people were oppressed by racism. The mythology simultaneously reinforces the element of the American dream that states if you work hard enough in our society, regardless of race, you will succeed. Unfortunately, the American dream strongly links success with virtue. This connection is essentially responsible for the aggressive omission of failure from the American dream and the black inventor myth. Failure is only referenced if it is a positive learning experience that leads one to future successes. If success in the American dream has connotations of virtue, then failure correspondingly can imply sin.[41] It is failure and sin—a powerful reference in a religious society—that the American dream and the black inventor myth must cover up and expunge. If American society is built upon never ending progress exemplified by new and better technologies, then failure has no place. Thus, the failures of black inventors are hidden. The successes, the inventions, and the patents are the focal points. Black inventor lists are a condensed version of the larger reduction of black inventors and can be seen as reestablishing the American dream within the historical narratives of African American people as well as reinscribing overly heroic black narratives into American history. By moving past what these lists represent and exposing black inventors to closer, and for some uncomfortable, examination, it is possible to destabilize the American dream and unravel inventive heroism of black inventors.

By examining the relationships between the technologies invented by African Americans and African American communities, the perception that African American inventors are race champions is called into question. Black people invented for some of the same reasons that other racial and ethnic groups invented. These reasons ranged from desiring to exploit a patented idea for financial gain, to becoming famous for someone with a social climbing agenda. Many black inventors were more interested in "getting paid" than in the racial implications of their patents. For example, by the beginning of the twentieth century most of the inventions made by African Americans only vaguely improved the lives of black people. Those inventions that made their way into the everyday lives of African Americans often had problematic effects. Several black inventors patented railway devices, but following the Supreme Court 1896 separate-but-equal decision in *Plessy* v. *Ferguson,* Jim Crow became legally embedded within railway cars, that is, unequal rail cars represented the inequalities of American society. Thus, one could interpret these inventions as providing a more efficient way to administer segregation and racism. One of the long-lived perceptions about technologies is that they benefit society by saving labor, increasing productivity, and subsequently freeing human beings from the contingencies of nature. But, the history of technology has shown that technologies often create more work than less, and increase the gulf between haves and have nots.[42] As a result, inventions by African Americans were far from instruments of societal uplift for the black community; they were regularly tools of white uplift and reinforced racial inequality and the hegemony of white American culture.

But the situation is not that black and white—that inventions by African Americans uplifted whiteness and denigrated blackness. Inventions by black individuals can be interpreted as subverting and resisting the dominant American society. The margin does not always have to be perceived as a site of deprivation, subjugation, and repression. Cultural critics like bell hooks have noted that the periphery is a key site for the production and sustenance of counterhegemonic discourse.[43] For instance, in the late nineteenth century, an African American showing that he or she possessed the God-given ability to invent could shake the very foundations of a racially stratified American society based on black intellectual inferiority. A black person shaping American material culture through the invention of technological artifacts was something potentially to cause alarm during the late nineteenth and early twentieth centuries. This act could result in the reformation of a dominant American culture that was not entirely constructed by the values, beliefs, and sensibilities of whites. Technological redefinitions based on black cultural priorities could leave black cultural imprints on the dominant American culture. These types of alterations to American material culture could not be avoided because of the inherent indeterminacy of technology.[44] Thus, technologies' inherent indeterminacy could enable black subversion and resistance of the dominant American culture.

In most cases, inventions by African Americans never wielded that much power. But inventive creativity by African Americans did contest the structural exclusion of black people from humanity in the late nineteenth and early twentieth centuries. As white American cultural hegemony intensified from Emancipation to the turn-of-the-century, the dominant American culture ignored, overlooked, and worse, demonized and pathologized black people. The dominant American culture constructed black people as this society's uncivilized other; and this construction left black people virtually nameless, faceless, and consequently, invisible. As Cornel West has indicated, this invisibility constructed "black people as a problem-people rather than people with problems; black people as abstractions and objects rather than individuals and persons; black and white worlds divided by a thick wall (or a "Veil") . . . black rage, anger, and fury concealed in order to assuage white fear and anxiety; and black people rootless and homeless on a perennial journey to discover who they are in a society content to see blacks remain the permanent underdog."[45] By creating artifacts, practices, and knowledge that were to become parts of American material and technological cultures, black inventors were becoming visible metaphorically and materially through their technological production. As black inventors received recognition for their inventive efforts in mass media, both black and white, they began to move out of the shadows, lift the veil, remove the mask, and solidify and develop decidedly positive representations and existences for African Americans within American society and culture.

FIGURE 2.1. Granville T. Woods as he appeared in *Cosmopolitan Magazine*, April 1895.

Chapter Two

Liars and Thieves: Granville T. Woods and the Process of Invention

The day is past . . . when a colored boy will be refused work because of race prejudice.
—Granville T. Woods, 1892

Granville Woods was the most prolific Negro inventor of the late nineteenth and early twentieth centuries. He was an exception among black inventors of this period in that inventing was his career. For Woods, invention was first and foremost an economic undertaking, a means to gain more capital to invest in future projects. But the grand ideas exemplified in his patents indicate that he also had a vision for modernizing America. It was this vision that led him to file numerous patents, and, by the turn of the twentieth century, he had become closely connected with the American electrical community. Woods's life, however, was not that of a triumphant and heroic inventor. He spent the majority of his adult life marginalized as an inventor, desperately struggling to secure funding and gain a respectable reputation for his work. In the most basic sense, Woods's day-to-day activities can best be described as surviving and even hustling, and in some instances, his tactics were rather suspect. But after the turn of the twentieth century, his hard work appeared to be on the verge of paying off. It was at this moment that powerful members of the American electrical community began to take notice of Woods and his work. Unfortunately, when success appeared to be within his grasp, a cerebral hemorrhage brought his life to an end in 1910.[1]

Throughout his career, Woods never fully capitalized on any of his patented inventions, and in this regard, his life refutes the patents-equal-financial-success component of the black inventor myth. Woods played the game aggressively, hard, and to win, but most of the time, he did not fare that well. For Woods patents did not produce economic rewards; they only represented unfulfilled dreams. Woods's life—at times closer to a nightmare than the American dream—clearly illustrates the harsh realities of being a black inventor at the end of the nineteenth century.

Woods Invents in Ohio

To begin a discussion of Granville Woods, it is necessary to go back to the beginning of his life and clear away some of the errors surrounding his birthplace and his early technical training. Many researchers have written that Woods's was born in Columbus, Ohio,[2] although no record of his Ohio birth exists. Granville Woods was born on April 23, 1856, in Australia. Four main pieces of evidence show this. The first is the United States Census Records of 1910, which reported that Woods was born in Australia.[3] The second is his death certificate, which stated that he and both of his parents were born in Australia.[4] Third are the biographical sketches written in New York area newspapers.[5] Fourth, a statement from *Cosmopolitan Magazine* in 1895 indicated that Woods's "mother's father was a Malay Indian, and his other grandparents were by birth full-blooded savage Australian aborigines, born in the wilds back of Melbourne."[6] It is important to note what was not written in *Cosmopolitan.* There is no mention of the racial background of Woods's other grandmother, which implies that most likely she was of African descent. This would have made Woods a quarter black—more than enough African blood to be considered a Negro by the racial standards of late nineteenth-century America. Regardless of whether Woods was part Aborigine and Malay Indian, the majority of both black and white societies viewed him as a Negro. Finally, Woods's combative spirit, the forthright manner in which he interacted with whites, and his fearless public challenges to white authority—all of which, because of the severe consequences, most African Americans avoided well into the twentieth century—indicate that he did not consider himself an American Negro.

As for Woods's early technical training, William J. Simmons, in *Men of Mark,* asserted that at the age of ten Woods began working "in a machine shop where he learned the machinist and blacksmith trades."[7] After this point, however, the accounts in *Men of Mark* are not supported by what Woods himself said about his life. Simmons claimed that some time in "November, 1872, [Woods] left for the West, where he obtained work as a fireman and afterwards as an engineer on one of the Iron Mountain Railroads of Missouri . . . In December, 1874, he went to Springfield, Illinois, where he was employed in a rollingmill." Simmons recounted that "early in 1876 he left for the East, where he received two years special training in electrical and mechanical engineering at college . . . [on] February 6, 1878, he went to sea in the capacity of engineer on board the 'Ironsides,' a British steamer."[8] In the *New York Recorder*, Simmons attested that instead of going West, Woods, "in 1872 came East and received two years special training in electrical and mechanical engineering."[9] Thus, there are obvious discrepancies in the reporting of the early events of Woods's life, to which Woods himself contributed. Nevertheless, from all the comments Woods made about his past, these dates and statements can be tied together to represent a reality.

First of all, it is quite likely that Woods engaged in some form of engineering or technical study. An article in the *Brooklyn Daily Eagle* stated that "Granville T. Woods, a coffee colored Negro . . . claims to be a graduate of the electrical department of Stern's Institute of Technology."[10] Another article commented that "Mr. Woods has a first-class English education, and is an experienced mechanic, having received special training in mechanical engineering."[11] These assessments of his technical education would mesh with the account that he was an "engineer" commissioned aboard the *Ironsides*. If Woods actually set sail in February 1878, as Simmons has written, it was slightly overzealous to pronounce that "while a sailor, he visited every country on the globe."[12] Woods would later testify that in 1878 he found employment with the Pomeroy Railroad Company, attending "to all of the pumping stations along the line of way and also to do the shifting of cars at Washington Court House, Ohio."[13] Hence, it would have been difficult for him to travel most of the world in less than eleven months. Woods worked for the Pomeroy Railroad for about eight months, after which he secured a position at the Dayton and Southeastern Railroad for the next thirteen months. The latter post was a significant improvement. As a full-fledged railway engineer, Woods was able to handle "every engine they had on the road" (Woods' Testimony in Surrebuttal, Interference cases #18,207 & #18,210, 282). By December 1880, Woods was no longer employed by the Dayton and Southeastern Railroad. Woods left this railroad because of its financial difficulties. Woods recounted that the railroad company "was in the hands of a receiver, and they paid us in script. No one cared to take the script at all, and if they did take it, they shaved it so that there was nothing left scarcely, and it was as much as I could do to get money to pay my board, lodging, clothe myself, without reference to patents" (Woods' Testimony in Surrebuttal, Interference Case #10,580, 8).

These jobs seem to have been better compared with the poor opportunities available in railway work for African Americans. Other sections of Ohio like the Western Reserve were known for their race tolerance, but the Cincinnati area was very "Southern" and enforced racial discrimination and segregation.[14] Woods was exceptionally fortunate to have those employment opportunities come his way. It is unclear how he was able to secure such employment; it may have been through his education, his trip on the *Ironsides*, or some other means. Nevertheless, he used these various opportunities as a training ground to become intimately acquainted with railway technology. He acquired some of his early electrical knowledge while working on the Dayton and Southeastern Railway. Since, as Woods has noted, he had "a great deal of leisure," a friendly telegraph operator in Washington Court House taught him how to operate a telegraph (Cases #18,207 & #18,210, 33). This statement by Woods does not help to corroborate his claim that he received two years of training in electrical and mechanical engineering in the mid 1870s, because if he had enrolled in such a program it is likely that he would have learned the basics of telegraphy and would not have needed further instruction. Regardless, this basic apprenticeship may have also included simple instruction in the fundamentals of electricity.

His frequent trips to the city of Washington Court House planted the seed for one of Woods's first inventions, his induction telegraphy system. On one of his regularly scheduled trips from Dayton to Washington Court House, he visited the Beckel House, a local hotel. The building's elevator piqued his interest. In his opinion, the signaling method used to communicate between the elevator and floors was inadequate. It occurred to him that the process could be improved through the use of induction—the transmission of an electrical information-carrying impulses through the air. The fact that Woods was thinking about inductive communication may indicate that he had received more technical training than anything obtainable from a friendly telegraph operator. In December 1880, he began to pursue the development of an elevator signaling system based on the principles of induction. The first idea he began working on was a system in which "a spool . . . with a primary wire wound around a core, and extending from the lower floor to the upper portion of the elevator . . . passed through the secondary wire, which was wound around a spool" (Case #10,580, 7). Each floor could signal by completing a circuit with the primary wire. That wire's impulse would inductively move to the secondary wire. Thus, when someone on a floor wanted to call the elevator, they would push a button and a signal would be transmitted to the car via the secondary wire, to which the elevator operator would respond. Woods began to make models based upon this uncomplicated idea, and through further investigations he soon developed a more sophisticated system. The improved system substituted a helix connected to the elevator car for the spools and wire. Woods made a few sketches of this device that he showed to his friends Thomas Schammel and James Barnett on December 29, 1880, both of whom affixed their signature to the drawings (fig. 2.2).[15]

From the technical complexity of this creative work, it is obvious that Woods had acquired a fairly decent command of electrical technology. How he came by this knowledge is still a mystery. A biographical sketch by Aaron Klein contends that he took up the study of electricity on his own. Klein intimates that Woods had such a voracious intellectual appetite for all works written on the subject of electricity and electrical technology that he had a white friend check out library books for him.[16] This may have been true, but Woods garnered much of his electrical knowledge as a practitioner rather than through a process of scholarly study. During interference testimony in 1886, Woods elaborated that he had been a mechanical engineer for fifteen years and a electrical engineer for fourteen. This answer perplexed the attorney cross-examining Woods, because this would have meant that Woods had been a mechanical and electrical engineer since he was fifteen years of age. Upon further questioning, Woods conceded that he only started working as a machinist at fifteen and that that was the beginning of his training as a mechanical engineer. Similarly, Woods stated that he only started studying electricity at the age of sixteen. So at that age he was only "laying the foundation" for the knowledge required to be a mechanical and electrical engineer (ibid., 21–22). If Woods had acquired his electrical knowledge through traditional educational routes, he most likely would have mentioned this fact when questioned about the origin of his technical knowledge.

So what ever came of his early elevator apparatus? Woods gave up on the device after showing it and several other inventions to patent attor-

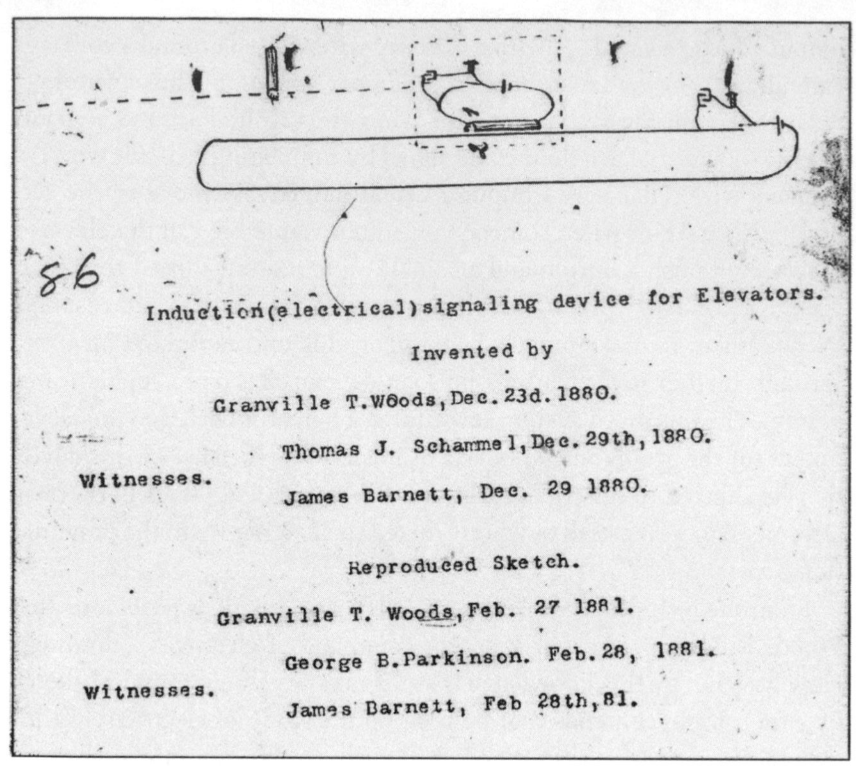

FIGURE 2.2. Woods's elevator signaling device intended to alert an elevator operator that someone was waiting to ride the elevator, although it did not indicate the floor the rider was on. This device was Woods's first success in inductive communications, December 1880. National Archives.

ney George B. Parkinson soon after his arrival in Cincinnati in 1880. Parkinson was not very optimistic about Woods's new method of elevator signaling because an "elevator could be signaled by the ordinary method very cheaply" (ibid., 29). Woods had hoped that this idea would have provided him with an escape from working on the railroad. By this point in Woods's life, he was becoming fairly disenchanted with the work. Moreover, as Jim Crow spread across the United States in the 1880s, it became even more difficult for him to secure railway positions. These difficulties propelled Woods to consider invention as a full-time occupation.

When Woods first moved to Cincinnati, he commented that he had quite a few inventions and inventive ideas available. Unfortunately, his financial situation was far from ideal. From 1880 until 1885 Woods did not have a steady source of income. Regarding this five-year period, Woods said, "I have been depending entirely upon daily labor and what money I could borrow, when I was short of money, of my friends" (ibid., 16–17). Woods dedicated a significant amount of time to his inventions because of these financial problems. His inventive ideas seemed to be a possible way out of his predicament or at the least a way to augment his meager income. In January 1881, Woods began to develop his ideas on inductive communication. He was beginning to think more broadly about the uses for inductive communication and began to devise a way to apply this knowledge to railways, his area of expertise. From his railway experience, Woods observed that there was a pressing need for communication between trains and railway stations. If he could invent a system that would enable trains and stations to communicate more efficiently, he believed that he would possess a highly marketable, as well as profitable, tool.

On this theme, Woods executed a group of sketches and produced two models loosely based on his elevator device (ibid., 8; fig. 2.3).[17] One of Woods's models intended to use the roofs of railway cars to communicate. Since telegraph lines existed near most railway tracks, it would be very simple to route the lines for Woods's induction telegraphy on telegraph poles. In this model, he constructed a miniature example of a section of track near a station. He described the model as follows:

> The telegraphic wire was represented as wound around an induction coil and carried over standards and grounded at the other end . . . For a ground I used a sheet of copper. The wire representing the telegraph wire was suspended high enough to let the car pass underneath. Instead of a car roof I placed a heavy wire running from one end of the car to the other, and cover this with tin foil. On this car . . . [was] a series of batteries an induction coil, vibrator, condenser, key, and telephone receiver, and also a telephone transmitter. The primary wire was held in close circuit by means of a switch, or could be cut out into open circuit . . . The secondary wire . . . is grounded, while the other end is intended to be connected to the roof of the car which is represented by a wire covered with tin foil. (Ibid., 9)

He based this model on a trolley system. With the contacts above the car, this apparatus could accommodate a system using magnetic, electri-

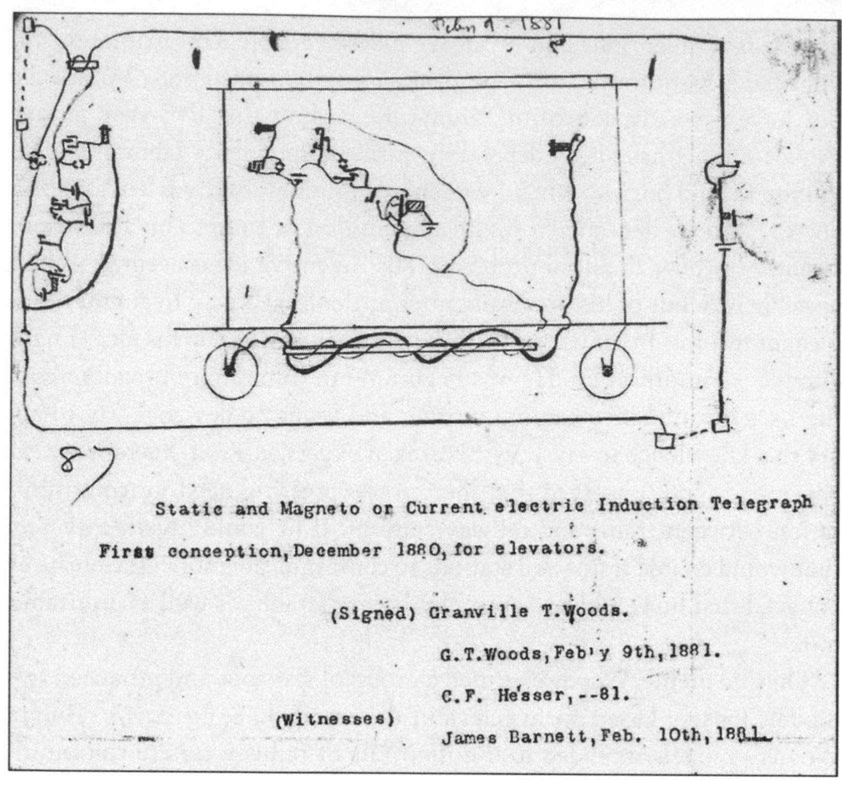

FIGURE 2.3. Railway communicator device, Woods's first version of his induction telegraph, based loosely on his induction signaling device for elevators. December 1880. National Archives.

cal, or static conduction. "The telegraph wire, which would be carried over the top of the car, or near the top, and supported upon ordinary supports, could be connected with a special wire, laid along the track, while the induction of the upper half of the coil would act upon the wire carried above the car" (ibid., 10). Woods was not just looking at this apparatus as a means of telegraph communication, but also as a method of transmitting telephone signals from trains (fig. 2.4). On this idea he cheaply constructed a second model that he displayed, along with his sketches, to several people in his neighborhood in East End (ibid., 11, 52). Woods sat poised to pursue this invention to the fullest, but two things contributed to his inaction. His financial situation had not changed, so he lacked the wherewithal to develop this device. In addition, he contracted a debilitating illness that aggravated his money problems.

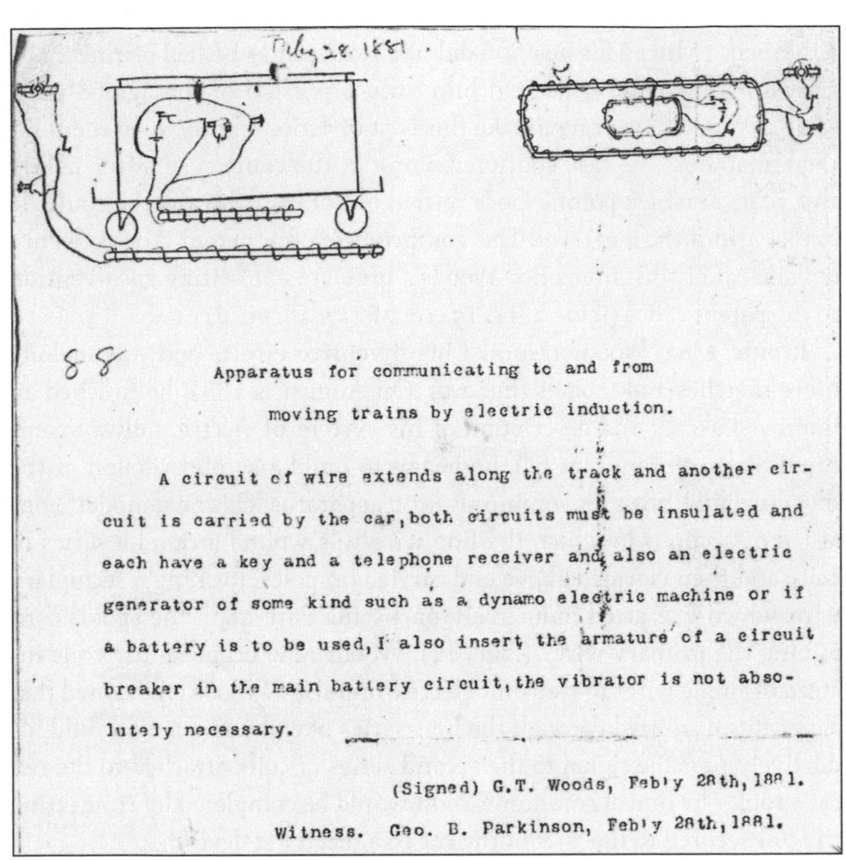

88 Apparatus for communicating to and from moving trains by electric induction.

A circuit of wire extends along the track and another circuit is carried by the car, both circuits must be insulated and each have a key and a telephone receiver and also an electric generator of some kind such as a dynamo electric machine or if a battery is to be used, I also insert the armature of a circuit breaker in the main battery circuit, the vibrator is not absolutely necessary.

(Signed) G.T. Woods, Feb'y 28th, 1881.

Witness. Geo. B. Parkinson, Feb'y 28th, 1881.

FIGURE 2.4. Woods's railway inductive communication device, attached under a car, provided a means by which stations could communicate with engineers on moving trains. February 1881. National Archives.

In August 1881, Woods came down with a severe case of smallpox (ibid., 2, 11, 15, 16, 28, 37, 38, 60, 61).[18] Woods commented that this disease hampered his activity for the next year (ibid., 2, 11). Woods lost much of his momentum during this ailment-induced moratorium. He was already living on a minimal income and "was reduced to extremities . . . to live and keep [his] family" (ibid., 2). The smallpox had Woods bed-ridden for several months, leaving him extremely weak for the next few years. For the remainder of his life he contended with chronic kidney and liver problems, both of which probably contributed to his death (ibid., 28). This malady magnified his inability to find regular work in 1881 and 1882. The only steady position he was able to secure was at the Queen

City Facing Mills. This position did not work out as he had planned. The Queen City Facing Mills paid him only a portion of the agreed upon salary. Woods, never one to take this sort of action lightly, sued them for the remainder. The case sputtered along in the court system for nearly two years at which point Woods settled out of court because he could no longer afford the legal fees. This compromise only netted Woods twenty dollars. All of this intensified Woods's problems of getting an invention to the patent office (ibid., 2, 11, 15, 16, 28, 37, 38, 60, 61).

In mid 1882, Woods resumed his inventive efforts and was making more sketches and models (fig. 2.5). On August 2, 1882, he finished an improved sketch and description of his system of electric railway communication; and by that fall, he began to build a second version of the model exemplifying his communication apparatus. This next model "consisted of sections in which the line wire was wound around a series of coils, and then elevated above and carried on poles, forming a secondary wire, which was acted inductively on by the wire upon the spools containing the primary wire" (ibid., 11). Woods now began to use coils instead of single wires to transmit electric impulses. Woods envisioned that a signal transmitted through the first series of coils, on a pole, would inductively pass the signal to the second series of coils, attached to the rail car's roof. The line of communication would be completed by connecting the coil secured to the roof of the car to a receiving device.

Woods did not construct this model entirely by himself. For this he employed the skilled workmen at C. E. Jones & Brothers, a company that specialized in manufacturing electrical appliances. The worker who spent the most amount of time fabricating Woods's model was August Fisler—whom C. E. Jones employed as a model maker. Woods did not necessarily need the help of Fisler and the C. E. Jones company to assemble the model, but he did need them to make the model's parts. Woods would instruct Fisler to machine the model's parts to his specification, after which Woods would assemble the different components (ibid., 41). Woods had the technical knowledge to make the models' parts himself, but he did not own the necessary tools required for the job—which is where the C. E. Jones company came into play. In the latter part of 1884, Woods constructed a third model (fig. 2.6) and by September 1885 he completed a fourth.

What differentiated the second model from the third was that Woods began to use a helix of wire which transmitted electrical impulses better than his other designs. In addition, this design placed the helix underneath the car. By doing this, it was necessary to lay a circuit of wire at track level and arrange the circuit so that the helix would be suspended

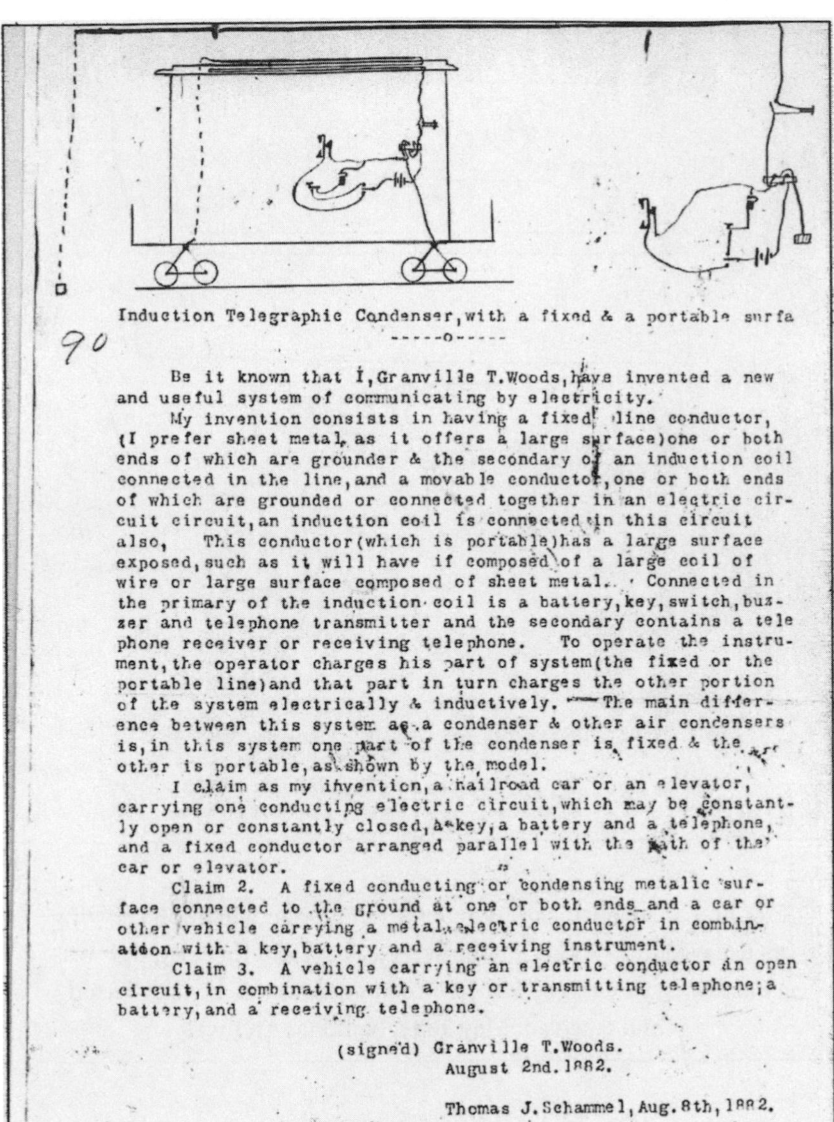

Induction Telegraphic Condenser, with a fixed & a portable surfa

-----o-----

90

Be it known that I, Granville T. Woods, have invented a new and useful system of communicating by electricity.

My invention consists in having a fixed line conductor, (I prefer sheet metal, as it offers a large surface) one or both ends of which are grounder & the secondary of an induction coil connected in the line, and a movable conductor, one or both ends of which are grounded or connected together in an electric circuit circuit, an induction coil is connected in this circuit also, This conductor (which is portable) has a large surface exposed, such as it will have if composed of a large coil of wire or large surface composed of sheet metal. Connected in the primary of the induction coil is a battery, key, switch, buzzer and telephone transmitter and the secondary contains a telephone receiver or receiving telephone. To operate the instrument, the operator charges his part of system (the fixed or the portable line) and that part in turn charges the other portion of the system electrically & inductively. The main difference between this system as a condenser & other air condensers is, in this system one part of the condenser is fixed & the other is portable, as shown by the model.

I claim as my invention, a railroad car or an elevator, carrying one conducting electric circuit, which may be constantly open or constantly closed, a key, a battery and a telephone, and a fixed conductor arranged parallel with the path of the car or elevator.

Claim 2. A fixed conducting or condensing metalic surface connected to the ground at one or both ends and a car or other vehicle carrying a metal electric conductor in combination with a key, battery and a receiving instrument.

Claim 3. A vehicle carrying an electric conductor an open circuit, in combination with a key or transmitting telephone; a battery, and a receiving telephone.

(signed) Granville T. Woods.
August 2nd. 1882.

(Witnesses) Thomas J. Schammel, Aug. 8th, 1882.
James Barnett. August 10th, 1882.

FIGURE 2.5. Woods's railway inductive communication device, attached above a railcar, would transfer signals from the top of a car rather than below as shown in earlier versions. August 1882. National Archives.

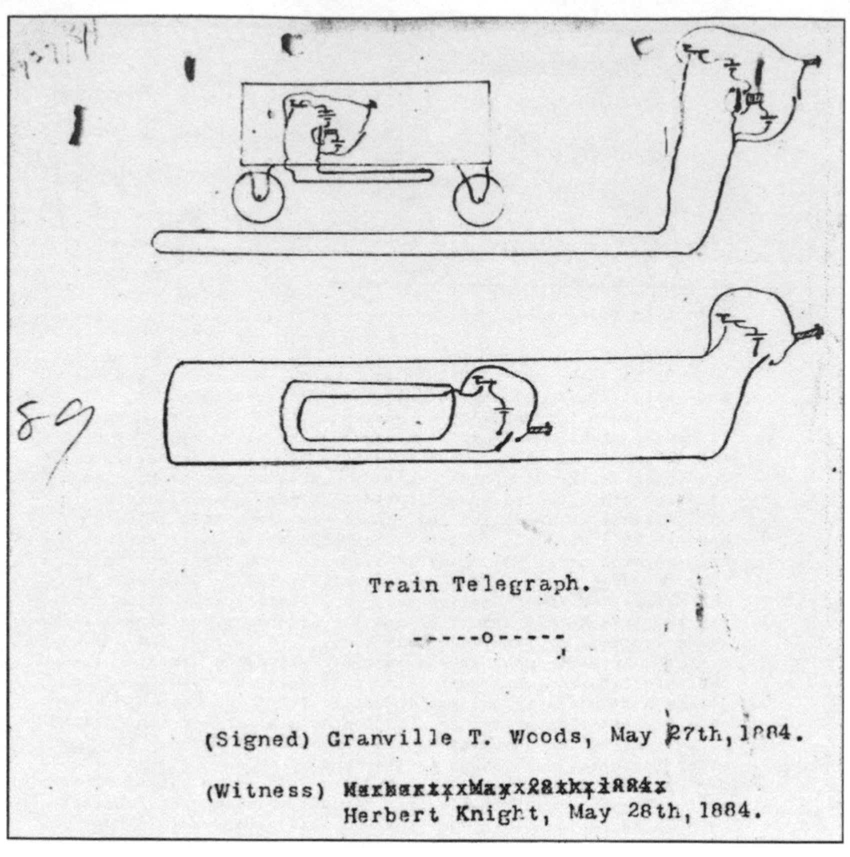

FIGURE 2.6. Schematic drawing of an induction telegraph showing its use within a railcar. In Woods's early system the telegraph was the primary means by which information was to be transferred and received. May 1884. National Archives.

in between the sending and returning wires. "[I]f a message was transmitted from the car the current passing through the helix would act inductively upon the wire on one side of the conductor arranged along the track, and, in passing up the other side of the helix, would act inductively upon the corresponding side of the wire arranged along the track" (ibid., 12) (fig. 2.7). The fourth model was the complete working system. In this model he added a telegraph key and the necessary communication devices (ibid., 18–21) (fig. 2.8).

Woods dedicated a great deal of his energy to this project; yet he did not focus exclusively on the development of this communication system.

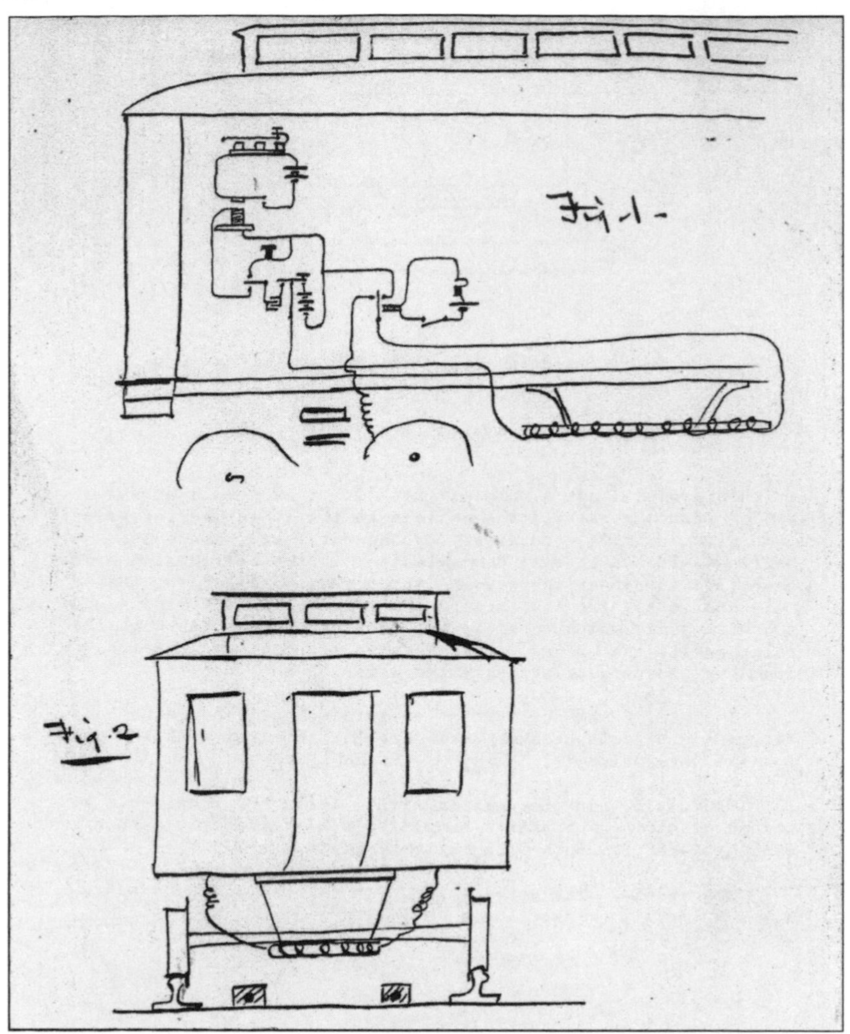

FIGURE 2.7. Schematic for planned application of Woods's 1885 induction telegraph device. National Archives.

After he regained his health, he began to work on other inventions that he hoped would bring quick financial returns to assist in the development of his system of inductive communication. During 1883 and 1884 Woods made several trips to New York City, the center of electrical activity in the United States in the late nineteenth century. The reason for these trips can only be speculated upon. Most likely they had a two-fold mission: to find work and solicit support for his inventions. These trips were

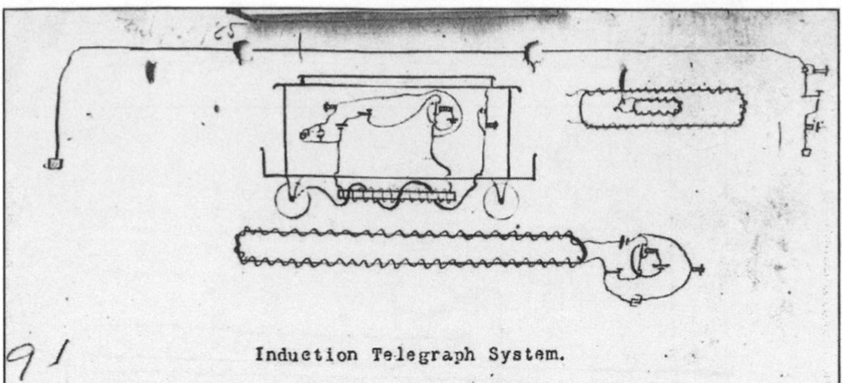

91 Induction Telegraph System.

Improvement on system invented Dec. 18880.

In this system I use a complete metalic circuit laid or suspended near the path of the vehicle so that I get better effect than with a single conductor. On the car I will suspend a helix of wire which will communicate with the battery, the telephone, the condenser, the key and the circuit breaker (of the main and local circuits) around the primary helix I wind a second wire gelix which connects the roof of the car (through the telephone) to the ground. Messages may be sent and received from the ordinary telegraph ~~xxxx~~ wires.

I claim. The combination of a telephone receiver, a battery, and a circuit breaker, which breaks and makes both, the main and the local circuit.

2nd. claim. In combination with a telephone receiver, a key and an electric generator, a complete metalic electric path extending along the path of a moving vehicle.

3rd. claim. The combination of a telephone, a condenser, a key, a circuit breaker and a battery.

Granville T. Woods, 2-17th, 85.

Witness. Donald D. McDougall,

Carl Spengel.

Feb'y 20th, 1885.

FIGURE 2.8. Woods's completed version of his induction telegraph system, which would enable both telegraphic and telephonic transmissions. February 1885. National Archives.

not successful on either account. He never was able to attract funding, but he almost secured a job. Woods attested that the last trip he made to New York City in 1884 was in November because a "Dr. Beckwith sent for me, stating that he had a situation for me; but after I arrived . . . I found that such was not the case, and in about a week afterwards Dr. Beckwith left for Europe" (ibid., 27).[19]

Woods endeavored to garner support for his inventive ideas by any means possible. During this period he wrote a few companies asking for assistance in the further development of his ideas or if they would buy his creations outright. Woods wrote the Westinghouse Air and Brake Company early in 1883, probably in reference to an idea he had for an electro-magnetic brake.[20] In their reply, Westinghouse wrote "that they would have nothing to do with [his] invention unless it was fully covered by a patent, otherwise they might be accused of appropriating ideas" procured through illicit methods. Woods also sent a letter of inquiry to the American Brake Company in St. Louis. Their response was slightly more encouraging, answering that if he ever received patents for his inventions they "would be glad to investigate them" (ibid., 17). He even asked Herbert Knight, one brother of the Knight Brothers law firm, to take out a patent for him since he did not have the necessary funds. Mr. Knight declined because that was not his standard business practice. Woods was thinking of innovative financing plans for his creative ideas, but these attempts usually did not prove successful.

Woods did not confine his inventions to electrical technology. On June 19, 1883, he filed a patent for a steam boiler furnace: it was for this device that he received his first patent (fig. 2.9).[21] Woods, of course, did not have the fifteen dollars for the application fee. Charles F. Hesser lent Woods a substantial portion of the money based on his optimism that the product would sell. Cincinnati's city government instituted a new ordinance that compelled owners of steam boiler furnaces to upgrade them to ones that would produce less smoke. Woods quickly realized that whoever produced a patented solution to this new technical problem could reap large benefits from the sale of the device. Such a success could provide him with the funds necessary to support his other endeavors and the additional income he needed to live.

Woods's invention was very similar to a reflux condenser, in which the steam and gases produced by the fire to heat the boiler are forced through a series of small openings by a partial vacuum created by spraying steam. The combustion gases combined with the steam and condensed when

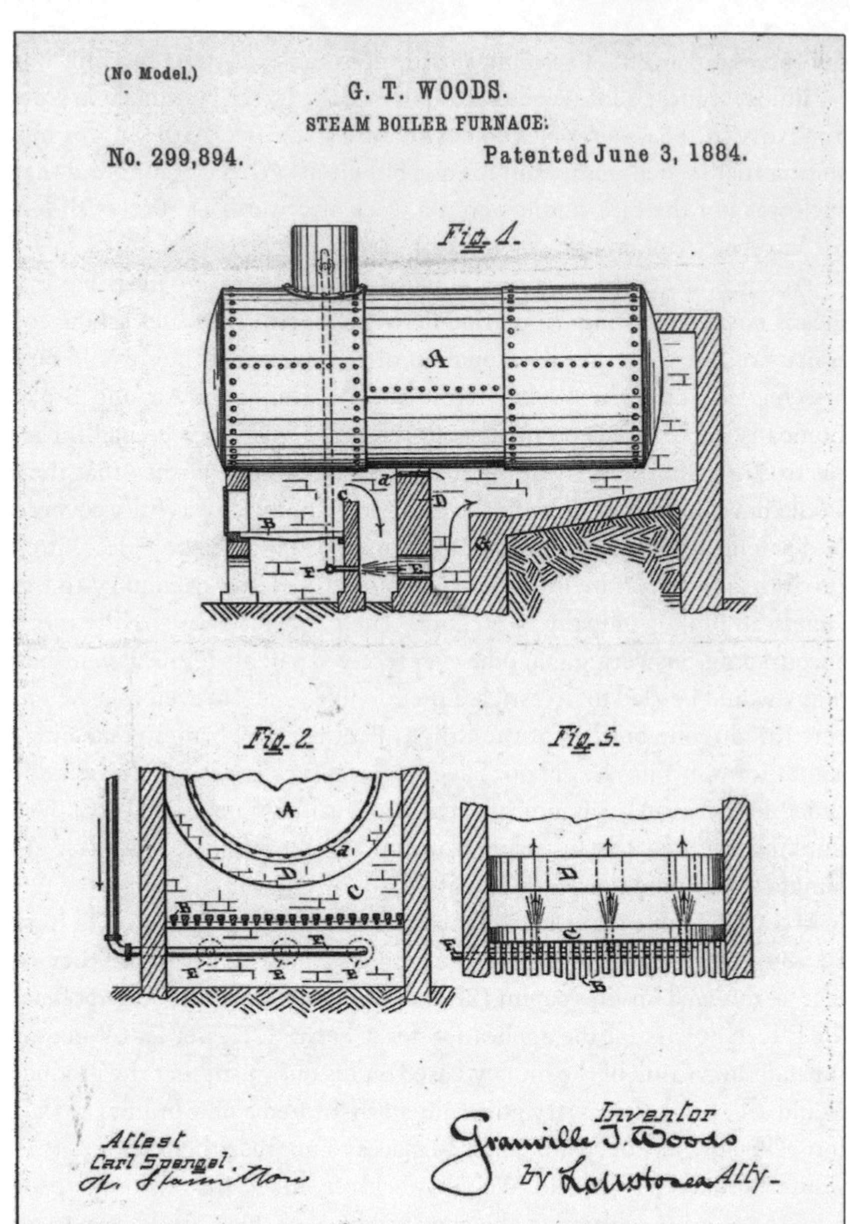

FIGURE 2.9. Steam boiler furnace, one of the patented devices that Woods referred to as "pot-boilers." June 1884. National Archives.

they came into contact with the cooler part of the boiler. The gases were then recycled back to the original point of the partial vacuum through a small vent, and the process started once again. This design does not seem to have significantly decreased the smoke production, it only postponed it. Potential buyers must have noticed this also, since Woods did not receive a single order for his furnace. When the patent was granted Woods did not have the money to pay the final fee, so he sold the patent rights to Ezra W. Vandusen for twenty dollars, which, coincidentally was the same amount as the final fee. Woods then took this money and reimbursed Hesser for the money he borrowed to file the patent application. Through much effort on his own, Woods had nothing to show for his inventive work except the most minimal financial gain (ibid., 84).

Woods also filed patent applications for two telephonic devices during 1883. One, a telephone transmitter, aimed "to produce more distinct and powerful effects than are attained by the undulatory currents ordinarily employed in telephonic apparatus, and capable of transmission to longer distances . . . by alternating the current, by means of varying pressure, upon two or more carbon or other semi-conductors."[22] The other, an apparatus that transmitted and received messages by electrical current, was a truly ingenious device. This apparatus which resembled a telegraphic key actually combined the function of a telegraph key with a telephone (figs. 2.10, 2.11). Woods felt that his device was superior to the standard telegraph key. A normal key worked as a sending and receiving device. This system of communication demanded that both the sender and receiver of the electrical impulses be quite skilled at both tasks. Woods also indicated that typical sounders did not respond well to weak signals like those used in telephony. He argued that his apparatus would overcome these problems. Since he designed the device to be used easily by an inexperienced person, he believed that it would have wide applicability. Moreover, he anticipated that it would be advantageous for telegraph stations to be able to communicate through Morse code and audible speech using one line. In addition to traditional uses, he saw his device being used as a teaching aid for Morse operators and by those who did not know Morse code. Woods explained that the device could toggle between telegraphic and telephonic operations easily. All the operator had to do was flip a switch to "cut the battery out of the main-line circuit and cut it into a local circuit, and then speak near the key." With that done "the sounder at the receiving station will cause the air to vibrate in unison with the electric pulsations that traverse the line wire" and transmit audible

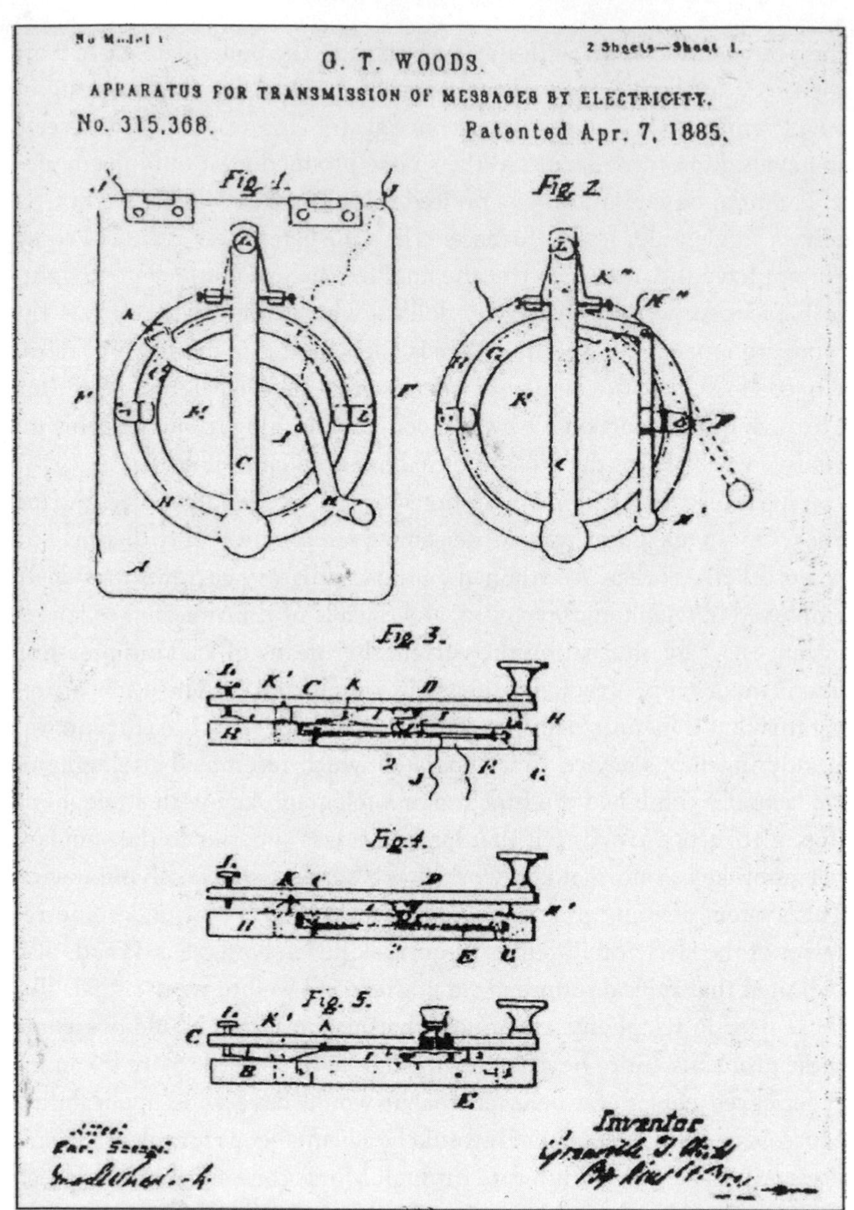

FIGURE 2.10. Woods's design for the telegraphony key, which could be used for telegraphic and telephonic communications. He invented this key specifically for his induction communication system. April 1885. National Archives.

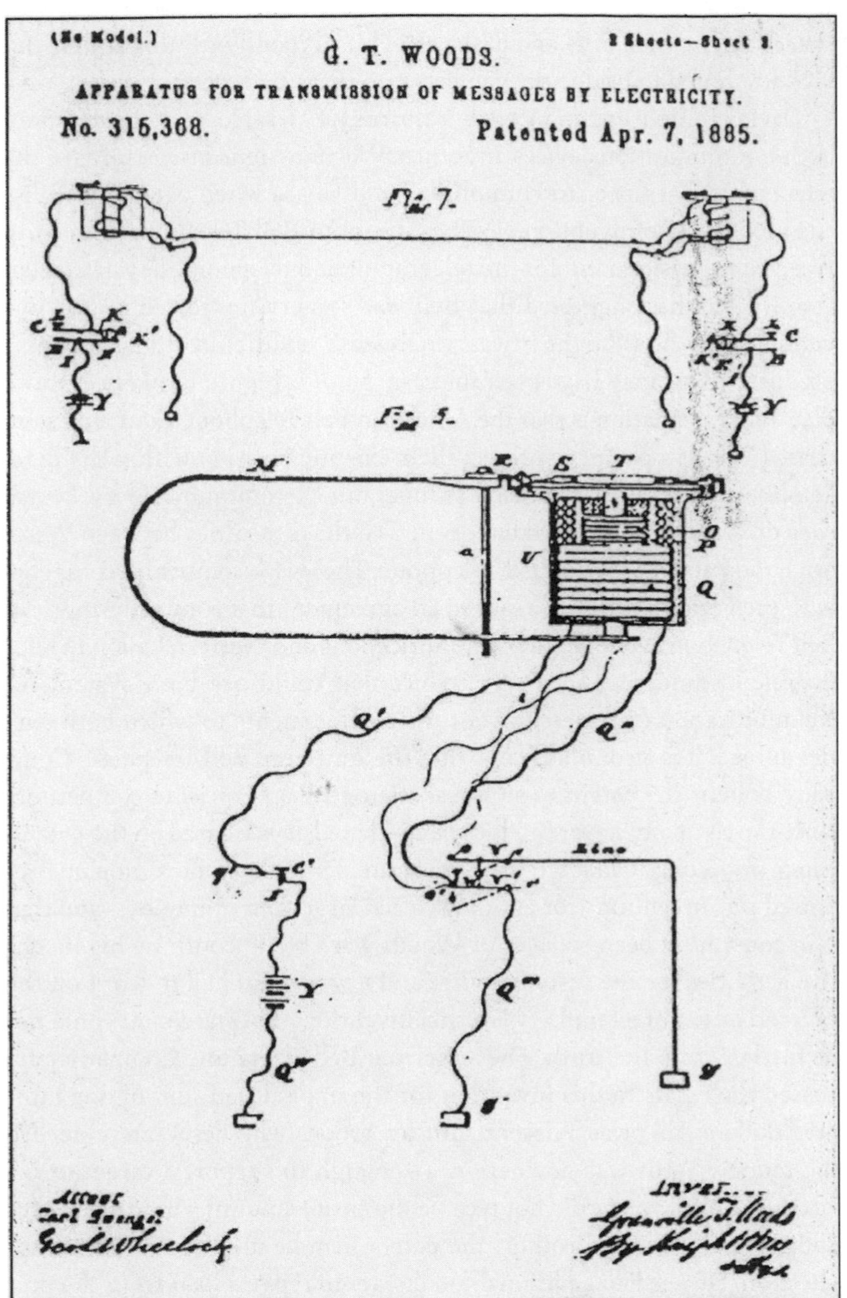

FIGURE 2.11. Circuitry for telegraphony system for communication between two stations. National Archives.

speech rather than dots and dashes.[23] Thus, Woods with this simple device attempted to bridge the gap between these two media.

David Humphreys and Woods's attorney, Lewis Hosea, helped finance both communication devices. In return, Woods assigned two-thirds of the telephone transmitter to Humphreys and Hosea when patents were issued for the two inventions.[24] The American Bell Telephone Company received the assignment for the telegraphic and telephonic key. Historian Aaron Klein has suggested that Bell was so very impressed by this invention, that he thought it was a necessary addition to the company's product.[25] This may have been the case, but it is highly unlikely. A more plausible explanation is that the American Bell Telephone Company purchased Woods's patent to protect their existing position within the marketplace. A device that enabled an operator to communicate by Morse code or verbal speech could have renewed the difficulties between Western Union and American Bell Telephone. These two companies competed with each other until they reached an agreement that confined American Bell Telephone to telephonic communications and Western Union to telegraphic communications.[26] A product that could use both systems of communication could circumvent the arrangements to which both parties agreed. It is also conceivable that the American Bell Telephone Company bought the patent to suppress its use by enterprising competitors since the company never produced a marketed device based on the patent. Klein also suggested that the American Bell Telephone Company acquired this invention "for an undisclosed large sum of money," and that "[i]t must have been sizable for Woods was able to continue his inventive activities for the rest of his life and never again had to work on the railroad or in a steel mill."[27] For this invention, that statement could not be further from the truth. The American Bell Telephone Company purchased the rights to this invention for the undisclosed sum of one hundred dollars. This was a decent sum for Woods who desperately needed the money. Yet it was nowhere near enough to support a career of inventing. Moreover, he did not receive the entire amount. Woods paid fifty dollars to the Knight Brothers the patent firm he used to submit his application. He used an additional ten dollars to repay a loan from the previous week given to him by Ed Gilliland. Coincidentally none of these expenditures included the money he probably owed to David Humphreys and Lewis Hosea (ibid., 84).

Woods planned for the all of these early patents, or what he called his "pot boilers," to provide him with immediate financial returns that he could use to proceed with patenting and developing his induction telegraphy system. Woods believed that this invention would change the mode and method of railway communication, but he also knew that to implement his system he would have to possess a great deal of money and have the support of influential individuals. Yet, as can be seen, the returns did not compensate Woods in the manner in which he hoped, nor did he make any substantial connections. Although these business ventures did not work out as planned, Woods did not get discouraged.

In February 1885, Woods finally had a breakthrough of sorts. In the February 21 issue of *Scientific American,* Woods ran across an article entitled "Recent Progress in Electricity—The Phelps System of Telegraphing from a Railway Train While in Motion."[28] The article described an induction telegraph system invented by Lucius J. Phelps which was extremely similar to his system. Phelps had developed his system much further than the model stage. The Phelps Induction Telegraph Company had been formed and they had exhibited the system on a twelve-mile section of the New York, New Haven & Hartford Railway. The article caught Woods off his guard, for he did not expect someone to have done enough work in this area to merit a review in *Scientific American.* It was at this moment that Woods awoke from a slumber. From that moment forward his inventive demeanor changed. For Woods, as an inventor who had not been particularly successful up to that point, this article provided timely motivation. If *Scientific American* was willing to publish an article on this device, he realized that his ideas obviously had to have some sort of relevance. But, the article did arouse his fears of not being able to capitalize on what he now considered to be his greatest invention to date. Woods, who had become at least somewhat familiar with the patent office, knew what this meant—he had to file for a patent quickly.

He believed that this technology was his personal domain, and was flabbergasted to see anyone working in his private area. He spent many years perfecting his system of inductive communication and was not ready to let it slip away to another inventor. Phelps, however, had a different vision for his device; it was a railway safety system. The existing system for signaling trains of oncoming traffic and other possible dangers relied on switchmen, signalmen, and station operators to alert locomotives of possible danger. No signalmen existed "who required neither sleep nor rest, who were not subject to fits and spasms, nor spirituous excesses, and above all, having eyes to pierce a fog."[29] Therefore, the reality of impending catastrophes could not be ignored. Woods did not go rushing to the patent office as one would expect. He poured more time and energy into the perfection of this invention because he had not reduced it to practice nearly to the level of the Phelps system.[30]

Woods also began to make contacts that were crucial in the future development of his induction telegraphy system. One such connection was with Donald McDougall, the Superintendent of the Cincinnati Medicated Mud Bath Company. He hired Woods in February 1885, as an engineer (ibid., 49). This was only a temporary position that Woods held until the middle part of that month. Woods spoke with McDougall about his ideas, his inventions, and probably the *Scientific American* article. This was in part to gain the confidence of McDougall, so that he could use the space and specific equipment in the possession of the Cincinnati Medicated Mud Bath Company. Soon Woods was performing experiments at the mud baths with the assistance of James Shane and John Oster, Jr. (ibid., 43–45).[31] The mud bath company owned a powerful Kidder battery which was of great use to Woods. The Kidder battery was necessary to test the strength of one of his first helixes. McDougall witnessed these experiments and was impressed that "at a distance of twelve feet we could hear the sound of the vibrator of the battery, and that was all . . . with the naked ear; but, by attaching a telephone receiver to this helix, we could hear it very distinctly, and much louder than with the naked ear" (ibid., 50). By March, Woods constructed another model which he tested thoroughly to prove that his system was a viable new product. Many "patients" of the Medicated Mud Bath Company viewed the device, minus the relay, in May and June (ibid., 13). Around this time Woods no longer needed the facilities of the Medicated Mud Bath Company because he made an important new contact, Dr. Lucius Robertson.

On March 23, 1885, Woods became acquainted with Dr. Robertson, a Cincinnati dentist. On March 25, Woods detailed the working of the helix, the many associated parts, and the flexibility of his system to Robertson. Woods explained that if one desired to suspend the helix from beneath the car, that the helix, housed within a box, needed to be within six or seven inches from the wires laid between the rails and above the railroad ties. If one affixed the helix to the roof of the railcar, the wires were to be at the same distance from the helix, but they would be suspended by poles above the railcar. One of the two wires coming from the helix would be attached to a device that would enable reception and transmission, while a railcar wheel grounded the other (ibid., 30, 31). Woods was proposing a substantial system. To fully implement his system, he would require a great deal of money, months of construction, and cooperation between cities and railways. It is clear that Wood now was thinking on a grand scale.

Robertson showed a great deal of interest in this idea, primarily from a financial standpoint. But, he did want to know if anyone had patented a similar idea, to which Woods provided a confident "no." It is unclear if Woods mentioned the work of Phelps. There are good reasons for him to have shared this information, and equally valid reasons for him to keep this fact to himself. The awareness of Phelps's work could have inspired Robertson to invest more money in order to reach the market faster, but most likely it would have scared him off. Regardless, Robertson and Woods entered into a business relationship. Roberston agreed to assist Woods in the cultivation and diffusion of his invention for a partial interest, which Woods accepted. Robertson's aid came in the form of financial support to build a new model, a place to display this model, and connections to his well-to-do friends. In June 1885, Woods perfected the relay at the Jones Brothers' office and by September Woods had built a fully communicating version of his model that was being shown at Robertson's office. In his office, the model rail car ran along a track "some ten or twelve feet in length, with batteries upon the car, with a wire running from the track connecting with the wire on the track, some fifteen or twenty feet from this track, which represented a station. Sounds were transmitted from this station to this moving car or model . . . that could be heard distinctly through a telephone at the ear, or upon the telegraph instrument upon the car." Robertson aggressively promoted this device during its three month stay at his office. In September, the *Cincinnati Commercial* published an article on the device, many telegraph operators tested the system, and Robertson was even able to entice "the chief experts from the Western Union Telegraph office" to evaluate the system (ibid., 12, 13, 14, 30, 31, 32).

Before Robertson and Woods became "partners" Woods had filed for a patent on his system on May 21, 1885.[32] McDougall advanced Woods the fifteen dollar fee to initiate an application for his "Induction Telegraph System" (ibid., 85). This patent application proceeded along normally for a complex patent, in that the Patent Office rejected it on both July 3, and October 3, 1885. It was not uncommon for the Patent Office to reject patent applications whose claim—or that which a patentee argues is new, novel, and innovative about their invention—were too broad and infringed on other patented inventions. While Woods and his patent attorney continued to fine tune the patent application's specifications, the imminent interference between Phelps—who filed for a patent on February 20, 1885—and Woods materialized on March 9, 1886.[33]

A patent interference occurred when two or more patentees simultaneously applied for patents on closely related ideas. As long the Patent Office did not grant a patent before the other parties applied for a patent, the applications would be in interference with each other. At that moment, the Patent Office stopped reviewing the patent applications and began a process of investigation. If one party did not concede, a court case before the examiner of interferences would begin. The interference that involved Woods, like all interferences, centered around the establishment of who conceived of this idea first. There was a great deal at stake; the person that could prove that they had the idea first—no matter how long each person had worked on the idea—would be able to continue through the patent process and hopefully receive a patent.

On this account, Woods had the upper hand. Woods provided evidence and witnesses to substantiate that he first conceptualized his system in February 1881. Phelps, on the other hand, could only confirm that he began working on inductive communication in October 1884. This did not deter Phelps's efforts to win. Phelps and his attorney, William Baldwin, attempted to prove that Woods did not merit a victory in the interference case because he did not show proper diligence in following his idea through to the state of an invention. They contended that Woods's work, prior to his viewing the story of Phelps's invention in *Scientific American,* could only be considered "abandoned experiments." They supplied as additional evidence three patents—#299,894, #308,817, and #315,368—that Woods received during the interim to illustrate that he had indeed abandoned induction telegraphy. They argued that if he was so interested in this idea, why had he spent his time patenting other inventions? To these challenges Woods responded that a severe case of smallpox disabled him for a considerable amount of time, which strapped his financial resources. Since he was in such financial duress, he had to do whatever possible to make ends meet. This was his reason for the other patents, none of which he financed himself. Woods argued that the reason it took him so long to get back to his induction telegraphy system was primarily because he could not find anyone interested in the idea until early in 1885, which coincidentally corresponded to release of the *Scientific American* article. Phelps's defense was not effective and the examiner of interferences decided the case in Woods's favor on October 7,

1886.[34] Phelps appealed unsuccessfully. The second decision handed down on February 9, 1887, was the same as before. The Examiner-in-Chief again concluded "that Woods did all which could be expected of him under the circumstances."[35] After much legal effort, Woods received a patent for this device on November 29, 1887. From this point forward, interference cases were to become a regular part of his life. In fact, of the forty-five American patents granted to Woods, no less than 17 were involved in interference cases.

Woods's efforts were being noticed by the general public before the end of the interference case. In fact, the January 14, 1886, issue of the *Catholic Tribune* enthusiastically commented that he was "the greatest inventor in the history of his race, and equal, if not superior to any inventor in the country . . . He had excelled in every possible way in all of his inventions. He is master of the situation, and his name will be handed down to coming generations as one of the greatest inventors of his time. He has not only elevated himself to the highest position among inventors, but he has shown beyond doubt the possibility of a colored man inventing as well as one of any other race."[36] The accolades did not stop there. They culminated in Woods being dubbed "the greatest electrician in the world" by the *American Catholic Tribune* in the spring of 1887.[37] This was extremely high praise for a black man with only a few patents to his name.

John A. Gano and Ralph Peters, two Cincinnati businessmen, noticed Woods, and more importantly Woods's economic potential, and were instrumental in founding the Woods Electric Company in Kentucky in June 1886.[38] Ralph Peters, the Superintendent of the Big Four Railroad, was not as well know as Gano. John A. Gano was a scion of the cultured community of Cincinnati.[39] He was extremely well connected within the city's financial community. He was the financial editor for the *Cincinnati Commercial*, secretary and president of the Chamber of Commerce, and held a financial interest in most of the successful economic enterprises in the area.[40] With an influential man like Gano at the helm, one would have expected success from the organization. However, the exact opposite was the case. Woods wanted to build a thriving electrical company that would begin with inventions. Conversely, Gano's plan was to put Woods's electrical patents on the market. He was organizing a patent holding company that would profit exclusively by selling the patent rights to the inventions that emanated from Woods's creativity.[41] In fact, shortly after Woods signed a working agreement with the Woods Electric Company, he desperately tried to extract himself from this contract and the shortsightedness of the company that held his name. He had relinquished his inventive life for the next few years. Woods, who was now branching out into electric railway propulsion, felt that they did not support him in his effort to patent his inventions in the way that he deserved (Testimony in Chief on Behalf of Woods, Interference cases #18,207 & #18,210, 45). In interference testimony, Woods explained how the company dealt with one of his electric railway inventions.

> They expected other people to come into the company and furnish the money to promote the invention. This money which they expected to obtain from other parties was to be for the sale of stock; I remember very distinctly that I went to Mr. George Kerper . . . the president of the Walnut Hill Railway System in Cincinnati. There was no electric railway in the West at that time, except the one that had been invented and used by Professor Sidney Short. The proposition which I made to Mr. Kerper was . . . as follows. He was to allow the Woods Electric Company the use of his road in Walnut Hill for experimental purposes . . . He was to furnish a car and power at the power house, while the Woods Electric Company [was] to furnish all the other matter which was to enter into the construction and use of the system. Mr. Kerper agreed to that, but when I made the report to the Company, John A. Gano . . . said as follows: "If he is willing to do that much, he is willing to do more. Now we have got a good basket of eggs, and people will run after us." But the people didn't run. (Ibid., 47)

As if the company's efforts to hold out to the highest bidder were not detrimental enough, the company did not uphold its end of Woods's contract. The contract he signed indicated that he was to receive a payment of fifty dollars per month for his services and an unspecified percentage of the company's stock. After eight months his salary was only sporadically paid, and the stock had yet to be issued (ibid., 59). Woods was having another financial crisis because the Woods Electric Company did not pay his salary. He tried to make ends meet by opening a small machinery repair shop in Cincinnati, but this venture only provided the most modest financial returns (ibid., 49). Meanwhile, Woods continued to construct models of his new railway ideas. The company's officials did not show a great deal of interest in these ideas, usually deeming them unworthy of their support. When one of the few railway devices on which the company granted Woods the permission to file for a patent interfered with a similar invention of two men named McElroy and Nicholson in

March 1886, the company decided it was not in their best interest to pursue the case on Woods's behalf (ibid., 7–8, 51). The financial backers of the company were looking for quick, easy, and substantial monetary gains. Woods built another model of a new method of railway propulsion in February 1887. Woods enticed some of the investors to come and personally inspect the model in an effort to create a support base within the company. But for the most part the investors agreed with Gano and Peters and had no interest in funding anything that they perceived to be risky. By mid 1887, Woods became extremely reluctant to discuss any of his new ideas with anyone associated with the company. He felt no compulsion to continue "forcing invention to their notice" (ibid., 58).

Woods now began hunting for a way to extricate himself from the contract he signed with the Woods Electric Company. He felt that since the company's officials were "neither electricians nor patent experts," they knew nothing "about what was required in a matter of this kind" (ibid., 62). Leaving the company would have been easy, but leaving the company with his patents was an entirely different matter. By 1890 all parties were beginning to get rather tense, as the company was having little success in selling Woods's inventions. In light of their lack of success, the Woods Electric Company allocated a small sum of money for Woods to travel to New York City in an effort to locate potential buyers. Woods departed in April 1890, and stayed for ten weeks (ibid., 96, 97). The result was far from what Peters and Gano anticipated. Of this trip, Peters wrote: "we made an assessment to raise funds to send him to New York for the purpose of introducing some of his inventions, but instead of doing this, he opened up an office and attempted to dispose of his patents" (ibid., 25). Gano mirrored Peters' animosity when he wrote: "[w]e found him at last in the act of perpetrating a gross fraud . . . I have reason to believe that with the connivance of a patent shark or pirate, he has perpetrated . . . frauds on our rights . . . He ought to be in the Pentitentiary [sic] and if he is still attempting to swindle people I trust he will get there" (ibid., 26).

Woods had a decidedly different account of his travels to New York City. He maintained that the Woods Electric Company only allotted him fifty dollars for his trip, of which his rail fare devoured twenty dollars. With only thirty dollars remaining for his ten week stay in New York, he soon ran short of cash; and when he requested more funds from the company, it refused. To alleviate his financial difficulties, Woods "hypothecated two of the inventions, one with Knight Bros. and the other with Mr. E. P. Thompson, a well-known patent attorney" (ibid., 30). From these individuals, he was able to pay his expenses and return to Cincinnati. Thus,

Woods argued that nothing happened that could be considered fraud. But upon his return, his relationship with the company was quite strained and was to get even worse. The fact that two Woods Electric Companies existed caused these complications to escalate to the breaking point.

Granville Woods had participated in the creation of two Woods Electric Companies, one in Kentucky and the other in Ohio. Woods had organized the Ohio company, whose president was John D. Gardella, prior to the formation of the Kentucky company, of which John Gano was president. But since Woods, Gano, Peters, and their attorneys were from Cincinnati, the United States Patent Office mistakenly assigned Woods's patents to the Woods Electric Company of Ohio. When Woods returned from New York in June 1890, he attempted to rectify the misunderstanding. He approached John D. Gardella to discuss his predicament on May 8. A Judge Hagans facilitated a solution to the assignment issue on June 27. He believed that the entire problem would be most easily handled if the Ohio company would reassign the patents to Woods, who would then transfer the assignments to the Woods company in Kentucky. This was all good in theory, but Woods did not notify Gano or Peters about the mix-up or how he intended to remedy the situation. When they received word of Woods's plan they proceeded to call Woods a fraud and initiate a legal complaint against him because the believe that he was stealing their intellectual property. Woods stated that Gano and Peters blew the entire situation out of proportion because he was not intending to do anything illegal. However, I am not so sure about that claim. Woods was far from pleased with the support he received from the Woods Electric Company, plus he spent ten weeks in New York City surveying the prospects for his ideas; when he received the rights and titles to several of his inventions, it most certainly crossed his mind to escape with his patents. The allegations forced Woods to procure the services of an attorney to fend off their attacks. From the reaction of Gano and Peters one can assume Woods was hatching some sort of plan with the Woods Electric Company of Ohio. Gano and Peters would not have reacted so antagonistically if they did not assume that this company was set-up to swindle them out of the money they put up for the development and patenting of Woods's inventive idea. Yet, Woods was a very shrewd character and even though this may have not necessarily been the case, a move such as the one Gano and Peters believed Woods was pulling, definitely was not beyond him.

In July 1890, Woods easily obtained a release from his contract with the Woods Electric Company of Kentucky. The two parties finally settled this ordeal on September 24, 1890, when Woods assigned the inventive rights and titles of the patents to the Woods Electric Company of Kentucky.[42] With nothing left in Ohio and his financial ties severely damaged, Woods departed for New York City on August 4, 1890 (ibid., 95, 97, 181).

New York City and Hustling Inventions

In New York, Woods had the freedom to apply for patents on his new inventions that the Woods Electric Company would not support. But once again he was without the financial resources to file patent applications. Times were extremely hard when he first arrived in New York City. In addition to supporting himself, he had the further burden of providing for his now ailing sister, Henrietta Wilborn, who still lived in Ohio (Testimony in Chief on Behalf of Woods, Interference cases #18,207 & #18,210, 115–16). His kindness aggravated his financial woes. Woods did whatever work he could find to make money, but the longest job he held was for three months as a porter on the Manhattan Elevated Railway, which paid only $1.20 a day (ibid., 50, 120). As soon as he arrived in New York City, Woods began to search for any form of aid to help him promote his railway inventions, but after a year, he had not discovered any support, whether because of racial discrimination or because his ideas were not in vogue or because he lacked business connections. In August 1891, in an effort to get his inventing career back on track, Woods cut out an intriguing advertisement for the American Patent Agency. This patent soliciting firm's ad claimed that "Invention promoted, and Companies Formed for Inventors" were its specialties (ibid., 63). Woods carried around the newspaper clipping for several days before he made his way to the World Building office of the American Patent Agency, around August 10. On that day, Woods met James S. Zerbe, the manager of the American Patent Agency. Little did he suspect that this encounter would begin a ten-year personal and intellectual property battle between the two (ibid., 108–11).[43]

Woods, the hopeful inventor, brought many sketches, including his electric railway inventions, an electric meter, and several electric lighting systems (ibid., 65). Zerbe was particularly impressed with a drawing illustrating a system "in which a divided or sectional conductor was employed and in which magnets were used to automatically energize the particular divided section" (Testimony on Behalf of Enholm, Interference case #15,666, 7). He suggested that he might be able to find someone interested in Woods's inventions and asked if he could keep one of the railway sketches for a short period and if Woods would return soon to talk further. Woods was very hesitant about leaving his drawing, but since this meeting was the first significant interest in months he agreed.

Woods returned within the week. Zerbe told him that he had found an individual, Calvin Bowen, a local preacher apparently with a great deal of money and influence who appeared very interested in what Woods had to offer in the line of electric railways. After discussing the prospects for Woods's inventions, Zerbe, speaking for both himself and Bowen, struck a deal to develop a simple electric railway based on a drawing Woods made in February 1887 (Woods' Testimony in Surrebuttal, Interference cases #18,207 & #18,210, 115–16). Zerbe would provide the legal expertise, Bowen the necessary capital, and Woods the technical skills. This partnership soon expanded to five with the addition of Henry Keim and Zerbe's son Arthur. On August 21, the five parties formally organized into the American Engineering Company. The partnership granted Woods 25 percent interest, the Zerbes a 25 percent share, Bowen 50 percent, and Keim received 10 shares—five from the Zerbes and five from Bowen (ibid. 130, 190). Woods was under the impression that the company only had the right to the one early railway invention and any other inventions outside of that specific railway device were his individual property. Zerbe and Bowen planned otherwise, however.

The company and a rudimentary workshop, which also doubled as a display room for prospective clients and investors, were set up in an office adjacent to the American Patent Agency. Woods felt he had finally become associated with men who could see the value of his work. When they presented him with business cards and letter head, he also believed they had the monetary wherewithal to follow through. Zerbe quickly began to write patent specifications for an application on a drawing Woods made on May 11, which was a slight improvement over the drawing of February 1887 (ibid., 36) and worked very hard to get this patented as quickly as possible. The company also allocated Woods $75 to build a model that would illustrate his system to potential investors.

Woods's railway invention was novel enough to receive a patent, but there were a few problems that needed to be addressed before it could supplant other electric railway systems, namely, that a railcar could not back up under power because he designed his system to move in only one direction. For the solution to this problem, Woods called on Oscar Enholm for help. One September night in 1890, after discussing some of their latest electric railway ideas, Enholm and Woods made a verbal agreement that if either one could find the necessary financial support, they would pool their inventive efforts to produce a marketable electric railway system. Not surprisingly, in September 1891, the American Engineering Company hired Enholm to assist Woods in testing the model and to assist in further development. Woods had completed the model by the time Enholm came on board; yet it shocked Enholm to see that the car moved in two directions and that the magnets that connected the sectional conductors were of his design (ibid., 35). When he brought this to Woods's attention, Woods, obviously somewhat embarrassed, explained what happened in the weeks before Enholm started working for the American Engineering Company.

Woods's design buried the magnets that controlled the sectional conductors in the road bed. Zerbe suggested that if there was any way to make the magnets more accessible, specifically in case of failure, the system would be even more marketable. Woods immediately thought of Enholm's work which placed the magnets above the road bed and arranged them in independent circuits. Woods spoke with Zerbe about how an invention by a friend named Enholm could provide a solution to their technical problem. Zerbe insisted that this information be used. Woods said that he felt uncomfortable about this line of action because he believed it was improper to discuss and use an unpatented invention of another man, let alone a friend. In response, Zerbe stated that the contract of August 21 bound the American Engineering Company to compensate Woods fully for any ideas he used and that consideration would include all outside settlements he would need to make with any other party. Moreover, Woods could validate this line of action because of the agreement that he and Enholm had made in the previous year (ibid., 226–28). The explanation satisfied Enholm; he trusted Woods. Woods assured Enholm that the electric railway patent filed in his name on August 31, 1891, would not claim Enholm's method of grouping magnets and that the company would support him in the filing of a separate patent application.

Everything appeared to be in order, until a day in mid October, when Enholm overheard Zerbe discussing the Woods patent on the telephone. As Zerbe read the claims to the caller, Enholm realized that his ideas had made their way into Woods's patent application. Enholm immediately went to Woods and confronted him with this information. Woods was as stunned as Enholm (Testimony on Behalf of Enholm, Interference case #15,666, 12–13).

At this juncture, Woods also began to realize something was amiss. Before the American Engineering Company filed for the patent, Zerbe submitted the specifications, of which Enholm had overheard, to Woods for review. Woods revised them because they were too broad and eliminated the intellectual property of Enholm. He returned the amended specifications to Zerbe, who appeared to have no problem with these changes. When Zerbe showed him a copy of the reedited claims, Woods did not let the matter enter his mind again. In this exchange, Woods and Enholm made one error; they gave affidavits stating that Woods invented the entire electric railway system without seeing the actual specifications submitted to the Patent Office (Woods' Testimony in Surrebuttal, Interference cases #18,207 & #18,210, 243). Zerbe took advantage of this mistake and filed a patent application with the wrong set of claims and used their affidavits to confirm that Woods invented the entire system (Testimony on Behalf of Enholm, Interference case #15,666, 19). Zerbe was in such a hurry to have this invention move through the Patent Office, that he paid an examiner a $150 bribe (Woods' Testimony in Surrebuttal, Interference cases #18,207 & #18,210, 126).

This incident confirmed Woods's growing suspicions; yet he continued to follow Zerbe and Bowen's instructions, hoping that once the American Engineering Company sold his invention, he would collect his portion of the profits and never have to do business with them again. Enholm now realized that if he were to have a chance to reap any benefit from his invention, he should patent quickly. On November 3, Enholm filed a patent application for his invention.[44]

During this time Woods started pulling together some of his previous work, along with some new ideas, to perfect a more sophisticated electric railway system—one that traveled in both directions and did not infringe upon the invention of Enholm. This latest invention became known as the multiple distribution station system. What made this system novel was that the working conductors were cut into circuit only when the car passed over a section, thus only energizing the specific section underneath the car—a system that was safer and more reliable than other systems. Woods based the model he began building for the American Engineering Company on the slightly improved sketch of the first drawing inspected by Zerbe in August. But, partially through Zerbe's prodding and his efforts to create "a system which . . . would give the best satisfaction to the largest number of people," the model was reconfigured to exemplify Woods's most current railway contrivance (ibid., 104). Once Zerbe viewed this set-up, he realized that this was the invention that he wanted to acquire. He repeatedly asked Woods for drawings, or any information relating to the most recent system. Woods insisted that he would distribute all the pertinent information to everyone concerned in due time. In reality, Woods, who was growing increasingly unsure of his partners, planned to file a patent application of his own and did not intend to assign any portion of his creation to the American Engineering Company until they proved their trustworthiness.

Unknown to Woods, the American Engineering Company had already begun to lay the foundation to acquire his inventions and push him out of the company. A few weeks after the company formed—when they planned to issue stock—Zerbe and Bowen called a meeting. They explained to Woods that they had not filed the previous assignment, which granted each member a percentage of his invention. They informed Woods that it would be better for all concerned if he reassigned the entire right, title, and interest of his electric railway system to the American Engineering Company. The reason given for this unexpected change was that the new assignment made "the stock of the company fully paid and nonassessable" (ibid., 111).

There was one catch, however: Woods no longer had the right to assign the entire invention to the American Engineering Company. He had assigned 1/19 interest to L. A. Mack, his landlady. Since Woods was still having financial problems, partially because the American Engineering Company paid him only occasionally, he bartered a 1/19 interest in his invention for his room, board, and a small loan. This assignment infuriated Zerbe and Bowen, who demanded that Woods go directly to Mrs. Mack and retrieve the missing interest. Zerbe communicated to Woods that the company was willing to pay Mrs. Mack $200 for her interest in the invention—which Bowen would supply as soon as Woods regained this stray interest. Woods did recoup the interest from Mrs. Mack, but Bowen did not deliver the promised funds (ibid., 122–23).

Zerbe and Bowen wanted the invention unconditionally assigned to the American Engineering Company because it was an integral step in the process of procuring Woods's invention. Unknown to Woods when he reassigned his invention to the American Engineering Company, the contract of August 21, which was to be the basis for the formation of the company, had not been "accepted." The American Engineering Company was in the process of accepting a new contract written by Zerbe. Zerbe structured this revised contract so that the resulting company would only be formed by himself and Bowen. Woods was to be a contracted inventor only and not a legal founder of the American Engineering Company. Additional changes in the contract were undertaken that would enable the American Engineering Company to gain control of all of Woods's inventions. No longer would the contract apply to a specific invention; it would, in fact, obligate Woods to turn over to the American Engineering Company any invention made or developed while he was employed by the company.[45] All of these maneuvers were an effort to gain control of Woods's most recent railway invention.

Various acquaintances began to tell Woods about Zerbe's reputation, warning him that if he were not careful he might regret it (ibid., 199). Unfortunately, Woods was no match for Zerbe at that point in his career. Woods summed up his experiences during this time of his life while testifying in a later interference case when he remarked, "the matter was juggled along, but the company never accepted the contract between Zerbe, Bowen, and myself, neither would the company enter into a new contract with me. In other words, as Zerbe stated, it was a clean steal of the whole system" (ibid., 88, 179).

Woods knew what type of men he was dealing with by late September, but at that point he had too much at stake to leave. One should not assume, however, that Woods was a fair-minded independent inventor who was doing no surreptitious plotting of his own. In fact, he intended to use the American Engineering Company's resources to build a model, secure financial supporters, and then leave the company behind. Sometime before August 6, 1891, Woods began secretly filing a patent application for his latest electric railway system. This invention was exemplified in the model he constructed for display in the office of the American Engineering Company. According to the Patent Office assignment index, Woods assigned this invention, as well as others, to James E. Chandler on August 6, and not to himself or the American Engineering Company.[46] These assignments make sense when it is understood that Chandler helped organize the Universal Electric Company—the company for which Woods worked after he ended his relationship with the American Engineering Company. Therefore, Woods was already scheming to start a new business relationship while still employed by the American Engineering Company.

Woods filed this application on October 14, 1891.[47] He executed the drawings himself in an effort to keep the application away from his American Engineering Company "partners." Since Woods was not a draftsman and did not possess the proper tools for drafting, the drawings he submitted were inadequate (ibid., 147). The unacceptable drawings were returned to him on Friday, October 16. After spending most of Friday getting the drawings into shape, Woods put them in a mailing tube, resealed it, and addressed it to his patent attorneys, Baldwin, Davidson & Wight. On Saturday, Woods came into the American Engineering Company office to show the model to prospective investors. He brought with him the drawings sealed in their tube. During the time he was explaining the working of the model, however, Zerbe and his son Arthur came into the office and noticed the mysterious tube on Arthur's desk. Not having any idea what the tube contained, the senior Zerbe opened it and found four sheets of the drawings for the invention that he had been pressing Woods to assign to the company. The Zerbes quickly scurried away with the drawings and copied them. That evening Bowen, Diebold, and Keim met at Zerbe's house to certify the tracings (ibid., 19–21, 302).

When Woods realized his drawings were missing, he had a fairly good idea of who had them.[48] Zerbe returned the drawings on Sunday when Woods was not in the office and according to Woods, this is what took place Monday morning when Zerbe arrived:

> He came into the office and went directly to his desk, and I followed him in there. I accused him of taking the drawings. He at once admitted the theft and stated that he was much obliged to me for leaving the drawings where he could take them and copy them. Thereupon I called him a thief and some other names and told him he was unworthy of the name man. He said nothing until I started out of the room and then he struck me [in the] back of the head. Instantly I responded. When Zerbe fell I ran around the table, and just as he was getting up, his son Arthur, who at that time was quite large for his age, ran in and leaped on my back, lapped his arms around my neck and used every effort to choke me. The row made so much noise at this stage that one of the janitors in the building ran in from the hall and separated us. There was no more conversation between us at that time . . . Zerbe only made [one] remark as follows "I will get even with you yet."[49]

That moment terminated Woods's association with the American Engineering Company, although he did return Monday evening and hastily remove the parts of the model that he paid for out of his own pocket. On Tuesday the model did not work and Enholm, who had not resigned, had to check each and every connection on the model. Woods commented, somewhat insincerely, that since he was in a rush to leave, he "may have made a mistake in reconnecting the wires."[50] Not surprisingly, shortly thereafter, the American Engineering Company fired Enholm.

Zerbe later charged that Woods had been deceitful by not handing over the inventive work that was the rightful property of the American Engineering Company. Woods, on the other hand, did not feel that the American Engineering Company held any right to this railway device because he invented many of the system's elements before he became associated with the company. In addition, based on the contract of August 21, the company had a legal claim only to the one simple railway invention based on the drawing of February 1887 (ibid., 175). Woods was now in a truly unpleasant situation. He left the company with only a small amount of stock and very little money; more important, he knew the situation with his latest railway invention was going to become quite complicated since Zerbe copied his drawings. He had to figure out a way in which to verify that his most advanced railway invention was not the property of the American Engineering Company. His first step was to attempt to sell his invention or organize a new company as quickly as possible so as not to lose any development time. In order to do this, he placed an advertisement in the *Street Railways News,* indicating that he "had certain territory for sale and referred to a sectional railway conductor system" (ibid., 77).

Woods seems to have received only one significant response to his advertisement. Two men by the names of Tryon and Chappell arranged to meet with Woods about the prospect of helping him further develop his inventions. Woods had met Tryon and Chappell previously at the offices of the American Engineering Company; they were two of the many potential investors that Zerbe brought by to examine Woods's model. Woods was extremely skeptical of two men who had obvious connections to Zerbe, but he needed the money to pay his debts and to initiate patent applications on his other inventions. Tryon and Chappell made Woods more uncomfortable when they demanded that if they were to reach an agreement Woods would have to transfer all of his American Engineering Company stock to them as a security deposit ensuring that he would carry out his portion of their arrangement. But when Tryon and Chappell informed Woods that they intended to purchase the invention he assigned to American Engineering Company and establish an enterprise of which he was to be an integral member, Woods disregarded his reservations. He signed a contract on October 29, 1891, then a revised version on November 4, formally uniting his efforts with Tryon and Chappell. In this contract, Woods granted them power of attorney to recover his property legally from the American Engineering Company. Unfortunately for Woods, his fiscal need allied with impatience led him into a trap carefully designed by Zerbe. Zerbe had already stolen Woods's drawings, but these sketches were not of much value to the American Engineering Company without the legal title to the invention. This is where Chappell and Tryon entered into Zerbe's plan. Shortly after Woods, Tryon, and Chappell signed the second contract, Tryon and Chappell sold everything acquired from Woods to Zerbe and the American Engineering Company. If this was not deceptive enough, Tryon and Chappell—but in reality Zerbe—paid Woods a salary of twenty dollars per week explicitly to keep him in the dark about their actions. Tryon and Chappell did quite well for themselves, receiving five thousand dollars for their effort.[51]

As these deceitful maneuvers took place, Enholm's work surfaced and created problems for the American Engineering Company. On October 20, 1891, the United States Patent Office approved the patenting of the only invention that Woods assigned to the American Engineering Company, the electric railway system that illegally incorporated Enholm's inventive work. But the Patent Office withdrew that patent because Enholm's patent application of November 3 interfered with the Woods patent containing the inventive ideas that Zerbe co-opted from Enholm. In the ensuing interference case the American Engineering Company put up a meager effort to win the patent suit. The company only submitted a lengthy brief without testimony, since it did not have Woods to testify on its behalf. Woods testified for Enholm, against the American Engineering Company and the patent in his name, stating that he did not invent certain devices claimed in the patent that was granted to the American Engineering Company. With such convincing testimony from Woods, the examiner of interferences decided the case in Enholm's favor on June 21, 1893.[52] The American Engineering Company did not take a financial loss as a result of the decision. Woods testified that the American Engineering Company was still able to make a profit of about $100,000 from his work (ibid., 196).

Early in 1892, Woods slowly began to discover that Tryon, Chappell, and Zerbe cheated him when he began to see newspaper advertisements placed by the American Engineering Company describing an experimental line built and eventually tested on the Coney Island Railroad, more commonly known as General Slocum's Road, that was incredibly similar to the drawings Zerbe had stolen (ibid., 139, 141). This project developed after Woods resigned from the company, but he was probably cognizant of this undertaking since Zerbe testified that the American Engineering Company began work on the project in October (ibid., 140).

The company initially planned to construct a test system from Brighton House to West Brighton on the King County Elevated Railroad on Coney Island because this line closed during the winter. But since the line closed in the winter, electric power was not available. Coincidentally, the Brooklyn & Coney Island Road, which carried passengers during the winter, ran underneath the King County Elevated. In order to get power, Zerbe had to negotiate with General Slocum, the president of the Brooklyn & Coney Island Road. General Slocum agreed to provide the American Engineering Company with power, as long as the test track was built on a section of the Brooklyn & Coney Island Road instead of the King County Elevated. The two parties signed this agreement in early December 1891 (ibid., 135). At the same time the American Engineering Company hired Joseph Sachs as a replacement for Woods (ibid., 307). Sachs, with youthful naïveté and exuberance in conjunction with his opportunism, was a perfect choice for Zerbe. Woods's ideas and drawings were not much use to Zerbe without a patent. Since it was obvious that Zerbe did not invent the elements of Woods's railway system, he needed someone to pretend that he had conceived these ideas and would assign the subsequent patents to the American Engineering Company. Sachs gladly filled that role (ibid., 313–19, and 114–15). Together Zerbe and Sachs filed for several patents relating to the Coney Island system (ibid., 138, 186–89). The construction began in January; the system was successfully tested on February 12, 1892, a date early enough for the system to be exhibited in March and April before the heavy summer traffic began (ibid., 249 and 135). Everything proceeded as scheduled until Woods disrupted their plan.[53]

But Woods was not inactive after he ended his relationship with the American Engineering Company. In early 1892, Woods, or more likely James Chandler, contacted Edison General Electric about purchasing or helping to promote the electric railway device, patent serial #410,129 for which Zerbe had pilfered the drawings.[54] On January 28, 1892, Arthur Kennelly, a consulting electrician and a well-known expert on electrical power systems, wrote to F. W. Hastings, Edison General Electric's treasurer, about the Woods inventions.[55] Kennelly's first impression was not very positive. Having only read a description of the system, without "drawings and specification," Kennelly concluded that Woods's inventions did "not . . . embody any novel principles . . . they are only applications of principles already in use. My opinion would be that these alleged inventions have little if any value."[56] Edison General Electric must have been somewhat intrigued or was at least investigating every potential option thoroughly because Kennelly was sent to meet with Woods and personally evaluate his inventions. Woods showed Kennelly three systems of electric railway propulsion, but pushed his sectional electric conductor system. Kennelly judged that the maintenance of the system, since it was quite complex and consisted of several potentially failing parts, would outweigh the benefit of significantly diminishing the electrical leakage over standard electric railways in use. Kennelly did not, however, completely write off Woods's inventions. He alluded to the fact that if testing and experimentation proved satisfactory the invention might hold promise.[57] Woods even enlisted the help of Tryon, who mailed additional supporting evidence to Edison General Electric for Kennelly to evaluate. Once again Kennelly's response mirrored that of his previous letter. "[T]he system could probably be made operative, but the expense and difficulty that would be met with are I think serious objections. It is true that these objections might be overcome by time and skill, but the systems should be successfully . . . [tested] for several weeks before they could be depended upon."[58]

Woods appears to have been somewhat optimistic about the evaluations Kennelly provided, and they directly influenced his attack on Zerbe. Initially, Woods seemed to have no interest in the work Zerbe had undertaken. But when Woods realized that Zerbe had, in a sense, reduced his invention to practice on a large scale, he hoped to swoop in and use the work of the American Engineering Company to prove the viability of his system. In effect, intentionally or unintentionally, he had induced Zerbe to build a testable exemplification of his system. Woods now had a clear picture of what was at stake, and so he proceeded to reengage the battle with Zerbe.

Woods struck out at the American Engineering Company and Zerbe by placing the following "warning" in the February 2, 1892, edition of the *Street Railway News:* "It has come to my knowledge that the American Engineering Company of New York City, is offering for sale an electric street railway system which is covered by patents, owned and controlled by the undersigned, who hereby cautions and warns the public against closing contracts with the above Company. The plans of this system have been purloined by J. S. Zerbe, manager of the above Company, who is now engaged in equipping a street railway according to the street plans and without the consent of the inventor" (ibid., 173). Woods consulted with an attorney, H. W. Smith, before he placed the warning in the newspaper. Smith advised Woods that if he were to place the article in the *Street Railway News,* he would most likely be arrested and have to prove that "the matter so published was true and that it was not published with malicious intent" (ibid., 265). But he intensified his attack on the American Engineering Company and Zerbe by publishing a more detailed full-page warning in the February 27 issue of the *Street Railway News*, and the March 5 edition of *The Electrical Age*.[59] Woods even instigated a public relations campaign when he provided information for a celebratory article in the *New York Recorder* of February 13, 1892, and when he published an ad in the March 19, 1892, *Street Railway News* for "Woods's Multiple Distributing Station Electric Railway," both of which confirmed that he invented the system tested at Coney Island (ibid., 237, 249).

When Zerbe got word of Woods's published statements, he retaliated forthwith and sued Woods for libel. The New York Police arrested Woods on Saturday, March 5, and detained him in jail at least until the following Wednesday because he could not raise the five hundred dollars for bail. Before the trial Zerbe was able to tell his version of the events to the *Brooklyn Daily Eagle*. He told a reporter that when he lived in Cincinnati he knew of Woods only as a promising inventor but had not thought about Woods until he showed up at his office in "rags" looking for work. Zerbe contended that he gave Woods direction and revived his career by not only suggesting that Woods should begin working on a system of transportation, but also by providing the conceptual framework for this system. Zerbe insisted that Woods "acted upon my suggestion and before long was granted the patent for an electric railway system upon which the electric railway at Coney Island is founded. The American engineering company [*sic*] paid him liberally to obtain absolute control of the result of his brain work. After accepting our terms, we discovered that he was playing us false."[60] Zerbe's statements did not hold up in court, of course. To counteract the chance of Woods's case being decided by a judge who could be bought by Zerbe or General Slocum, Woods's council demanded that the case be tried by a jury. This request was granted and the trial at Brooklyn's Gates Avenue Police Court began on April 3. The standard cast of characters testified for and against each party; however, it probably helped Woods's case substantially that Tryon testified on his behalf (ibid., 172). After the witnesses gave their testimony, the jury passed down a verdict of "not guilty" for Woods in less than seven minutes. They decided that the drawings Zerbe appropriated were Woods's property and that Woods had a right to publish the warnings (ibid., 47). The jury allowed Woods to regain control over the intellectual property contained in the drawings Zerbe had stolen because the Patent Office never granted a single patent to Zerbe or Sachs or, for that matter, to the American Engineering Company after Woods's departure (ibid., 222 and 138).

Zerbe did not give up easily, for he now used the warning of February

27, 1892, as the foundation of a civil suit against Woods in the City Court of New York. This case dragged on for several years before eventually being dismissed (ibid., 174–75, 236).

Zerbe fought so vehemently for the right to control Woods's railway invention because a great deal was at stake for him and the American Engineering Company. The company was capitalized at $1 million and the only property the company "owned" was the electric patent #463,020, withdrawn as a result of the Enholm conflict. Zerbe viewed the lost interference to Enholm as only a slight setback. Zerbe had the Woods drawings and he wanted to parlay them into monetary success through the testing and selling of the system on the Coney Island Railroad. Furthermore, Zerbe had already patented the invention, that included the work of Enholm, in England, France, Belgium, Germany, Italy, Austria, Spain, and Russia (ibid., 78, 189–90). Zerbe understood the invention to have the potential of being extremely valuable. He stated, "I would not have considered the invention worth $1,000,000 at the time that the company was organized, but after the application . . . and after the tests had been made, I would of course have considered it even more valuable" (ibid., 155–56). Clearly, it was a project worth fighting for.

At the end of the libel suit Woods went to Judge Connelly, who presided over the case, to initial the stenographer's minutes, the charge, and the decision. Woods received an interesting response when Judge Connelly commented that Woods should have been the one to have filed a complaint against Zerbe (ibid., 47).

A few days after the libel suit ended, Judge Thomas J. Kenna requested a meeting with Woods at his home.[61] In addition, Kenna asked William Safford, Woods's attorney, and Zerbe's counsel, a Mr. Patterson, to be present. Judge Kenna, one of the primary stockholders and a director of the American Engineering Company, called this meeting because he was distressed by what he had heard during testimony. Kenna noted that "Zerbe might be an angel with wings growing out from under his coat, but the evidence at the trial did not point that way" (ibid., 48). He did not want to get swindled either. These talks instigated an effort to have Zerbe disbarred, and Judge Kenna resigned from his position on the board of directors on April 25, 1892 (ibid., 193). In the following months a group organized to strip Zerbe of his power within the American Engineering Company and of his legal credentials. As their investigations began to uncover the seedy past of James Zerbe, Woods saw the true colors of the man he had hoped would turn his fortunes around.

A long list of complaints trailed Zerbe, beginning as early as 1888 when he resided in Cincinnati. On September 8 of that year, he was arrested, charged with "obtaining money under false pretenses," and jailed. This trial did not reach completion because Mr. Hirley, the man who brought the charges against Zerbe, did not appear at court on October 31, the date scheduled for the trial (ibid., 41). Zerbe contended that this fact absolved him of any wrongdoing. But his relationship with the American Engineering Company brought more of his shady dealings to light. Zerbe argued that the company's stockholders' personal disagreements led them to attack him unfairly. Zerbe explained that the stockholders undermined him:

> There were about 60 stockholders, two-thirds of whom were Germans on the East Side and who were all pretty closely related to each other, and as the different ones had obtained stock at different prices, dissensions arose between them of a personal and family character, so to speak, until it had reached such an acute stage that as secretary and manager of the company I was compelled to take sides in the controversy, until finally, when the trouble arose with Woods, the members of the company antagonistic to me began a fight against me personally. This fight was a most virulent one extending into a period of nearly two years and during that time resort was had to every species of disreputable practices on their part in order to injure me. (Ibid., 42)

This "virulent" attack, unfortunately for Zerbe, uncovered several people he cheated over the years. This anti-Zerbe faction enticed his draftsman, C. Fred Buchman, with a better drafting position in return for information relating to Zerbe's improprieties. On November 4, 1892, Buchman passed along a list of six "Zerbe victims": Mrs. Headifin, Mr. Raines, E. E. Hardy, George Elliott, G. W. Staples, and Mr. Kling (ibid., 42–43). The angry group of stockholders, who felt that Zerbe was attempting to swindle them, also began to write letters to all of Zerbe's present and former clients for whom he had done patent solicitation work. Zerbe commented rather proudly that only three people, Mrs. Headifin, Frank M. Ashley, and Woods, filed complaints against him. Mrs. Headifin and Mr. Ashley had similar complaints; Zerbe had taken money from them to secure patents for their ideas, but instead he "used the money for his own benefit" (ibid., 245). Meanwhile, as the Patent Office complaints proceeded, George Elliott, Reverious Marsh, and Frank Ashley had Zerbe arrested on criminal charges. The charges by Elliott and Marsh were dismissed, but the court indicted Zerbe on the Ashley charge. This case never made it onto the docket and the district attorney eventually dismissed the charge. Frank Ashley did not let Zerbe slip away; he brought another action against Zerbe for money he had paid to obtain patents on inventions. Zerbe argued that in this civil suit his attorney, Mr. Hallen, who was sentenced to eight years for forgery in 1899, ineffectively represented him by settling out of court with Ashley (ibid., 44).

Zerbe's situation went from bad to worse: Henry Keim, the vice-president of the American Engineering Company, also had Zerbe arrested because he borrowed from Keim the five thousand dollars that he used to purchase Woods's stock from Chappell and Tryon and never repaid him. Moreover, Zerbe made a profit from these transactions, and in order for Keim to recoup his investment, he took Zerbe to court in February 1893. Since a contract existed between Zerbe and Keim, the jury decided in Keim's favor awarding him $14,500. Zerbe also received a six-month jail sentence. But a month later Keim recanted, with one important caveat—that they reorganize the American Engineering Company. They both needed each other. Zerbe needed Keim to get out of jail and Keim needed Zerbe because he still owned the railway system. They soon came to an agreement and reorganized on February 10, 1894 (ibid., 45–46).

After Zerbe left jail, the Patent Office passed judgment on the complaints of Headifin and Woods by dismissing them. But it took the Ashley complaint more seriously. The evidence compiled by Ashley was quite strong. It appears that Woods and Ashley had been building their case against Zerbe as early as December 1891. On December 2, Mr. C. H. Lawton forwarded a letter of complaint to Commissioner of Patents W. E. Simmonds describing his relationship with Zerbe. Lawton was the Eastern agent of the American Patent Agency—Zerbe's patent solicitation company when he lived in Cincinnati—from late January until early March 1891. In March, Lawton realized that American Patent Agency was more interested in cheating people than advising and helping inventors to patent and sell their creations. After severing his connection with the American Patent Agency, he received further evidence in the form of false Patent Office correspondence. Woods and Ashley most certainly used this information to their advantage, since Lawton sent them the incriminating evidence.[62] Woods and Ashley worked quite hard to have Zerbe disbarred, and their effort finally paid off when the Patent Office disbarred Zerbe on November 18, 1893 (ibid., 47, 205, 221, 222).

While Zerbe faced this battery of legal actions in late 1892, Woods became involved with the development of a new firm, the Universal Electric Company. Woods probably began making arrangements with this

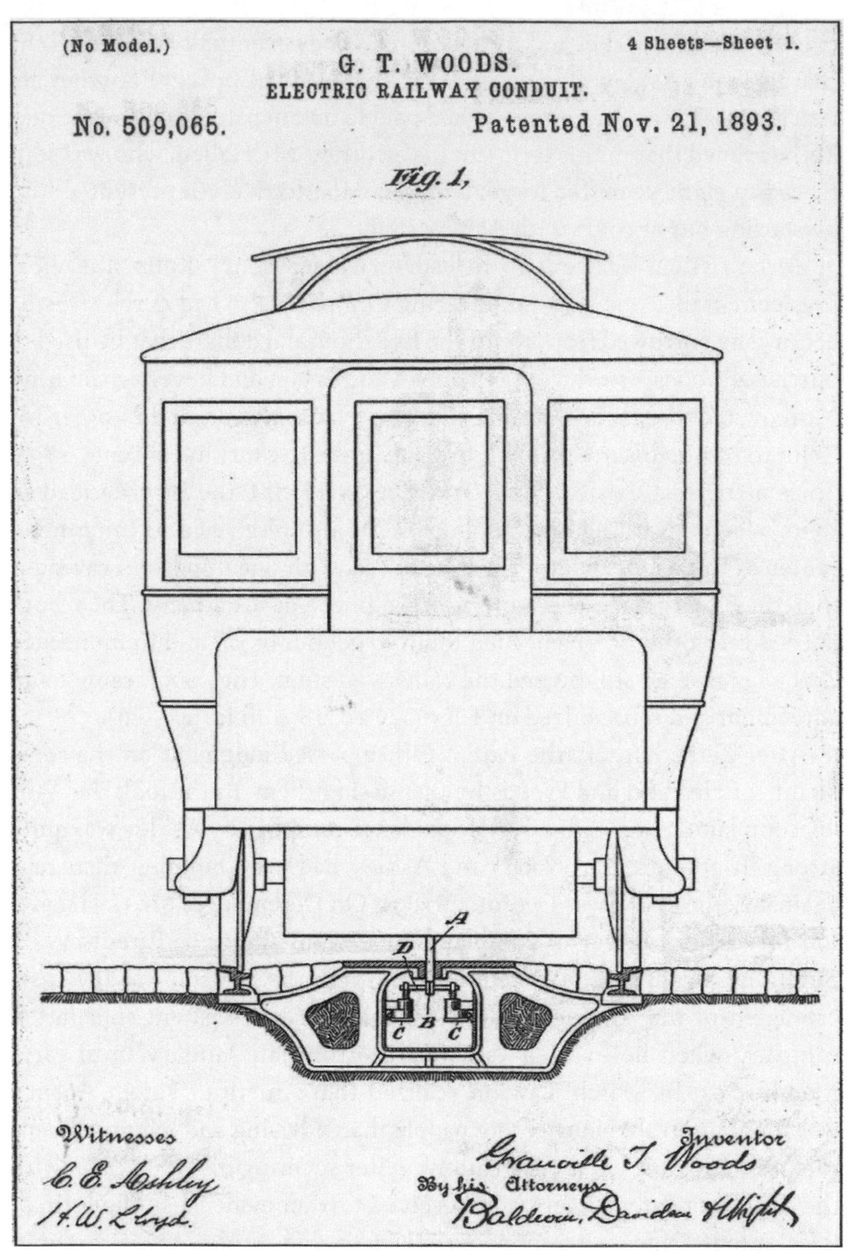

FIGURE 2.12. Woods's conception of how to safely transfer electric power to a railcar through an underground conduit system. Rear elevation of car and view of the track, roadbed, and conduit in cross section. July 1893. National Archives.

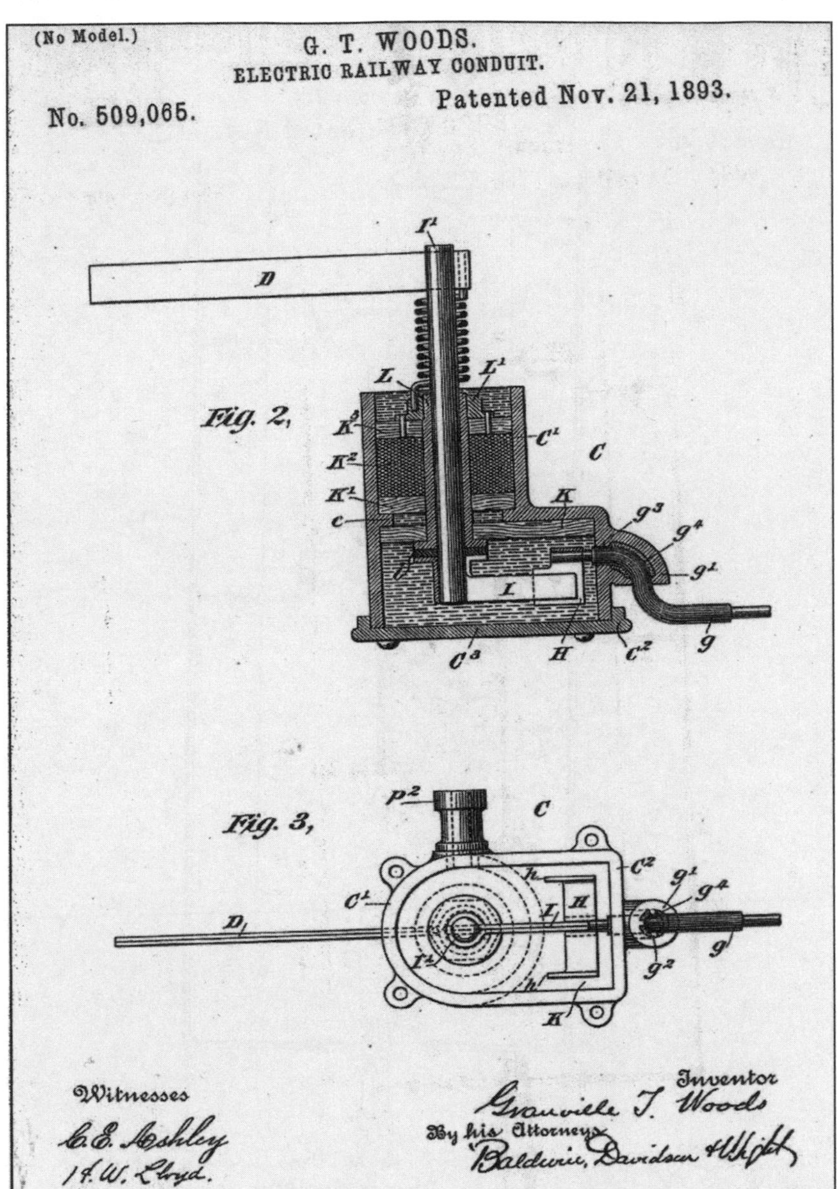

FIGURE 2.13. Vertical central section through one of the boxes. National Archives.

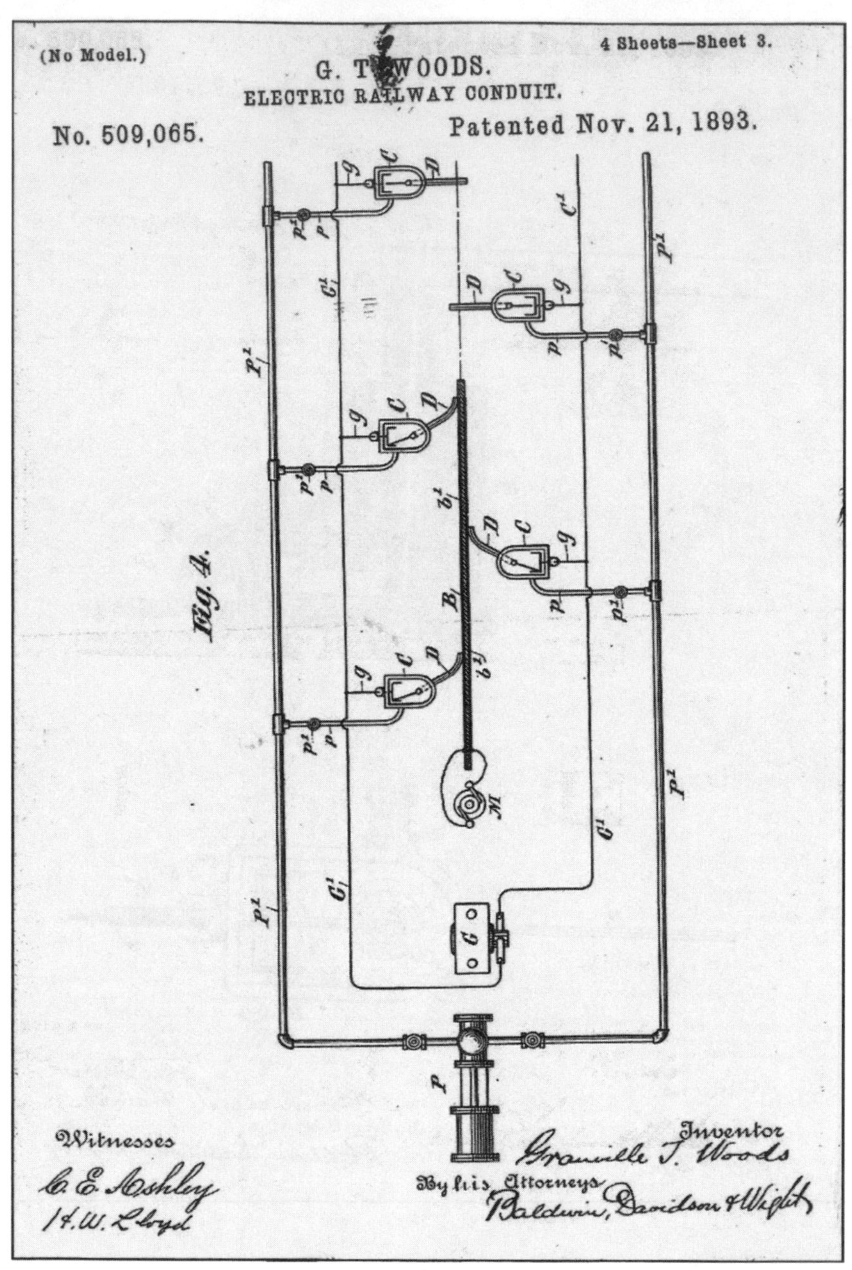

FIGURE 2.14. Diagram of railway conduit system. National Archives.

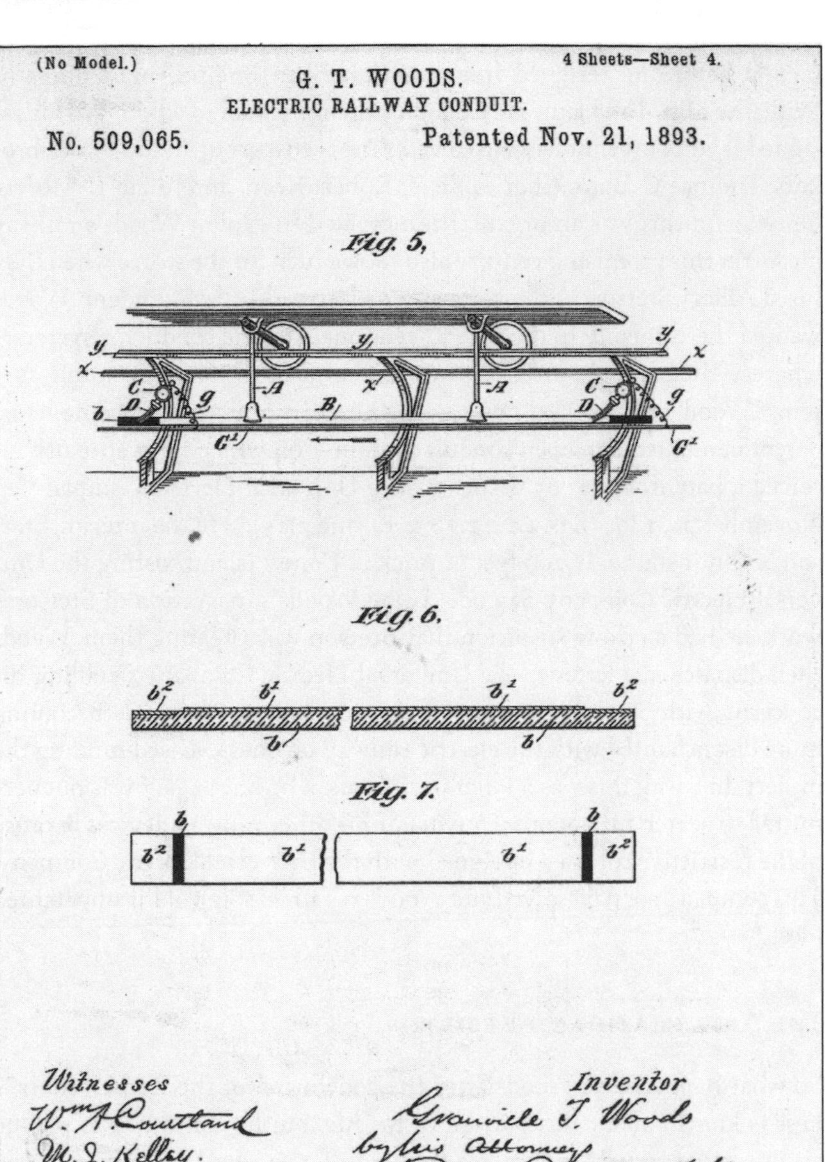

FIGURE 2.15. View of the arrangement and action of the brush of contact plates carried by the car. National Archives.

faction before he resigned from the American Engineering Company. William Safford and James E. Chandler, an individual to whom Woods assigned several inventions, introduced Woods to a group of four stock brokers: Thomas C. Buck, Charles Keep, Robert Keen, and Julian L. Morris. Once again this was an organization created to exploit Woods's railway ideas. Yet this promising venture also took a turn for the worse when they hired Albert Stetson as the company's electrical superintendent. Woods wanted the company to produce a "sectional electric conductor system," whereas Stetson supported the construction of an "open-conduit system." Woods was not too upset with this turn of events, since he had a patent pending on an open conduit system—on which he eventually received a patent, #509,065, issued to the Universal Electric Company on November 21, 1893 (figs. 2.12, 2.13, 2.14, and 2.15).[63] In the interim, Stetson began installing 1,200 feet of track at Coney Island costing the Universal Electric Company $22,000. Upon Woods's inspection of Stetson's work, he had a strong suspicion that Stetson was cheating them. Woods then dispatched a letter to the Universal Electric Company detailing his concerns with Stetson. The four financial backers, who were becoming more disenchanted with the electric railway business, ceased funding the project. In a way this was a relief for Woods, who once again was not permitted to search for potential buyers of his other railway devices because of the restrictive contract he signed with the Universal Electric Company. This company soon dissolved and Woods regained some of his unpatented ideas.[64]

The Aftermath and Rebirth

So what happened to Woods after the conclusion of the Zerbe "affair"? Less is known about this portion of his life, but he continued to pursue an inventive career. In fact, by the end of 1893 he had only received twenty of the forty-five patents that would be granted to him before his death. Woods evidently did experience a modicum of success during this period which enabled him to purchase a farm in Monsey, New York, in 1896 (ibid., 3, 32). He still continued to hold out hope of obtaining a patent for his system of electric rail transport that he developed and exemplified in the model assembled in the offices of the American Engineering Company in 1891. Woods recast this invention and reapplied for a patent on July 24, 1895. Yet by this time Woods was not the only inventor who was attempting to patent this type of electric railway. As

Woods's invention was making its way through the Patent Office's procedures, he received a letter on July 14, 1896, informing him that the Patent Office was suspending action on his application because of the probability of an impending interference.[65] This potentiality became a reality on September 17, 1896, when Woods became involved in two interference cases—#18,207, between William Chapman, Frederick Esmond, D. Mac Therell, and Woods; and #18,210, between Esmond, Woods, and Malone Wheless.[66] Another interesting twist came about shortly thereafter. Woods assigned this invention, given the serial #557,045, to the Electro-Magnetic Brake Company. Yet the assignment was sent to Charles S. Terry, whose address of record was the Westinghouse Electric and Manufacturing Company in New York City. This assignment makes more sense when one understands that Esmond had been working intimately with General Electric in Schenectady.[67] Even though this was nearly seven months after both General Electric and Westinghouse had signed their patent cross-licensing agreement, they were still competitors and potentially interested in maintaining defensive patent positions.

This case progressed rather slowly, partially due to the number of participants and the fact that testimony was taken from February 1898 through August 1899. The one person who caused the testimony to be so lengthy was James Zerbe. He was somewhat of a witness on Esmond's behalf, yet most of his testimony attempted to clear his name by refuting much of Woods's testimony. It was effective in bringing Woods's testimony into question, but it did not alter the examiner of interferences' decisions on January 26, 1901. Woods did not receive a favorable decision in either case. The examiner of interferences did not contest the fact that the idea germinated in Woods's mind before any of the other applicants, but he did fault Woods's diligence to apply for a patent. Woods again supplied his financial duress as an explanation for his sluggishness in applying for a patent. But, the examiner did not feel that Woods had established his poverty with sufficient evidence. Moreover, the World Building model did not qualify as a reduction to practice, nor did the Coney Island system constructed by Zerbe because Woods never actually saw the system and Zerbe testified that this system varied substantially from Woods's invention. Regardless, the deciding factor was that Woods did not show proper diligence in filing a patent application.[68] Woods was not a complete loser because the interference decision only disallowed six of the patent application's initial claims and the Patent Office granted Woods the patent #678,086 on July 9, 1901, on the remainder[69] (fig. 2.16).

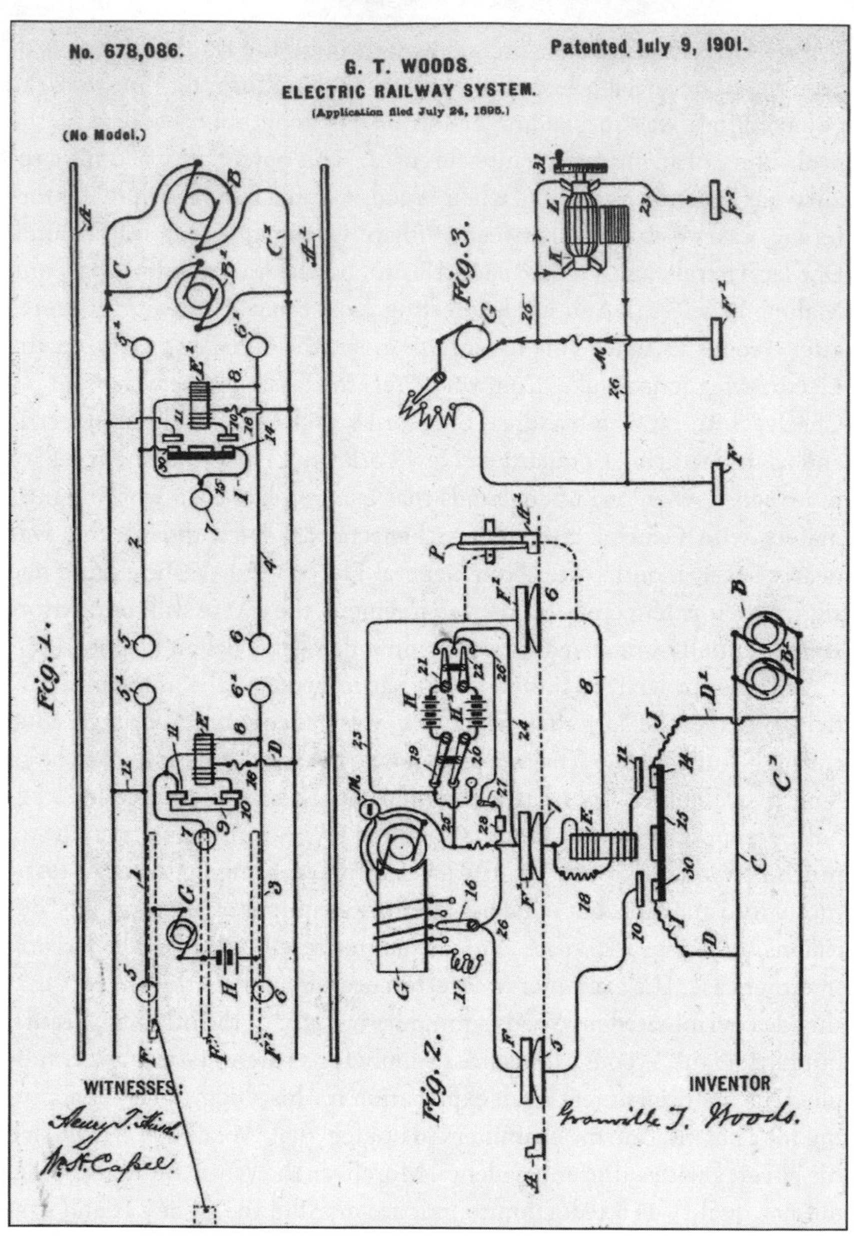

FIGURE 2.16. Wood's system of powering an electric railcar. July 1901. National Archives.

As these two interference cases played themselves out, Woods's inventive career began to truly flourish. In July 1896, Woods began to foster an inventive relationship with General Electric and Westinghouse—the two most prominent electric companies of the period—and those closely associated with these two companies. A few years after the turn-of-the-century, Woods had become a part of the dominant technological and inventive culture's apparatus. Between 1900 and his death in 1910, Woods patented twenty-two inventions (see appendices A, B, and C). Of those only two were not assigned to General Electric, Westinghouse, or H. Ward Leonard. Leonard, a major inventor in controlling systems, is known to have supplied General Electric and Westinghouse with controlling devices.[70] Not coincidentally all the inventions Woods assigned to Leonard were controlling devices. In particular, his relation with Leonard is most telling about his integration in the dominant corporate electrical culture. On September 20, 1899, Woods made a patent assignment with Leonard that was in effect a contractual agreement. This assignment reads as follows:

> Territory Assigned: Assigns all inventions, discoveries, methods, and apparatus, conceived developed or produced by him [Woods] in whole or part, either before or after this date, and for *twenty years* next ensuing, in or relating to control of speed or torque of electric motors by all means other than Ohmic resistance, and agrees to execute papers for applications, etc., on terms stated. Woods declares that he has not now pending, alone or jointly with another, any applications covering apparatus or methods of motor regulation by any means other than Ohmic resistance. Should any United States Letters patent be granted upon applications made by him either solely or conjointly with another, and claiming or disclosing a method or methods of motor regulation other than by Ohmic resistance, he hereby grants to said Leonard license to make use and vend same free of payment of royalty or other obligations. Woods declares that he has no applications for letters patent now pending in the Patent Office for inventions concerning the regulation of electric motors of which he is not sole owner.[71] (Emphasis added)

Thus, Woods had finally reached a point uncommon to most inventors. With this substantial agreement, he could no longer be viewed or consider himself on the margins of the dominant electric culture of this period.

Woods was now on his way to attaining the level of success for which he had worked all of his life. But, the historical fragments do not give a clear reason or ensemble of reasons why, from a patenting perspective, his fortunes drastically changed for the better at the turn of the century. It can be speculated that Woods's legal battle served to provide him with positive publicity. That is, the libel case that Zerbe brought against Woods was a forum for Woods to speak publicly about his inventions and inventive skills. This potentially could have attracted the interest of companies like General Electric and Westinghouse. Woods could have also made some yet undiscovered contacts who could have assisted him in building relationships with these companies. On this account, Lewis Latimer is a fairly decent candidate for a contact. As the chief draftsman for the General Electric/Westinghouse Board of Patent Control, Latimer was potentially an important player in the patent acquisitions of these companies. In this position, he could have helped to sway higher company officials to purchase the patents of an associate, like Woods. But, it is still completely uncertain that Woods and Latimer every personally knew each other. Albert Davis, General Electric's patent attorney, was another potential contact.[72] Davis handled all of Woods's patent related matter with General Electric.[73] This may have been because he was General Electric's patent attorney or because he or a closely associated colleague was taking special interest in Woods's work. One could also speculate that Arthur Kennelly, H. Ward Leonard, or a host of others were partially responsible for the improvement in Woods's fortunes. The most probable reason for his success was that Woods had learned how to play the inventive game.

Woods, late in his career, had learned how to invent within that time period's electrical environment. Through his years of trial and error, he had found a place and had become a knowledgeable independent inventor. He was no longer an outsider, but he was no longer aiming to construct large technological systems. Nevertheless, for Woods, becoming a system builder was the goal, and anything short of that was a disappointment. Many of Woods's difficulties do not appear to be racially connected on the surface. But, was the dominant late nineteenth-century inventor culture or the dominant American culture ready to accept a Negro system builder shaping the material fabric of America through technology? This is doubtful. Even with the high quality of his inventive ideas, American society would not allow him to fully flourish as a system builder. As a result, he began to focus on supplying parts for the system. He began to concentrate on solving reverse salients in larger technological systems—case in point are his controlling devices.[74] These reasons, in addition to those yet to be revealed, all contributed to his very relative success.

This brief portrait of the inventive career of Granville Woods is valuable for several reasons. It illustrates the complexity of inventing on the margins of a dominant technological culture, as well as the complex negotiations between various parties and institutions that determine one's inventive success. The experiences of Granville Woods have shown how complicated and difficult it was for unestablished inventors to participate actively in developing new technology. A great idea does not necessarily guarantee success. Marginal inventors had to navigate a sea of problems—animate and inanimate—before they could get their ideas patented, let alone built and used on a large scale. Such well know inventor-entrepreneurs as Thomas Edison and Elmer Sperry had similarly trying times in their early careers.[75] But, what is at issue here, is the understanding of what it was like to be an African American inventor, and whether the negotiations necessary to participate in American technological development were different for a black man. From historical documentation recounting the racial discrimination during this period, it is easy to assume that race adversely influenced how people perceived and interacted with Granville Woods. Yet, several articles referred to Woods as a great Negro inventor, the greatest inventor of his race, or some other descriptive phrase that emphasized his racial heritage. These seemingly complimentary statements indicate that Woods was viewed as something different.

The role that race played in his inventive career is quite elusive, and it would be naive to suggest that race was the sole reason for his difficulties. Direct documentation of racial discrimination, while Woods was trying to patent inventions, is relatively non-existent. Yet one article did recount that Woods had "been frequently refused work because of the previous condition of his race, but he never despaired."[76] This statement is interesting in that the author wrote of the "previous condition" of the black race, as if black people had uplifted themselves and were no longer considered the uncivilized other. Indirectly, there are instances where Woods is treated less than fairly. When Woods placed the warning in *The Electrical Age,* Zerbe had Woods arrested on the libel charge. Prior to the trial, the press only solicited Zerbe's opinion about the incident. The white press probably assumed that it was highly unlikely that an African American invented such a sophisticated technological device. At this point he was not an inventor, he was a Negro and treated accordingly. But, this does not address what happened to Woods in a professional setting. Was he treated similarly? Possibly, but one cannot automatically assume that everyone Woods met reacted negatively because of his race. For instance, I do not think Zerbe attempted to steal Woods's inventions specifically because he was black. Zerbe had quite a history of cheating anyone he could: white men, women, whomever. As far as his business was concerned, he was an equal opportunity swindler.

Even though Woods did not achieve inventive and financial success, he used invention and his inventive skills for financial gain. There was never an instance where Woods considered his technological work anything more than a financial opportunity. This of course does not mean that he did not take great pride in his inventions; but they were economic projects. In his quest for financial stability, and at best success, Woods was very conscious of what he had to create. Woods attempted to invent new "systems" of railway communication and later railway propulsion.[77] Woods was very ingenious in his inventive efforts. He regularly worked to build a system held tightly together by his patents. He wanted to patent all the parts together and sell or produce the system as a unit. He believed that this was an important aspect of becoming a successful system builder. When Woods realized that this was not possible, he showed great malleability and adaptation by selling his inventions separately rather than as an entire system. Moreover, late in his inventing career, he had learned a great deal from patenting and his interactions with shady patent solicitors. These unpleasant experiences prompted Woods to perform most of the preliminary legal work on his later patent applications.[78] Nevertheless, Woods's marginalized standing within a racialized late nineteenth-century corporate electrical culture made his goal of system building unattainable.

In a few instances, Woods may have used racial tension to his benefit. In an early interference case, he alluded to the fact that he was poor because of the lack of opportunities available for Negroes (Woods' Testimony, Interference Case #10,580, 3, 18, 19). Woods may have used his race as a ploy to create a small amount of sympathy for himself. The fact that Woods was black may have also created interest in his work, if not curiosity, which helped to separate him from other inventors. So being a Negro did not necessarily have to be completely harmful. It should also be noted that in certain environments there was room for an African American to succeed, as will be seen with Lewis Latimer in the next chapter. Woods did find a niche for himself by the turn-of-the-century through his connections to General Electric and Westinghouse. This does not mean he was now a member of the electrical inventor's inner sanctum or became wealthy. When Woods signed the twenty-year agreement with H. Ward Leonard to invent controlling devices, he was definitely no longer an inventor on the fringe. Granville Woods led a complicated life; and the ups and down of his life illustrate one way in which race, technology, and dreams about success in America met within the late nineteenth century.

Chapter Three

Lewis H. Latimer and the Politics of Technological Assimilationism

The Negro must acquire culture, polish, and refinement, he must acquire an aristocratic, high-bred feeling. We must improve the racial stock. We must produce a high-minded, high-spirited, high-toned race of men and women, who will walk with head erect, lift their feet and strike the ground with a firm elastic step.
—William H. Ferris, 1913

By the time of his death in 1928, Lewis Latimer had more polish and refinement than William Ferris could have hoped for any black man. This was not without cost; that cost was to cloud his connections with the general black population. For Latimer, it was a fair price to pay. The only way to raise members of the black race to be strong, productive, and useful members of society was through assimilation. The union of black American culture and white American culture would have only lowered the standards of American society, thus integration was not a worthy option. The post-Reconstruction program of racial uplift and progress to which Latimer subscribed deemed that for black citizens to advance toward civilization they had to transform into, or at the least emulate, white American society. This ideological stance was partially responsible for Latimer's ambivalence to black movements throughout his life. He considered the efforts to reassemble a black culture futile. His conservative politics did nothing to change the racial conditions of the time and he would

FIGURE 3.1. Lewis Howard Latimer in 1882.
Queens Borough Public Library.

have been misguided to think that his position on the race question did not affect his life as a black man in America.[1]

Latimer's technical work also exemplified his world view. He was neither an inventor nor inventor-entrepreneur in the mode of Edison, Maxim, and others for whom he worked. He was a technical expert to whom the creation of new technical artifacts, practices, and knowledge was not a fundamental goal. The irony of Lewis Latimer is that he is not the race champion that the black inventor myth has made him. Latimer did not invent for the race; he invented for himself. If inventing had had a negative effect on his standing within his technical environment, he would certainly have given it up. Inventing and patenting merely played the role of a credential. They were tools used to enter and to solidify his position within corporate electrical culture and the associated social and economic order. They also enabled Latimer to gain access to a world closed to most black men. Latimer wanted to fade into this technical world to the point where he was no longer seen as a black man, but as a raceless member of this environment.

The Acquisition of Technical Skills

To understand the foundations of Latimer's relation to the elite black community, as well as to invention and technical development, it is necessary to examine the ordeal of his parents, in particular the experiences of his father, George W. Latimer, which significantly shaped his conceptions of and interactions with white society. George Latimer was born on July 4, 1818, in Norfolk, Virginia. He was the son of a white stonemason, Mitchell Latimer, and Margaret Olmstead, a slave owned by Mitchell's brother Edward. George spent his first sixteen years as a house servant for Mr. and Mrs. Edward Mallery; Mrs. Mallery had been the wife of Edward Latimer. The Mallerys treated George quite well during these years, allowing him to hire himself out as long as he paid a quarter a day for food, clothing, and shelter. This flexibility did not last long. Because of the Mallerys' financial problems in the 1830s, the freedom to work for his own monetary gain ended. Over the next eight years George was hired out, jailed for the Mallery's debts, sold several times, and generally mistreated.[2]

George did not intend to take this pernicious treatment for the remainder of his life. In 1840 he ran away for the first time, only to be recaptured shortly after his escape. Latimer wrote that upon his return

James B. Gray, George's current owner, treated him "with . . . more severity, as he had a dislike for me."[3] George escaped again in October 1842, but he was not alone. In this run for freedom, George had much more at stake than his personal liberty. In January 1842, he married Rebecca Smith, who soon became pregnant.[4] With the abuse that Latimer experienced after his recapture, he did not want to bring a child into the world of slavery. Rebecca, being owned by someone other than Gray, added an undesirable complexity to his predicament. As bad luck would have it, the Latimers encountered a man who had worked for Gray, William Carpenter, when they arrived in Boston on October 7. Not surprisingly, Gray appeared in Boston on October 11 in order to reclaim his property. But to Gray's dismay, Latimer had gathered the support of many of the Boston area's most avid abolitionists, such as Dr. Henry Bowditch, William Francis Channing, Frederick Cabot, and William Lloyd Garrison. This group helped publish six issues of the abolitionist paper, *The Latimer Journal, and North Star,* which significantly helped to publicize Latimer's plight. Latimer spent a short time in jail and became a free man on October 17. After a day of negotiations by various parties, a black minister, Reverend Samuel Caldwell, raised four hundred dollars and paid the attorney representing James Gray to compensate him for his lost property.[5]

George Latimer became relatively famous in the northeast after this episode. He attended abolitionist rallies, meetings, and conventions throughout Massachusetts as a living example of Northern abolitionists' successes. It was written that he "was the . . . fugitive slave whose emancipation guided and influenced the American abolitionists of the 1850s."[6] At one event reported in the *Salem Observer* and *The Liberator,* his attendance was quite an occasion. "George Latimer, the lion himself, was present. His appearance caused a sensation among the audience . . . At the close of the meeting, by the request of several present, Latimer stood in front of the rostrum, that those who wished might pass along and shake hands with him, as is the custom when the president and other distinguished men receive the attention and civilities of the sovereign people."[7] George Latimer had become larger than life. He was no longer a runaway slave but a "lion" and a distinguished man whom sovereign citizens wanted to meet.

In 1894, Frederick Douglass wrote to Lewis Latimer about the impact his parents had on Northern abolitionists after their freedom was won. Douglass stated that one "could hardly imagine the excitement the attempts to recapture them caused in Boston. It was a new experience for the

Abolitionists and they improved it to the full extent capable."[8] This reconstructed image of his father is important. Young Lewis probably grew up with this heroic construction of his father. He saw his father as a valuable participant in the fight against slavery. This exultation assisted his family in gaining cultural acceptance. But even more important was the racial tenor of the environment in which he grew up. White citizens greatly aided his parents' freedom. His father's freedom resulted directly from abolitionist efforts, so Lewis did not grow up seeing the white population as a homogeneous malevolent foe. He saw many whites as benevolent citizens working for the betterment of an underprivileged race. An entry in one of Latimer's Logbooks referred to some of his childhood racial experiences. Commenting on his surroundings after his family moved into a predominantly Irish neighborhood, Latimer wrote that "the greatest enemy the Negro had was the Irish boy but if you lived right among them you could have no better neighbors."[9] Latimer carried this agreeable view of racial intercourse with him throughout his life.

Lewis was born in the backdrop of George's abolitionist-related activities in Chelsea, Massachusetts, in 1848.[10] His early years in primary and secondary school were quite normal. He also helped out in his father's barbershop—a well-respected business for an African American man in the nineteenth century. If the clientele was white—a definite possibility—he would have had another occasion to interact in a familiar environment with white men. When George became a paper hanger, Lewis assisted him in the evenings as well. Helping his father came to an end in 1858, when Lewis was ten years old; George left his family and from then on was "an unknown quantity."[11] Regardless of the reasons for George's disappearance, it placed the Latimer family in a difficult financial position because Lewis's mother could not provide for her four children.[12] When Lewis was thirteen, he found employment working as an office boy for an attorney and became familiar with legal practices at an early age. After a stint waiting table for a Roxbury family, he secured a job as an office boy for Isaac H. Wright, a distinguished local attorney.[13]

During the Civil War, Latimer enlisted in the Union Navy on September 16, 1864. He served for a little less than a year and was discharged on July 3, 1865.[14] The Navy discharged Latimer in Boston and shortly thereafter his mother "appeared," and as he puts it, "they went to housekeeping." Where his mother appeared from is not known, but it made sense to combine her efforts with those of her youthful son. The housekeeping work only lasted a short time and he had very limited success in finding another position until luck intervened. According to his recollections, the firm of Crosby, Halsted & Gould, Solicitors of American and Foreign Patents, were looking for "a colored boy with a taste for drawing."[15] Latimer heard about this position from a black woman who cleaned the firm's office. Crosby, Halsted & Gould was a reputable establishment, particularly with men such as John J. Halsted, a former principal examiner of the Patent Office, as a partner in the firm.[16] Since Latimer was looking for work at the time, he applied; when they offered him the job, he gladly accepted.

While working for Crosby, Halsted & Gould, Latimer acquired his drafting skills. As he performed his duties as an office boy, he carefully watched the draftsmen at work. Drafting intrigued Latimer and he soon began making a concerted effort to master this skill's techniques. He wrote in his Logbook that "whatever a man knew he had put in a book." Latimer put this maxim to use when he proceeded to buy second-hand books that explained the techniques of drafting. Soon thereafter, he purchased a complete set of drafting instruments. Latimer commented that he "looked over the draftsman's shoulder to see how he used his instruments."[17] He would go home and practice until he felt he could replicate the manner in which the draftsman used these instruments. This process of emulation, an informal apprenticeship, was the basic training that many craft, technical, and engineering people received in the nineteenth century.[18]

When Latimer was confident of his drafting abilities, he asked the draftsman to let him execute a few drawings. This indicates a level of familiarity with the draftsman. It would have been out of the question for an office boy to make such a request if he did not have an informal relationship with the draftsman. The draftsman initially took this appeal less than seriously. But eventually he agreed to let Latimer do some sample drafting in order to see if he possessed any drafting skills. Latimer's efforts obviously pleased the draftsman because he occasionally allowed Lewis to complete some of his work after that episode. Higher officials of the firm recognized the quality of his work and when the draftsman resigned, they appointed Latimer to the vacated position. It is important to note that most likely Crosby & Gould only had one draftsman; therefore he was not appointed the *chief* draftsman as some have stated, but *the* draftsman. Before their draftsman left the firm, Crosby & Gould had two men drafting cheaply. Latimer's promotion confirmed his competency; from 1866 to 1878 his wages increased from three dollars to twenty dollars a week, as he rose from an office boy to draftsman. Even though Crosby & Gould paid him five dollars less than the previous draftsman, he was not upset with the fact. Latimer wrote that he was quite pleased because "twenty dollars a week was large wages then."[19] As the draftsman, he was responsible for "making drawings for, and superintending the construction of, the working models . . . required by the U.S. Patent Office."[20] Thus, Latimer engaged in more than merely drafting for this firm.

Drafting required the close coordination between the inventor and draftsman, in an almost symbiotic relationship. The act of drafting was a crucial step in the visual representation of a technical artifact.[21] From this intimate interaction a draftsman could learn a substantial amount of technical information. According to Latimer's description of his responsibilities as a draftsman, this position required an individual who possessed a great deal of technical knowledge. In Latimer's eleven-year tenure, he had become very skilled and knowledgeable in a variety of technical areas. So much so, that in later years he "took entire charge of the business when Mr. Gregory was absent, receiving cases, making necessary drawings and writing specifications to be forwarded to Mr. Gregory for his guidance in making out final papers."[22] In addition to these duties, he performed patent research for the firm in the Boston area. It is quite evident that Latimer had a firm handle on the technical and legal aspects of patenting by the late 1870s.

His increasing technical knowledge manifested itself in the form of his first patent in 1874. This device, copatented with Charles W. Brown, was an "Improvement in Water-Closet for Railroad-Cars." Instead of having a toilet opening to the ground, where "dust, cinders, and other matters [could be] thrown up from the track," Latimer and Brown devised a commode with a trap door activated by the toilet lid. They "constructed the apparatus with an earth-closet mechanism; by which a supply of dry earth, sand, or equivalent material is lodged upon the . . . receiving or discharging plate whenever the seat-cover is raised, and before the apparatus is used" (fig. 3.2).[23] The utilization of this apparently useful appliance is not known. An early letter of rejection forwarded by the United States Patent Office, in reference to the invention, stated that parts of the device had been "substantially anticipated by Wm. E. Marsh . . . and J. H. Seymoser."[24] It is possible that this patent was a small augmentation on a preexisting device.

Even though this invention was not a marketable success, it was important because it showed that Latimer was thinking creatively about

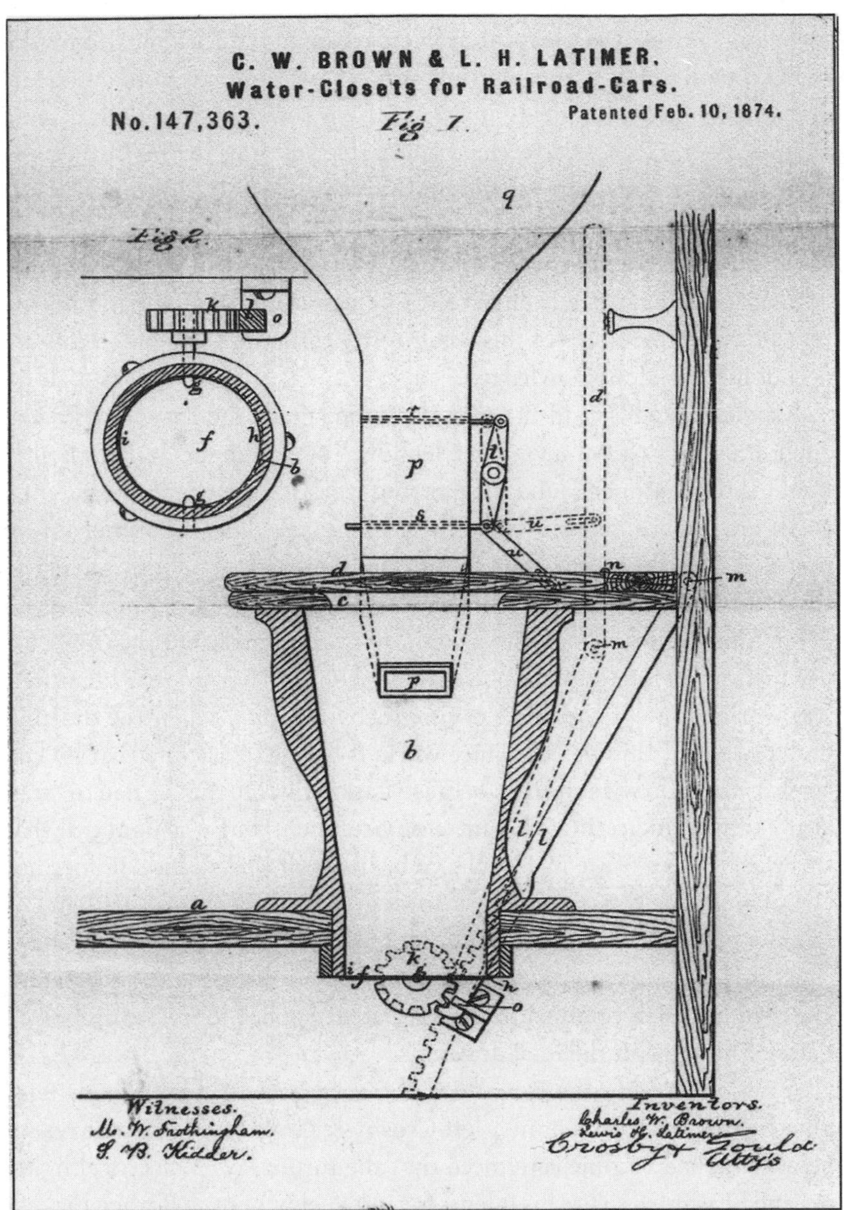

FIGURE 3.2. Water-closets for railroad cars. An on-train toilet and Latimer's first patent. February 1874. National Archives.

technical solutions to practical problems. Moreover, Latimer followed a familiar path to inventing. Drafting was a basic skill taught to engineers and others in technical fields; in fact, many inventors began their careers as draftsmen. Hence, he received applicable training for his future endeavors. Yet, this was a relatively basic inventive effort for his surroundings. Boston was one of the centers of electrical work and many electrical inventors certainly passed through the offices of Crosby & Gregory. Latimer must have been conversant in electrical technology and his interaction with members of this community certainly augmented this aspect of his technical knowledge.[25]

Latimer stated that in the mid 1870s he "made the drawings for the application for a patent upon the telephone" of Alexander Graham Bell.[26] It seems that Latimer found the drafting work for the telephone patent a slight annoyance because of Bell's teaching schedule.[27] Latimer wrote that Bell "had day classes and night classes and I was obliged to stay at the office until after nine p.m. when he was free from his night classes to get my instructions from him as to how I was to make the drawings for the application for a patent upon the telephone."[28] It is unclear if Latimer was working under the auspices of Crosby & Gould when the drafting took place or if this was freelance work. It is safe to assume that he had some connection with the firm because Latimer wrote that he had to "stay at the office," indicating a business environment; but it is doubtful that this was his own office in a freelance business or Bell's office. It does not appear that this was a special assignment, requiring the skilled hand of Latimer or that Bell requested Latimer's services, as some historians have suggested.[29] It was merely that Latimer was the draftsman of the patent law firm that Bell retained to file his patent application which required Latimer to perform the final drawings.

A few years after the Patent Office issued Bell his now famous telephone patent in 1876, Latimer left Crosby & Gregory. He did not resign because he had become convinced that the future lay in electrical lighting and he wanted to use his talents for its development.[30] Rather, his resignation centered around the managerial changes at Crosby & Gregory. Gould had died and Crosby retired, leaving the firm most likely in the hands of Gregory. Latimer stated that since he "could not agree with the man in charge of the office, he left" Crosby & Gregory in 1878.[31] This was an important point in Lewis Latimer's life. He had risen to a meaningful position within the firm of Crosby & Gregory, but then he quit. Why? He obviously enjoyed drafting and his additional responsibilities, but something caused conflict between Lewis and the new management. The explanation he provided is vague at best. Did he leave for personal or professional reasons? The explanation quite possibly could have been racial, but the evidence does not confirm or contradict this likelihood. The next few months were not the best of times. Latimer found a position similar to the one he held at Crosby & Gregory working for another Boston patent solicitor, Joseph Adams. But, the adverse business climate forced Latimer to support himself as a painter and a paper hanger. Again he changed jobs and began working in the pattern shop of the Esterbrook Iron Foundry in South Boston.[32] This transient lifestyle was not to his liking and when his sister suggested that he move to Bridgeport, Connecticut, where she and her family lived, Latimer heeded her advice.[33]

Upon arriving in Bridgeport in 1879, he was able to find employment again as a paper hanger. Sometime during this year he obtained a job drafting for the Follandsbee Machine Shop.[34] The outcome of this work was a stroke of luck. One day while Latimer was working, Hiram Maxim, the inventor of the machine gun, entered the machine shop and to his surprise discovered a colored man drafting. During this chance meeting, Maxim remarked that he had yet to encounter a colored person who drafted so admirably. Intrigued, Maxim asked Latimer how he acquired his drafting skills. Latimer told him about his experiences drafting for various patent law firms in Boston. This fact intrigued Maxim. In fact, he was familiar with some of Latimer's former employers.[35] Latimer stated that Maxim had been searching for weeks to find a draftsman to execute patent drawings before Maxim stumbled upon him. This statement is a bit strange because other skilled draftsmen probably practiced in Bridgeport. Latimer wrote that Bridgeport was "perfectly alive with inventors and it would be impossible to throw a stone into any company of men gathered anywhere about in the street without hitting one." He further described Bridgeport as "a perfect hornets' nest of industries."[36] With Bridgeport's saturation of inventors and industries, it is highly unlikely that the concentration of patent lawyers, patent solicitors, and draftsmen was not comparable. Maxim's selection of Latimer to execute patent diagrams, in a location that did not have a shortage of draftsmen, can be regarded as a confirmation that Latimer possessed a high level of technical knowledge and drafting skills. In February 1880, Maxim's United States Electric Lighting Company hired Latimer as a draftsman and as Maxim's general assistant.[37]

Latimer had now entered the heart of the electrical community of the late nineteenth century. At this point he had reached a level of success foreign to most black men, let alone those working in electricity. Yet, Maxim hired Latimer as a draftsman and not as an inventor. Latimer possessed a substantial amount of technical expertise, but he was not in a position to use it to produce new technological artifacts. Nevertheless, this job was not devoid of creative thinking. Latimer was able to express his creativity by interpreting other inventors' ideas, for which he then was responsible for providing the technical drawings. Latimer knew this job's limitations well and made the most of his opportunity at the United States Electric Lighting Company. From this point in his life, Latimer became increasingly accepted by the corporate electrical culture that held a position of prominence in the development of electrical technology. He slowly but surely assimilated into the fabric of this technical environment.

Soon after arriving in Bridgeport, Latimer began to make important social connections. He was an active enough member of the cultured community to have presented a paper on the "Practical Relation of Art to Science" before the Bridgeport Scientific Society. A reviewer wrote that "Mr. Latimer showed the relation between art and science as exhibited in the delineative portion of art. Art in this connection, serves to treasure up and transmit the results of the labors of science in its various departments, and also to serve as a universal language for the diffusion of scientific knowledge."[38] By art, the reviewer was not speaking of mechanic arts, the terminological precursors to technology, but the art of representing the scientific and technological. Obviously Latimer was very adept at explaining the complexities of science and technology through his drawings. His drafting work was not merely a part of the patenting process, but an art form that disseminated the scientific and technological in a manner that literate society could comprehend. In a sense, art was a mechanism to quell technological fears and repackage technology for fearless consumption.

Around this time, Latimer's artistic eye and keen aesthetic sensibility began to emerge in his public writings. For instance, he offered a critique of the larger than life-size statues proliferating in public parks during the late nineteenth century. He contended that these grandiose statues exhibited very skillful casting but were not aesthetically pleasing. He wrote that if society wanted to "indulge in the heroic, in size, and be so scrupulous in detail, we should, at least, endeavor to offset this painful exactness, by placing the work at a distance from the beholder sufficient to blend these exaggerations into a dignified and harmonious whole."[39] Latimer also wrote articles about recent science and technology. In an article entitled "The Progress of Invention," Latimer described the work of local inventors like Henry House, "the Edison of Bridgeport," and the electric lighting lecture and exhibit by Maxim and a Professor Sterling before the Bridgeport Scientific Society.[40] To be such a public voice, it is quite evident that, regardless of his race, the Bridgeport social, scientific, and technical communities had accepted Latimer.

Latimer and the Electrical World

The United States Electric Lighting Company was a stimulating place for Latimer to be in 1880. The company came into existence in 1878 with funds from the Equitable Life Insurance Company and the help of S. D. Schuyler.[41] The company aimed to exploit the incandescent lamp patents of Hiram Maxim and William Sawyer. Sawyer soon left the organization under less than amicable terms, which placed the company in Maxim's hands.[42] With Maxim at the helm, the company concentrated its efforts on the production of an improved incandescent lamp. The company was on the forefront of incandescent lamp technology at this time. Their incandescent lamp was the second lamp on the market, only to be preceded by that of the Edison Electric Light Company. The Edison Company announced its incandescent lamp in the fall of 1879 and the Maxim lamp appeared in the fall of 1880.[43] In June 1880, when the United States Electric Lighting Company's factory moved to New York City, the Latimer family also transplanted itself.[44] The United States Electric Lighting Company installed its first commercial incandescent lighting system in the fall of 1880. The recipient of this lighting system, the Mercantile Safe Deposit Company, was located within the Equitable building that housed both the Equitable Life Insurance Company and the United States Electric Lighting Company. This installation took place about six months after the *Columbia* steamship had been fitted with Edison's incandescent lamps.[45] This was a very busy time for Latimer; he wrote regularly about the long hours. When he was not drafting, he was helping to manufacture lamps. In the evenings he would either assist in the installation of new units or go to one of their existing installations and make sure everything ran properly. This regularly required him to be on hand at least until midnight and sometimes even later.[46]

The United States Electric Lighting Company's primary competitors were the Edison companies.[47] Both organizations entered the market at about the same time, with the United States Electric Lighting Company having a slight advantage because it produced a longer lasting filament. But it did not reach the level of success achieved by the Edison companies, and it did not have the technical and scientific capabilities of the Edison Companies.[48] Since the company had not devised a mathematical method of determining the electrical loads of lighting systems nor did it possess precise electrical measuring devices, the wire choice decisions during installations could be called educated guesswork at best. Latimer wrote that at the company's early installation the workmen would speculate as to what "size wire would carry a certain number of lamps without over heating. A number of mysterious fires about this time were probably the fruit of our ignorance."[49] In stark contrast, the Edison Company hired Francis Upton, a mathematical physicist, to perform the difficult calculations for determining voltages, lamp resistances, and conductor sizes.[50] Upton's contributions, as well as those from Edison's large number of assistants, such as Charles Batchelor and John Kruesi, were crucial in helping the Edison Company find effective solutions to critical technical problems.[51] The two companies had different industrial plans of action. The United States Electric Lighting Company focused on the production of a quality incandescent lamp, whereas the Edison Company aimed to build an entire electrical system that included everything from the filament to the dynamo.[52] From the outset the United States Electric Lighting Company did not structure itself to build an incandescent-lighting system and by the time they began to move in this direction, the Edison Company had gained a distinct advantage.

The United States Electric Lighting Company also lagged behind in market competitiveness because of the lack of team cohesion and Maxim's personality. In 1889, Latimer testified in a patent interference case on behalf of Charles G. Perkins and provided some insights into the internal workings of this organization. Perkins, as the general foreman, had the responsibility of managing the production of lamps. Perkins and Maxim had a less than cordial relationship that dated back to the company's Bridgeport days. Latimer recounted an argument in which Perkins charged Maxim with stealing his inventions. Maxim retorted by claiming that it was not Perkins's job to make inventions, and since it was not what they employed him to do, he no longer had any legal right to his creative ideas. Perkins explained to Maxim that Schuyler hired him and instructed him to do everything humanly possible to "improve the devices . . . manufactured by the company."[53] Perkins made it abundantly clear to Maxim that there was nothing in the agreement with Schuyler requiring him to give up the rights to his inventions. Maxim turned this exchange against Perkins. Maxim relayed their conversation to Schuyler and distorted their argument to make it appear as if Perkins was neglecting his responsibilities to spend time inventing. Soon afterward, Schuyler came into the factory and "upbraided" Perkins for not having his priorities in order. This incident substantiated the workers' opinion that Maxim "was exceedingly jealous of anything of the nature of inventive ability, being displayed by any of the workmen."[54] Regarding this working environment, Latimer commented that these activities had a stultifying effect on the company's creative environment. He indicated that no one ever publicly discouraged the workmen from pursuing creative and innovative work, but after the treatment Perkins received, most felt that it was not in their best interest to submit suggestions and invent. The company had sent a clear message that if you intended to contribute ideas, no matter how brilliant, you would not be credited or compensated.

Besides stunting creative growth, Maxim did not appear to be very optimistic about the prospects of incandescent lighting. In fact, Perkins was primarily responsible for installing the United States Electric Lighting Company lamps in the vaults and reading rooms of the Mercantile Safe Deposit Company. Latimer commented that at that time Maxim was "out of conceit with the incandescent lamp, and we were expecting every day that branch of the company's manufacture, to be abolished."[55] When the Mercantile Safe Deposit opportunity presented itself, Maxim was only lukewarm about the project. Latimer contended that if Perkins had not pursued this possibility and taken it solely under his direction, the installation would never have occurred. This lack of team cohesion was not as widespread in the Edison enterprise. He had a well-trained team of loyal men who gladly helped build his empire. Even though Edison patented many devices that did not arise from his creative output, his researchers believed that they were building upon his ideas, which was a critical difference between the Edison and Maxim organizations.[56]

Maxim's lack of interest contributed to Latimer having to take on new responsibilities. Moreover, this was not a large enterprise in any manner. The 1880s were the genesis of the incandescent lighting industry and there were many companies competing in this technical field, most of which had small staffs. When the United States Electric Lighting Company moved to New York City, there were initially only eight men working at the factory. These eight were Charles G. Perkins, machinist and general foreman; Gustav Muller, Emil Pflock, a Mr. Rosenbaum, and Joseph V. Nichols, all glass blowers; Joseph E. Lockwood, risking carbons; J. A. Vandegrift, pump operator; and Latimer, as a draftsman.[57] Because this organization was small and Maxim's enthusiasm was waning, it is understandable that Latimer had to become a vital member of this enterprise if the company intended to survive.

Latimer was on hand at all the lighting installations undertaken in 1880 and 1881. Besides the project at the Equitable Building, he assisted at the installations at Fiske & Hatch, Caswell & Massey drugstore, and the Union League Club. He was solely in charge of the operation of the latter two plants with great success. When the company expanded its operations to Philadelphia, Latimer was one of the valued men brought along to assist in the implementation of a lighting system in the Philadelphia Ledger Building. Upon returning from Philadelphia, he directed the installation of a lighting system in Montreal, Canada. This trip took place around the middle of 1881. He supervised the installation of an incandescent-lighting system for a railroad station and an arc-lighting system for the accompanying railway yard. The French-Canadians were very receptive to Latimer because of his willingness to learn their language in order to communicate instructions to the workmen more effectively. This high level of responsibility was reserved for only the most capable electrical men. Valorized inventors like Nikola Tesla helped install lighting systems before branching off to become independent inventors.[58] To supervise an installation of the size of the Montreal project, Latimer had to be knowledgeable in all aspects of artificial lighting. The United States Electric Lighting Company had come to the point where they had complete faith in Latimer's ability, soon placing him in charge of producing carbons for lamps and dispatching him on foreign installations.[59]

While involved with the new lighting installations of the United States Electric Lighting Company, Latimer also had the time to invent products that were fundamental to the development of the company. It is likely that the company's commercial lamps by late 1881 benefited from Latimer's work and were essentially of his design. The United States Electric Lighting Company probably began serious production of incandescent lamps in the fall of 1880. In October 1880, Maxim received a patent for a process that treated filaments with a hydrocarbon vapor so as "to equalize and standardize . . . resistance."[60] A filament treated with Maxim's process burned longer than a filament used in an Edison lamp. Concurrently, Latimer had begun perfecting a way to mass produce these filaments and eliminate filament breakage and deformity, commonplace with preexisting procedures. Existing manufacturing techniques used plates to confine the blanks, or filament material, which had different chemical properties than the blanks. During heating, the blanks would expand and contract at a different rate than the confining plates. Latimer's primary suggestion was that the confining plates, used during carbonization, be made of a fibrous material with a similar rate of expansion and contraction as the blanks.[61] The advantage of this procedure was that it produced highly resistant filaments that could be formed into new shapes. The shape that was chosen for most of their lamps was an "M," conceivably for Maxim. He reduced this new procedure to practice prior to July 20, 1880. This patent application went through a few amendments because sections had been anticipated by a Maxim patent and a British Edison patent, but on January 17, 1882, the Patent Office granted Latimer a patent for a "Process of Manufacturing Carbons" (fig. 3.3).[62]

Latimer and a United States Electric Lighting Company associate, Joseph Nichols, also patented an improvement in incandescent lamps in September 1881 and assigned it to themselves. This technique produced a cleaner attachment from the filament to the wire connections. The bottom of the filament was widened, and into this enlarged section was cut a rectangular slit. A copper or platinum contact would be placed through this slit and bent down around the remainder of the filament. This system dispensed with all forms "of clamps, . . . nuts, screws, or pins, and similar accessories" (fig. 3.4).[63] Latimer had now produced two fundamental innovations that the United States Electric Lighting Company introduced into the production of its lamps, making its lamps a viable competitor to those produced by the Edison Companies. Latimer was in no small way responsible for the limited success the company experienced. In addition to these inventions, Latimer and another associate, John Tregoing, created a new type of globe supporter for arc-lamps (figs. 3.5, 3.6).[64] By the summer of 1880 Latimer divided his time between drafting and supervising the manufacturing of filaments, sharing this latter responsibility with Joseph E. Lockwood.[65] By the summer 1881 Latimer had become the superintendent of the incandescent lamp department of the United States Electric Lighting Company. In this capacity, he directed the production of filaments, commonly known as carbons, for Maxim lamps. This job also required him to supervise the forty men working in the division.[66] Latimer was now in an extremely unusual position, not just for a black man, but for anyone attempting to become a member of the electric lighting industry. The position of superintendent of the lamp

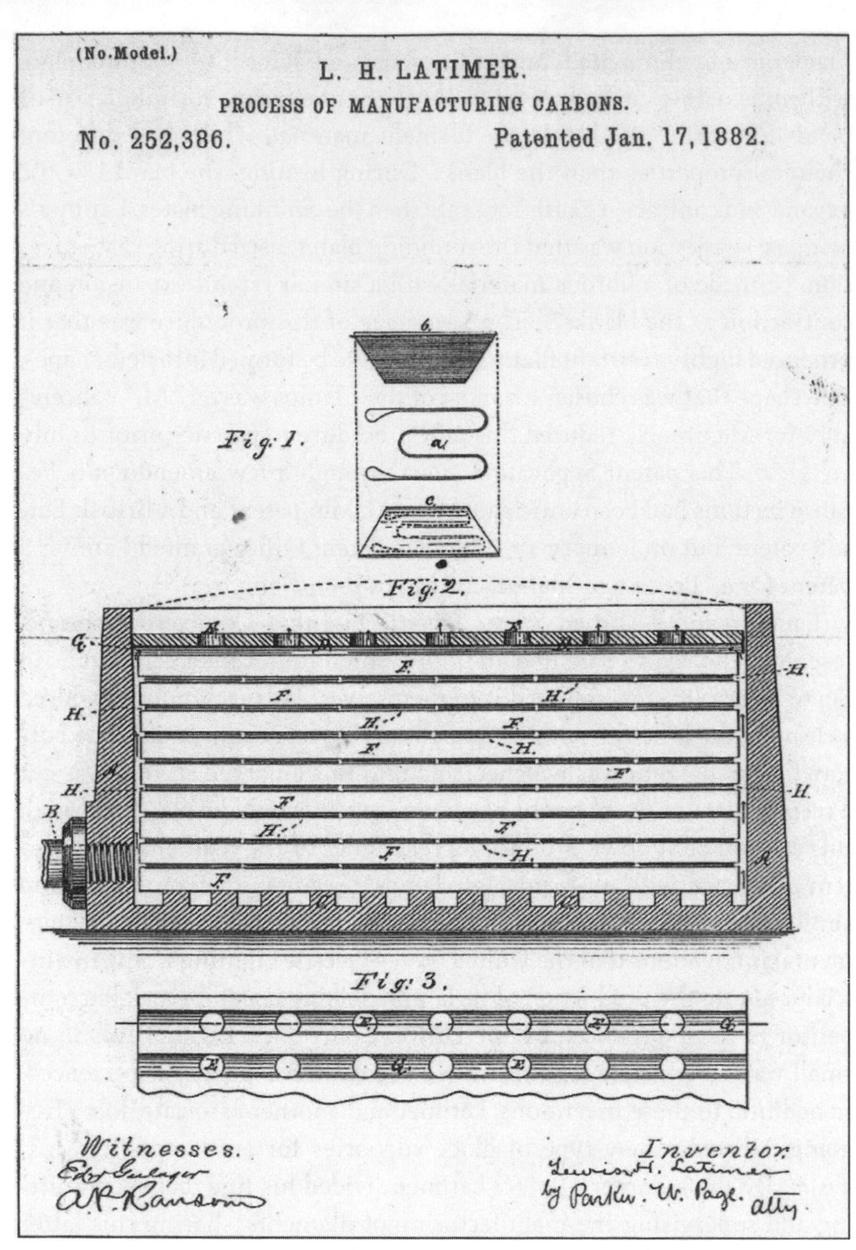

FIGURE 3.3. Latimer's process for improving the manufacture of lamp carbons. January 1882. National Archives.

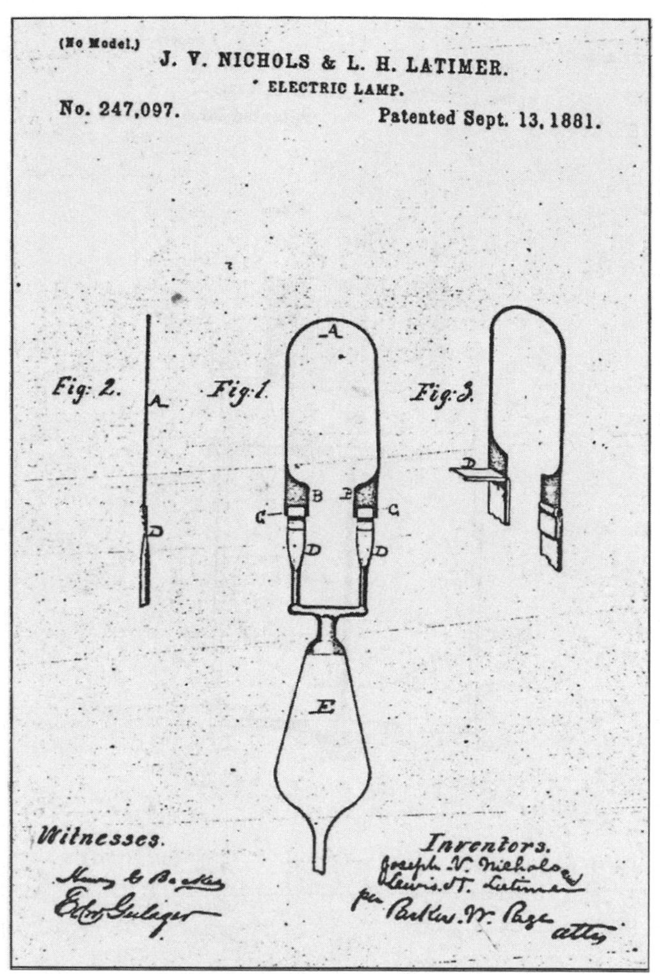

FIGURE 3.4. Latimer's electric lamp patent created a new way to attach lamp carbons to electric power sources. September 1881. National Archives.

works was a position of industrial importance. Latimer had not only assimilated into this developing electrical culture at this stage in his life, but he had risen to the point where he was a fairly prominent member of this community.

Latimer had obtained a vast body of knowledge of all types of electrical lighting systems and was an expert on the Maxim system by this point in his life. When a new British concern, the Maxim-Weston Electric

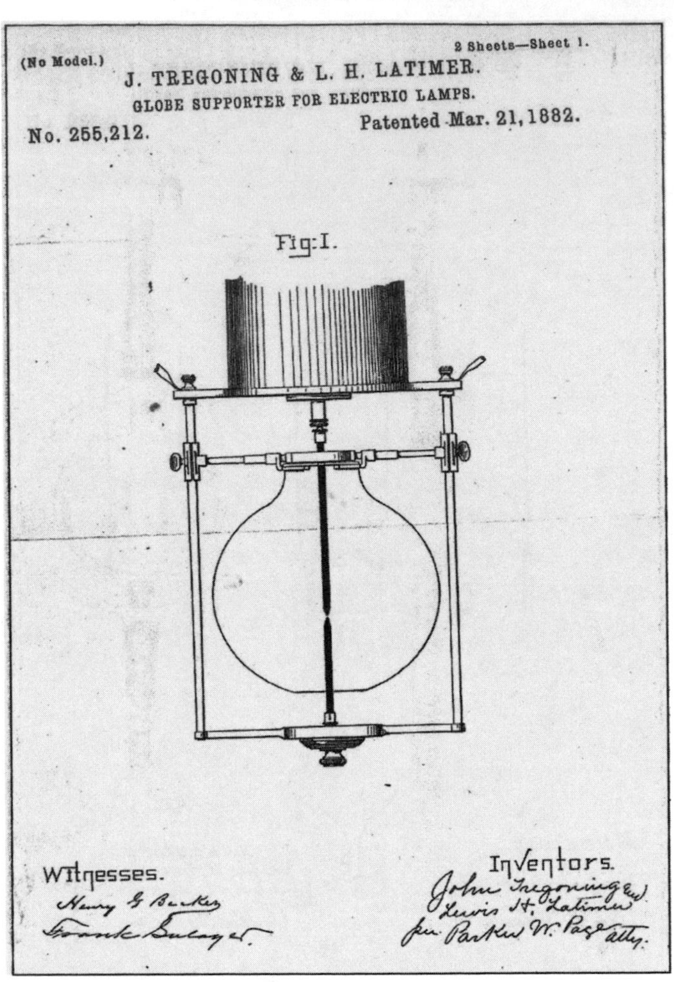

FIGURE 3.5. Latimer's design for supporting a globe covering an arc-lamp. Front elevation. March 1882. National Archives.

Lighting Company, needed accomplished electrical men to establish a factory producing incandescent lamps in London, Latimer was one of the obvious choices. It probably did not hurt that Latimer "had . . . chumy [sic] relations with Hiram Maxim."[67] This new company came into existence when the United States Electric Lighting Company merged with the Weston Electric Lighting Company in England and the United States. In England this union yielded the Maxim-Weston Electric Company, and in the United States, the United States Electric Lighting Company absorbed

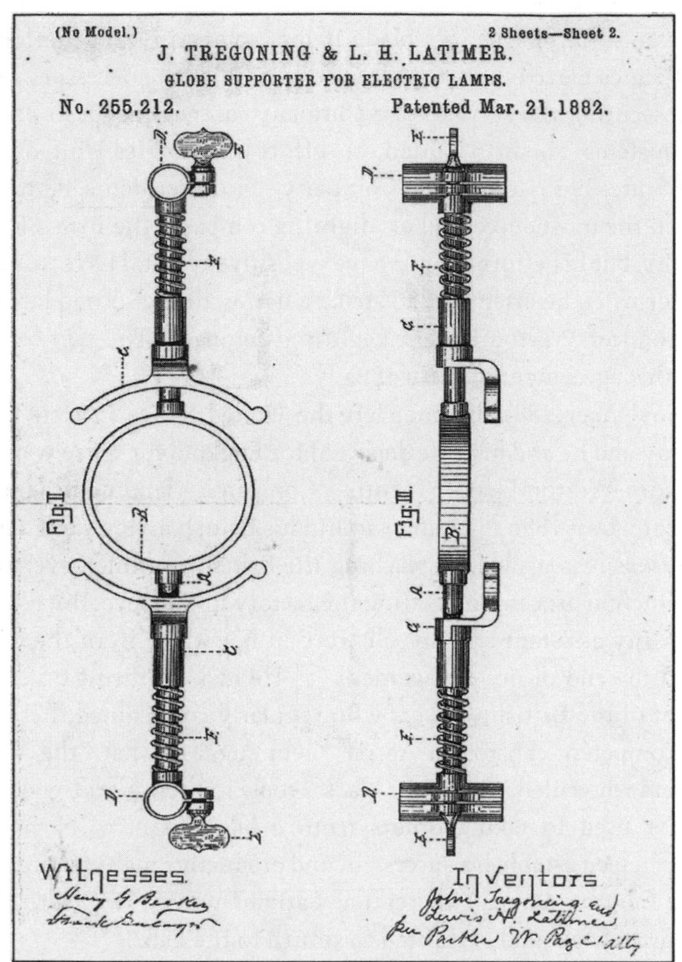

FIGURE 3.6. Elevation of globe supporter or holder.
National Archives.

the Weston Electric Lighting Company. Both of these enterprises were distinct entities. The merger was a way for the Weston company to eliminate its United States branch and for Maxim to expand into England. Both of these new factions became more potent players in the electric power game because each now had control of the Farmer, Maxim, and Weston patents in their respective countries.[68] The merger was brought about by the difficulties of the previous years. United States Electric Lighting produced an incandescent lamp, but did not possess a supporting power system. This fact made it less competitive in the long run. United States Electric Lighting decided to acquire the necessary technology by securing the services of a company that was adept in producing power systems. The man behind this effort was Charles Flint, one of the United States Electric Lighting Company's vice-presidents. Flint first approached the most successful arc-lighting company, the Brush Electrical Company, but his effort did not have a positive result. His fortunes were far better when he attempted to strike a deal with the second largest arc-light producer, Weston Electric Lighting Company. The two companies signed this agreement in early 1882.[69]

In November 1881, Latimer left the United States Electric Lighting Company and he and his wife departed for England for his new post with the Maxim-Weston Electric Lighting Company—landing in London on New Year's Day 1882.[70] Latimer found his British assignment a difficult one. He was responsible for teaching the British workmen every part of the production process and getting the factory up to speed. But as Latimer puts it, "my assistant and myself were in hot water from the first moment to the end of my engagement."[71] He had a difficult time gaining the trust of the British workers who regularly complained that Latimer was incompetent. Historian Aaron Klein suggests that "the Victorian Britishers who ruled millions of black people in their world-wide empire were not used to taking orders from a black man."[72] Nevertheless, Latimer helped establish a successful and productive manufacturing plant in nine months. Shortly thereafter, Latimer wrote, "we were released from our contract and permitted to return to the U.S."[73]

Upon his return from England in 1882, the employment situation was not the same as when he left, and he spent the next few years moving from company to company. Because Latimer's activities in these years are not well documented, this period of his life is open to a great deal of speculation. It appears that after the Maxim-Weston Company prematurely released him from his contract, he returned to the United States without a formal association to any company. His lack of connection with the United States Electric Company or any other organization negatively affected his job search upon his return. Latimer, with his exemplary experience, did not think it would be difficult to find employment, but the racial climate in the United States had begun to change significantly after President Hayes's "Compromise of 1877" ended Reconstruction and the legal protection of black people throughout the United States.[74] Perhaps the electrical industry had become saturated with quality men.

Latimer did state that "we found the ranks closed up and every place filled" when he returned.[75] With the job opportunities being so limited, Latimer was fortunate to find employment for a short stint at the Weston factory in Newark, New Jersey.[76] Late in 1882, Latimer secured a better situation with the Olmstead Electrical Light & Power Company in Brooklyn as a draftsman and manager of lamp fabrication.[77]

It was around this period that Latimer began to fully pursue economic stability by attempting to assist this company in the development of a profitable incandescent lamp. This was important because by the end of 1882 his wife was pregnant with their first child; therefore financial security was becoming more critical. Latimer could see that the more he assimilated into the dominant electrical world the better his chances were to succeed. It was this company that manufactured the Latimer lamp (fig. 3.7).[78] This lamp indicates that Latimer was potentially thinking about moving toward the inventor-entrepreneurship side of the electrical lamp industry. As with many incandescent lamp designs of the late nineteenth century, the Latimer lamp never received a patent and did not prove to be successful. Eventually in 1883, the Olmstead Electrical Light & Power Company failed. Latimer moved on to work for the Acme Electric Lighting Company in 1883 and 1884. This company also failed. Latimer found another appointment with the Excelsior Electric Company. This position was short-lived because by the fall of 1884, Latimer was working for the Imperial Electric Light Company.[79] Charles Perkins, whom Latimer worked with at the United States Electric Lighting Company, hired him as a draftsman and his general assistant.

Latimer spent a significant amount of his time in search of suitable employment. In regard to securing his position at the Imperial Electric Light Company, Latimer said that since he "was not promised employ[ment] by the Imperial Company, I had made several applications to Mr. Perkins, and on calling on him one day, was engaged there . . . without any previous agreement."[80] Thus, when Latimer showed up, Perkins hired him on the spot. Latimer remained with Imperial into 1885, at which time both he and Perkins migrated to the Mather Electric Light Company located in Hartford, Connecticut.[81] This appointment, like all the others since his return, was short. But in the same year when the Edison Electric Light Company procured his services, Latimer's situation began to look brighter.

In 1884, the Edison Electric Light Company began to alter its corporate strategy. Edison had recently regained control of the board of direc-

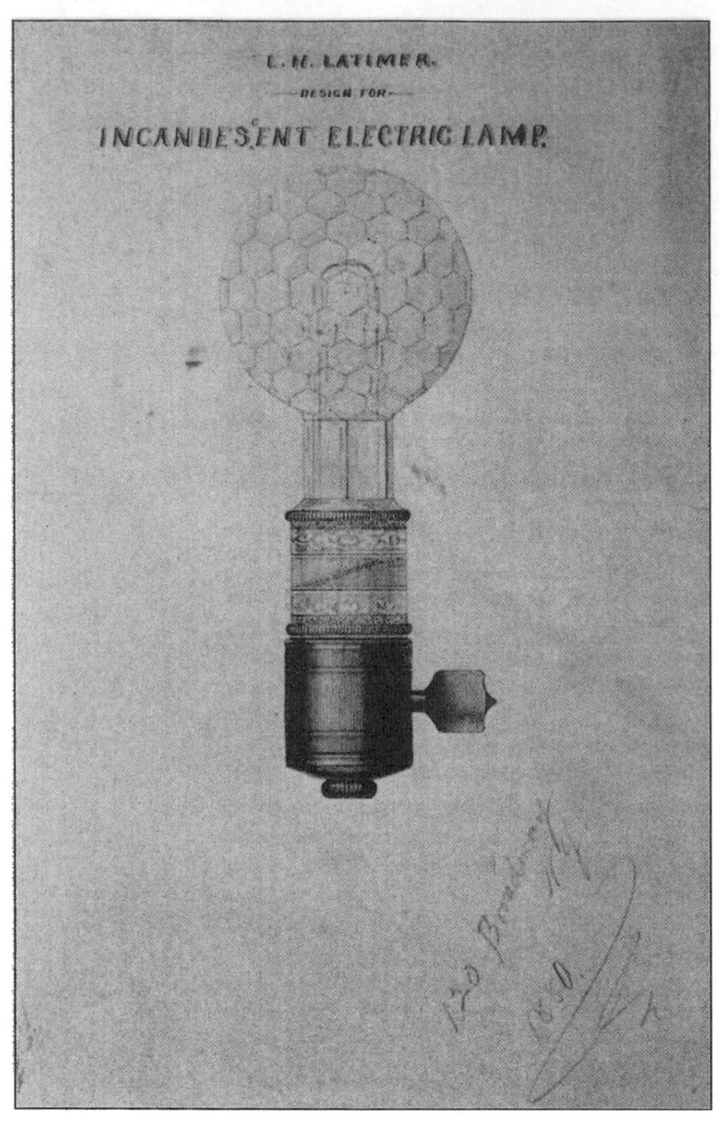

FIGURE 3.7. Latimer's design of an incandescent light bulb. Queens Borough Public Library.

tors and the company had just won an important legal battle against the Swan incandescent lighting patents in Germany. This Swan decision greatly motivated Edison. He remarked that "the effect of the decision is in the highest degree important, not only there but here and in every other country, for it practically affirms that every other incandescent lamp is an infringement upon the Edison patent."[82] On May 23, 1885, the Edison Company circulated a booklet listing the twelve patents that in some fashion contributed to the production or were an actual part of an Edison lamp.[83] This pamphlet's intent was to notify infringers that more potent legal actions would be taken against them. From this point onward, the Edison Company began to prosecute infringers aggressively. In that same month, the Edison Company initiated patent litigation against United States Electric Lighting, Consolidated Electric Lighting, and several other incandescent lamp manufacturers. The centerpiece for these battles was the Edison patent of 1880, #223,898, for an incandescent lamp.

It can be argued that the Edison Company hired Latimer to help expedite the infringement process. Soon after he began his tenure with the Edison Company, he was transferred to the engineering department under the direction of J. H. Vail.[84] Latimer's task was to be a "draughtsman inspector and expert witness as to facts in the early stages of the electric lighting business . . . [traveling] extensively, securing witnesses' affidavits, and early apparatus, and also testifying in a number of the basic patent cases to the advantage of his employers."[85] Latimer was an excellent choice for these assignments. His knowledge of the state of the electric lighting industry and his acquaintance with many of the actors in the field would have been exceptional, considering his movements since he returned to the United States. He would have been an important addition in view of his close relationship with the Edison Company's most formidable competitor, the United States Electric Lighting Company. In addition to being an expert witness called on behalf of Edison Company's interest in patent litigations, it appears that he was also an in-house technical consultant—another reason that Latimer became a member of the Edison system. Latimer stated that "the Edison people sent for me."[86] His phrasing is important: they "sent" for him; he did not apply for the position. This indicated that they needed him for some specific reason and this reason probably had a great deal to do with his previous business associates and his craft and technical knowledge.

Of all the patent infringement suits, the only case carried out to completion was the one filed against the United States Electric Lighting Company. The hearing did not begin until 1889. This infringement case was not easily won by Edison General Electric. Many manufacturers were not convinced that the Edison lamp patent, #223,898, would be upheld since similar patent applications for incandescent lamps by Goebel, de Changy, De Moleyns, J. W. Starr, and others had been filed prior to that of the Edison application.[87] The United States Electric Lighting Company, which owned the patents of Farmer, Maxim, and Weston, was confident that it held a strong patent position because Farmer and Maxim had started working in incandescent lighting before Edison.[88] Nevertheless, Judge William Wallace validated the Edison patent on July 14, 1891, by deciding that Edison was the "first to make a satisfactory high-resistant illuminant out of carbon," thereby making incandescent lighting a commercial reality. The United States Electric Lighting Company did appeal, but on October 4, 1892, a higher court upheld the prior decision.[89]

It should not come as a surprise that Latimer became a member of the legal department in 1889, the year in which the United States Electric Lighting infringement case began.[90] His reassignment took place after June 7, 1889. On that date, J. H. Vail wrote a strong letter of reference for Latimer commenting that "his services have been performed in the most faithful and efficient manner, and have been of the most satisfactory character."[91] His entrance into the legal department corresponded to his acquiring legal credentials, which may have been partially responsible for this transfer.[92] His title still remained that of draftsman, but Latimer's responsibilities went well beyond that of merely drafting. The definition of a draftsman within the Edison corporate environment, as far as Latimer was concerned, was quite broad. He "made drawings for court exhibits, had charge of the library, inspected infringing plants in various parts of the country, testified as to facts in a number of cases, . . . did considerable searching . . . in the historical filament case and others of this period, involving basic patents."[93] Exactly how important Latimer was to the infringement case against the United States Electric Lighting Company and other legal conflicts is not known, but the implications suggest that his role was far from trivial.

After his return from England and before he became a member of the Edison enterprise, Latimer had worked for and had connections with many of the lamp manufacturers that were forced to close when the Edison patent became a clearly enforceable legal reality. He was very familiar with Charles Perkins, from whom the Perkins Electrical Company received its name, and had worked for the Mather Electric Company. These were two of the first plants where lamp production was forced to end.[94] It is difficult to imagine that Latimer did not assist in closing these operations. During the period between 1882 and 1885 Latimer was rather transient. Yet these ephemeral positions enhanced his knowledge of the second and third tier of incandescent lamp manufacturers, with whom the members of the Edison companies were less familiar. His travail through various electrical companies was one of the features of his life that made him valuable to a larger electrical manufacturer.

Latimer had become a fairly well-connected member of the electrical lamp community, but the manner in which he wove himself into the fabric of the dominant electrical culture is not as obvious. A few historical documents exist that provide clues to Latimer's life below the surface. Latimer considered himself to be an aspiring poet—an example of proper education and cultural status. On June 16, 1888, Latimer penned the following letter to Thomas Edison in regard to one of his writings.

> Dear Sir
> As the fourth of July is near at hand, I venture to hope that you may deem the enclosed lines, a fit and proper speech for the Phonograph to make on the celebration of that day.
> Trusting that you will not be wasting valuable time reading them,
> I am Very Respectfully
> Yours
> L. H. Latimer[95]

The humble tone of this note makes it clear that Latimer definitely did not have a close personal relationship with Edison as has been suggested. To send a poem directly to Edison for a Fourth of July celebration was a bold move, but one that paid dividends. He received a reply on June 20, from Edison's private secretary, Alfred Tate, in which Tate transmitted a thank you from Edison for the poem and a confirmation that Edison himself would place Latimer's poem on a cylinder for the Fourth of July celebration.[96] Within the next year Latimer's poetry became more familiar to Edison. In July 1889, Latimer submitted another poem to Edison, who "read it over very carefully and said it was d——n good."[97] The author of this piece of correspondence, John Randolph, finished the letter in a very friendly tone intimating that he and Latimer were more than corporate friends. Randolph even goes to the length of adding that "when I go home this evening I will mail you one of my photographs taken a short while ago." To have been on such friendly terms with a close Edison assistant further illustrates the extent to which Latimer had become a member of this corporate electrical culture and that he had become one of the boys. Latimer's poetic efforts also show that he was attempting to become a true civilized man. He endeavored to succeed in two areas associated with civilization—technology and literature—both of which, based on the standards of the dominant culture, had very few black representatives.

Latimer's knowledge of the electrical lighting industry was known beyond the walls of Edison General Electric's legal department. On March 31, 1891, S. B. Eaton—the former president of the Edison Electric Light Company from 1882 to 1884—wrote a memorandum for the meeting of the patent litigation committee in which Latimer's name appeared. Eaton mentioned Latimer in reference to the litigation surrounding a Brush arc-regulator patent. The issue was of importance because it had implications for Edison General Electric's merger and acquisition strategy. The Brush Electrical Company, Western Electric Company, the Sperry Electric Railway Company, and the Sperry Mining Machine Company initially contested the case, but the numbers of companies involved would soon be cut in half. After Thomson-Houston purchased the Brush Electric Company in 1889, it owned the legal right to the Brush arc-regular patent.[98] Only Western Electric and Thomson-Houston remained after Thomson-Houston bought the Sperry Mining Machine Company and the Sperry streetcar patents on May 10, 1892.[99] Regarding these events, Eaton wrote, "The Western Electric Co. wishes to examine our Mr. Latimer as a witness to help break down the Thomson[-Houston] Regulator Patent. QUESTION: Shall we consent?"[100]

Whether or not to allow Latimer to participate in this case was certainly an important point of discussion because the financial backers of Edison General Electric had been interested in merging with Thomson-Houston since 1889 and certainly would have wanted Thomson-Houston to maintain a strong patent position. After the two companies merged in 1892 to form General Electric, a decision to allow Latimer to contest any Thomson-Houston patent would not have been in the company's best interest.[101] It is apparent from information such as this, that Latimer was far from just a draftsman.

Not only was Latimer a source of legal information for the Edison companies and later General Electric, he also participated in Edison publicity while enhancing his own literary credentials. In 1890 he published a book entitled *Incandescent Electric Lighting: A Practical Description of the Edison System*. This volume was not an original manuscript created by Latimer but a revised edition of William Sawyer's *Electric Lighting by Incandescence, and Its Application to Interior Illumination: A Practical Treatise*.[102] In Latimer's short version of this book he discussed Edison,

Edison's incandescent lamps, and the Edison system in the most complimentary way. He wrote that incandescent light was "like the light of the sun, it beautifies all things on which it shines, and is no less welcome in the palace than in the humblest of homes."[103] He was equally flattering about Edison: "Mr. Edison is the fortunate possessor of that rare combination of faculties, superior inventive ability, supplemented by unusual business qualifications and, to his intimates, the fact that he has invented a device is a sufficient guarantee of its commercial success."[104] Latimer had become a part of the Edison system.

Although Latimer's value and responsibilities increased within the Edison enterprises, he did not give up inventing. The Edison General Electric Company partially facilitated Latimer's patenting activities by showing interest in a device that potentially had "points which will be useful in the future of electrical fireworks."[105] But there were occasions when his corporate connections stunted his inventive activity. For instance, Latimer had been developing improvements for elevators since around 1882 (fig. 3.8).[106] In 1898, Latimer began to initiate patent applications on these augmentations. Since he was a member of the General Electric–Westinghouse Board of Patent Control, these companies had the first opportunity to purchase his invention. Latimer received a letter from Frederick Fish, General Electric's general counsel, indicating that the company had examined the inventions and had "no objections to [Latimer] submitting the matter to the Otis Company." Fish also intimated that Latimer should speak with a Mr. Terry, the representative of the Westinghouse Company before Fish would write him a letter of introduction to the Otis Elevator Company. Fish also wrote that "[i]f there should be anything in your inventions that interests the Westinghouse Company, it is better that we should find the matter out now than later."[107] At this point in his life, Latimer had little flexibility in his patenting efforts. As a result of this situation, his patent production decreased (see Appendix D). Latimer was not the only one feeling the corporation's influence. Beginning in the late nineteenth century, most technical industries experienced growth in corporate control. It was this control that resulted in a narrowing of the patenting flexibility for most aspiring inventors working within corporate institutions.

The restriction on Latimer's patent applications contrasts distinctly with the experiences of Granville Woods. The corporate connections that sometimes hindered Latimer's inventive efforts were the contacts that Woods tried all his life to make. As an independent inventor, Woods

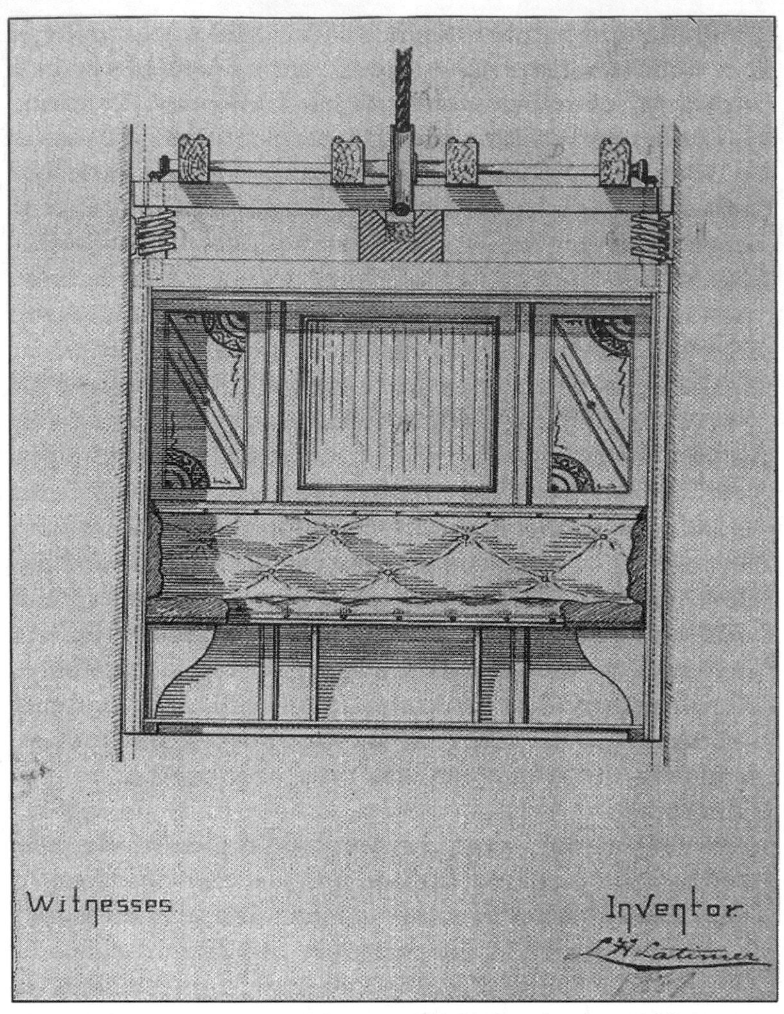

FIGURE 3.8. Latimer's design to provide suspension for elevator cars. Queens Borough Public Library.

wanted nothing more than for a company the size of General Electric to take an interest in and support his work. Eventually, General Electric and Westinghouse did purchase some of Woods's inventions, but each man followed a different path to his goal within the electrical community: Latimer made his connections from the inside and Woods built his contacts from the outside.

Within the constraints that existed, Latimer did invent several patentable devices. In 1886, he received a patent for an "Apparatus for Cool-

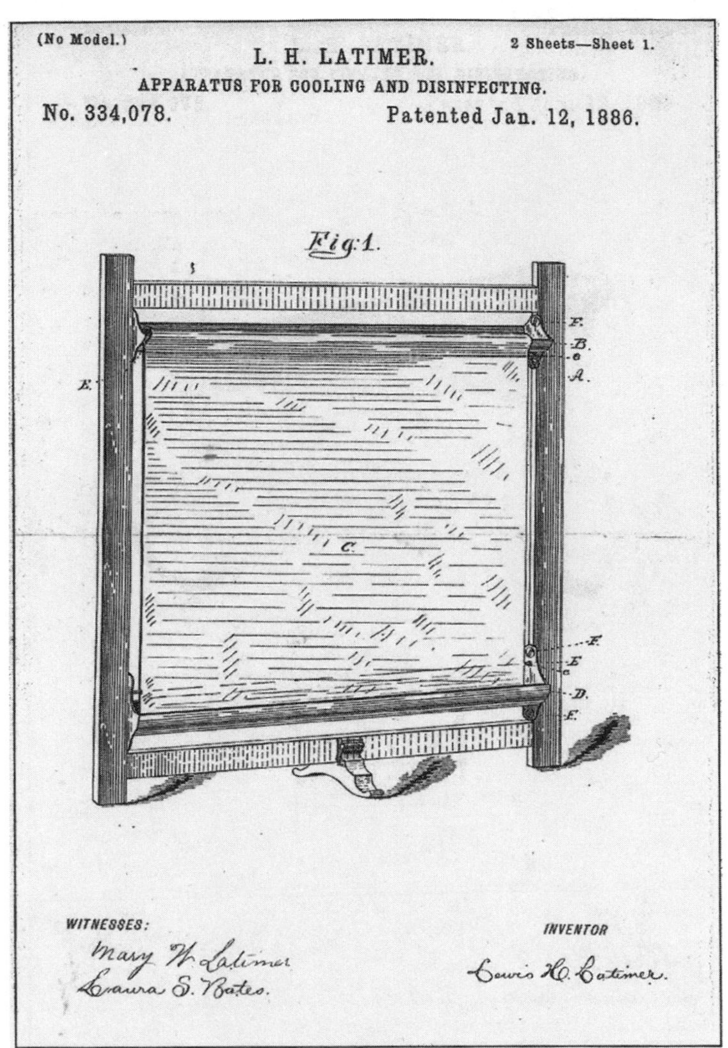

FIGURE 3.9. Latimer's design for a screen that would either disinfect or cool air entering through a window. January 1886. National Archives.

ing and Disinfecting."[108] This device consisted of a fabric screen, saturated with a disinfecting liquid, that would cool and disinfect the air as the wind blew through it (figs. 3.9, 3.10). He also patented a "Locking Rack for Coats, Hats, and Umbrellas" (fig. 3.11). These devices—neither of which was particularly revolutionary or successful—were important because they show that Latimer was still inventing. These patents fur-

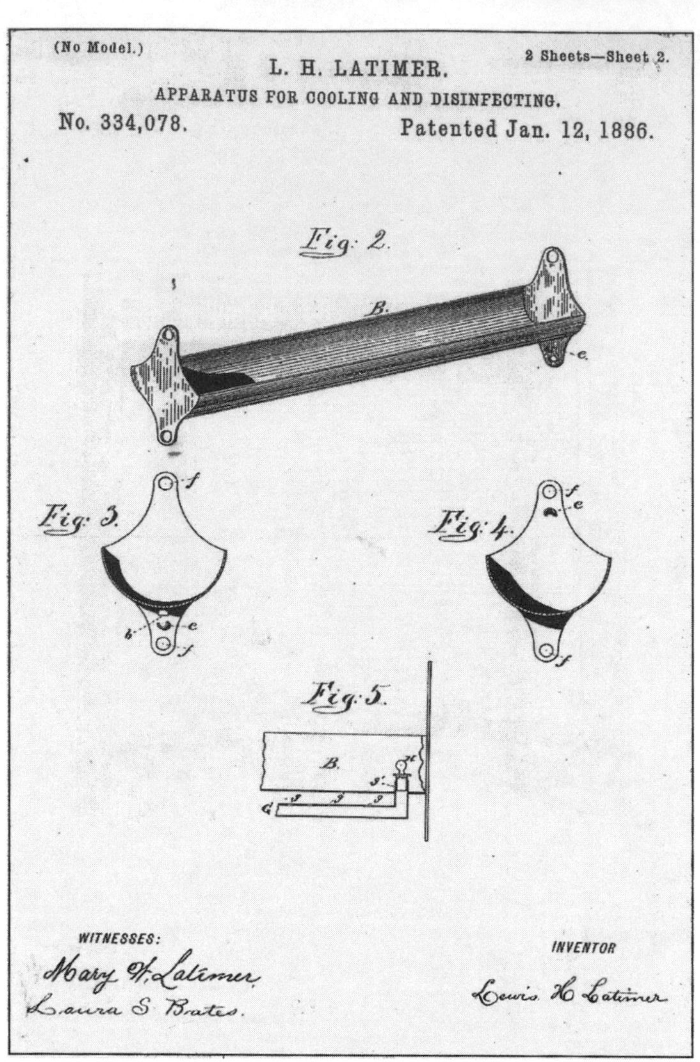

FIGURE 3.10. Trough for disinfectant or cooling liquid. National Archives.

ther legitimated him within the corporate electrical culture, which placed a high value on inventing and patenting, a mandatory exercise to remain firmly entrenched.

The last major move for Latimer within General Electric came when he was made chief draftsman of the General Electric/Westinghouse Board of Patent Control in 1896.[109] The formation of General Electric and later the General Electric/Westinghouse Board of Patent Control were

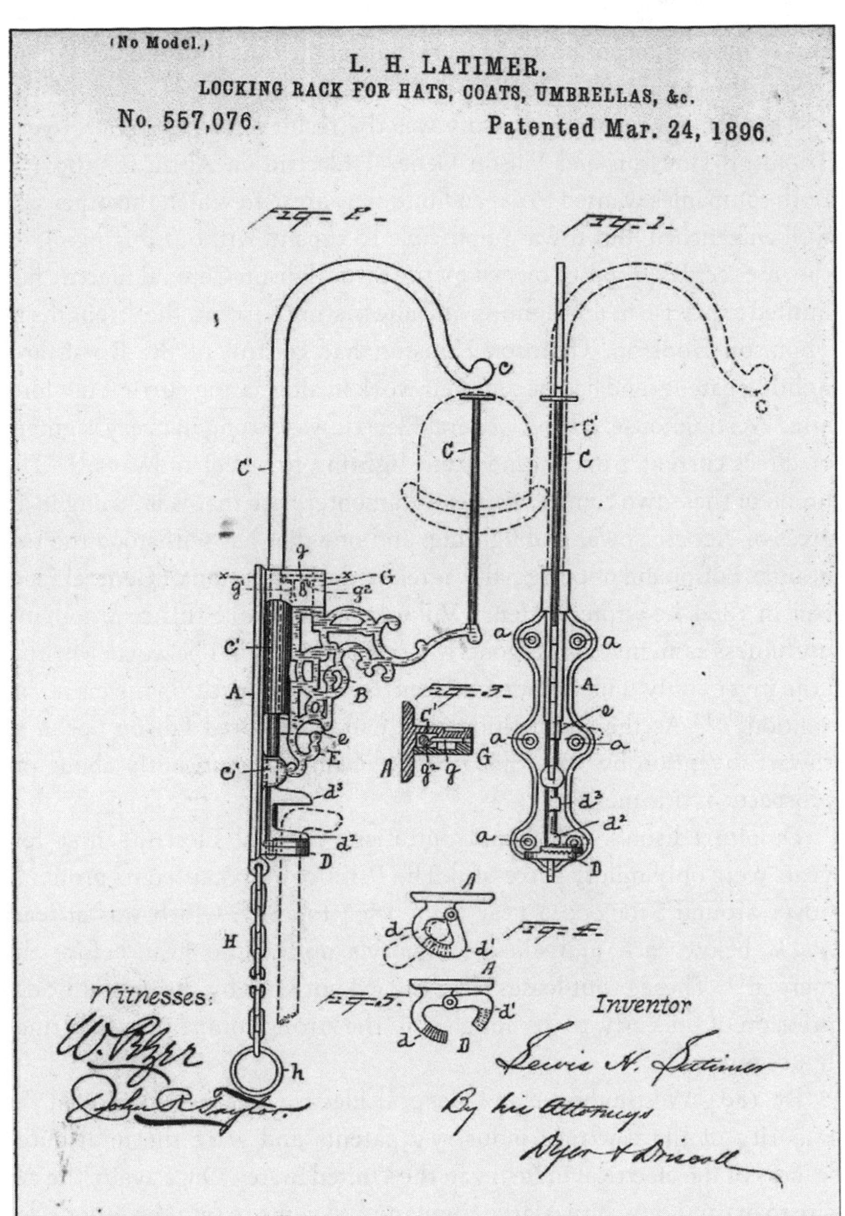

FIGURE 3.11. Latimer's design for a locking rack for personal items. March 1896. National Archives

two significant corporate maneuvers that set the tone for the electrical industry throughout the 1890s.

The General Electric Company was the result of the merger between Thomson-Houston and Edison General Electric on April 15, 1892.[110] Both companies wanted to expand into new areas in which the other was well entrenched. But it was impossible to expand without infringing on the intellectual property owned by the other. Edison General Electric had limited expertise in arc-lighting and alternating current, the strengths of Thomson-Houston. Thomson-Houston had control of the Brush arc-lighting patents and had begun their work in alternating current not long after Westinghouse. Edison General Electric was strong in every segment of direct current from incandescent lighting to street railways.[111] The union of these two companies created an enterprise that was strong in all areas of electric power and lighting, and one that has withstood the test of time. Edison did not originally agree with the creation of General Electric. In 1889, he wrote to Henry Villard, "if you make this coalition, my usefulness as an inventor is gone. My services wouldn't be worth a penny. I can invent only under powerful incentive. No competition means no invention."[112] As the competition that had so inspired Edison began to thwart invention by 1892, his attitude changed significantly about the prospects of this merger.

Despite Edison's new-found optimism General Electric's first few years were only mildly successful. The Panic of 1893 caused its profits to hover around $500,000 a year from 1894 to 1897, which was at least 400% below each individual company's profits the year before the merger.[113] These profit losses were caused not only by the economic depression of the early 1890s but also by the strong competition Westinghouse provided.

By 1894, Westinghouse and General Electric together controlled the majority of the electrical industry's patents and were the undisputed leaders of the electrical industry in the United States. Once again, the desire to expand caused two large companies to venture into the other's domain. Westinghouse held an advantage in polyphase power and General Electric's strength was in electric railways. Neither believed the other had a strong enough patent position to inhibit expansion. Consequently, both companies initiated sharp legal action in 1894, spending a great deal of time and effort fighting each other. During the spring of 1895, rumors of an agreement were floating about. These negotiations soon dissolved, and by 1896 there were more than three hundred patent-related suits pending between the two organizations. As their combined legal strain intensified, infringers were able to capitalize on the escalating battle. Both companies reached their breaking point and signed a patent cross-licensing agreement on March 12, 1896, with only one exception: General Electric did not place its incandescent lamp patents into the pool. A Board of Patent Control had the responsibility of managing the cross-licensing arrangement. The agreement had a profound effect on the rest of the industry. By pooling their patents, both companies cemented an even stronger position in the market. They were now free to attack other infringers, resulting in the rapid purchase of many smaller electrical companies by General Electric or Westinghouse.[114]

The activities of the Board of Patent Control—outside of protecting the financial interests of General Electric and Westinghouse—can only be speculated upon because very few documents relating to its functions exist. As for Latimer's responsibilities, he probably continued to engage in work similar to that which he performed for Edison General Electric in the early 1890s. A minuscule glimpse of this work is attainable from documents surrounding the use of Heinrich Goebel electric lamp work by Edison Company competitors. Goebel, a watchmaker from New York City, became well known in the electric lamp industry after 1892 for purportedly manufacturing carbon filament incandescent lamps from 1854 until 1872. Edison Company competitors like Boston's Beacon Vacuum Pump & Electrical Company began to invoke Goebel's legacy to invalidate the Edison patent by arguing that Goebel's carbon filament lamps preceded Edison's. The only problem with that tactic was the lack of evidence supporting Goebel's work. He did not receive a single patent or proceed through the necessary channels to disseminate his work. Moreover, Goebel had unsuccessfully attempted to sell his inventions to the Edison Electric Lighting Company in 1882. Thus, Beacon Vacuum Pump & Electrical Company failed to obtain an injunction against General Electric, but the Columbia Incandescent Lamp Company of St. Louis succeeded.[115]

Latimer's knowledge and skill helped to eliminate General Electric's Goebel problem. He was directly involved in the litigation when complainants used Goebel as a defensive strategy. Latimer submitted an affidavit for the Edison case against the Columbia Incandescent Lamp Company that referred primarily to Charles Perkins, who had become the chink in the Goebel defense armor. In a memo entitled "Mr. Latimer's Theory on the Goebel Lamp Case," Latimer showed that the purported Goebel lamps, the critical pieces of evidence, were not originals, but reproductions. Latimer's relentless research had traced the imitation lamps to Charles Perkins, who had instructed Gustav E. Muller, a glass blower he employed (whom Latimer also knew since he and Muller had worked at U.S. Electric Lighting) to fabricate the fraudulent lamps. Latimer carefully examined the witnesses' affidavits and met with and questioned several glass blowers in reference to the lamps in question. Latimer relied on his thorough understanding of lamp making, along with the information gathered from interviews to reach his conclusion. He was able to determine who had produced a lamp from observations based on his knowledge of the art of incandescent lamp making in conjunction with his connections in the industry. This ability was indispensable for Edison General Electric. His investigative skills were a vital tool in the preservation of Edison incandescent lamp patents. This work confirms that Latimer had reached the core of the electric lighting community.[116]

Another equally intriguing portion of this memo was his new attitude toward Perkins. In 1889, Latimer had testified favorably on Perkins's behalf, but by the mid 1890s he contended that Perkins, as far back as 1879, during their Bridgeport days, had "commenced [a] career of deception and trickery in connection with electrical lighting matters which he has ever since consistently followed out whenever and wherever it appeared to him that a criminal course would advance his personal interest."[117] Had Latimer been playing along until he reached a position where he no longer had to associate with men like Perkins? Or was he now falling in line with his new employer? Either way, his political savvy helped seal his position within General Electric.

Latimer remained the chief draftsman of the General Electric/Westinghouse Board of Patent Control until 1911. The breakup of this organization in 1911 forced Latimer to make another important career decision. Very uneasy about his future at his advanced age, he preserved his trepidation in an illustration entitled "My Situation as It Looked to Me in 1912" (fig. 3.12). In this sketch Latimer depicts himself as tenuously perched on the "ragged edge" that led to an "uncertain future" with "E. W. Hammer, consulting engineer." He could stumble from the ruler-edged tight rope to either "the wide wide world," or the "General Electric Co. Feathers," and an unsteady Latimer apprehensively asked, "which way will he fall?"[118]

The most intriguing aspect of this sketch is the name tag affixed to the bottom of Latimer's jacket. It resembles a price tag. Was Latimer alluding

FIGURE 3.12. My Situation as It Looked to Me in 1912.
Queens Borough Public Library.

to the commodified nature of his existence within American society? Latimer undoubtedly understood the value of his services to General Electric, Hammer & Schwarz, and a host of other organizations interested in his skills. Was he making a statement about how those who might compete for his services viewed him as a purchasable asset? This drawing can also be interpreted as Latimer deemphasizing the importance of his race in his pursuit of economic success, while simultaneously reinscribing the understanding of black people as commodities to be bought and sold, whether they were slaves or consultants, onto the dominant American culture. All of the options Latimer sketched were appealing to him. General Electric would most certainly have found a position for Latimer, but he was past his prime. If he could have moved into the managerial hierarchy, that promotion would already have taken place. Similarly credentialed men had already made their way into upper management. Latimer must have fully understood the limited opportunities for himself at General Electric. Yet a token position may have been better than journeying blindly into the "wide wide world." Latimer eventually decided to join the patent consulting firm of Hammer & Schwarz, which proved to be a very shrewd move. When the Board of Patent Control dissolved, most of the engineering department went to work for Hammer & Schwarz. With the overt racism of engineering circles during the early twentieth century, a firm where he "was . . . liked and respected by all of his associates" was a very good place for Latimer to be.[119] He remained with the firm until he became ill in 1924.

In the interim, Latimer became a founding and the only African American member of the Edison Pioneers. On January 2, 1918, Charles Wirt, William J. Hammer, Sidney Paine, and Frederick A. Scheffler sent an inquiry to all the men associated with the Edison company before 1885 suggesting that they meet on January 24, "for the purpose of renewing acquaintances and perhaps to form some sort of organization."[120] As the organization became a reality, the constitution and bylaws clearly defined the group's objectives: "The objects of this Association are to bring together for social and intellectual intercourse the men who were associated with Thomas A. Edison in the days prior to and including the year 1885 in his work of invention and experimentation in the arts and sciences; to revive and perpetuate the memories of those pioneer days; to pay tribute to Mr. Edison's transcendent genius and achievements and to acknowledge the affection and esteem in which we hold him."[121] This was a group of early electrical innovators attempting to preserve their legacy. Moreover, it was a way for this group of men, most of whom did not have technical degrees from colleges or universities, to professionalize. But for all of its formalism, this group was nothing more than an exclusionary elite social organization, which makes it all the more exceptional that Latimer was a member. This was the coup de grâce of Latimer's assimilation. He had become so much a part of white civilization and the corporate electrical culture that this institution willingly accepted him as a member.

Latimer and the Politics of Assimilation

By the mid 1890s, Latimer started to become more visible in the elite intellectual circles of the African American community. This should not come as a surprise because his rise to a position of prominence in a white male-dominated industry had become fairly well known. On December 6, 1895, Latimer received an invitation to the National Conference of Colored Men from a close personal friend, Richard T. Greener, a long-standing member of the black aristocracy.[122] The previous National Conference of Colored Men had been held in 1873, but the deterioration of African American rights and freedom merited the call for another meeting. The organizational committee stated "that the time had come when the leading and active colored men should meet together and confer and deliberate upon principles and measures important to the welfare and progress and general improvement of the race."[123] Disenfranchisement, Jim Crow, and lynching were the main issues of discussion. The primary goal was to form a national committee that would pursue equality through a unified political platform that would be presented at the 1896 Republican National Convention. Latimer was not involved in the organization of this meeting. In fact, he received his invitation after the fact. The original call for the meeting was September 10, 1895, three months before Greener extended Latimer an invitation. In the formal call sent to Latimer, Greener wrote nonchalantly that "this is sent to you that you may send an acceptance, and a letter on general principles, or some particular principle to be read at the convention." Greener does not seem to take the meeting very seriously. His only purpose in attending was to "lay out some of the lines of the conventions."[124] It is questionable whether Latimer would have received an invitation if Greener had not planned to attend; even if Latimer had received an invitation, it is doubtful that he would have accepted. Latimer carefully controlled his affiliations with potentially politically radical black groups, all of whom certainly would have had a deleterious effect on his professional standing.

Latimer did respond to Greener's request. He transmitted a lackluster reply listing five reasons for having a National Conference of Colored Men, in just enough time to be read before the conference participants. The fact that his letter was read is significant because it demonstrates the black community's knowledge of Lewis Latimer. If he had not been considered a prominent man, it is unlikely that his comments would have been read and printed in the *Detroit Republican*. It would be accurate to assume that Latimer had parlayed his electrical success into social distinction. Latimer's rationales for the congress were far from radical, but they are very informative about his position on the race question at the time. He began his response by stating: "1. It is necessary that we should show the people of this country that we—who have by our martyrdom under the lash; by our heroism on the battle field; by our Christian forbearance beneath an overwhelming burden of injustices and by our submission to the laws of our native land, proven ourselves worthy citizens and conscientious patriots—are fully alive to everything which affects the interests of our common country." In this first point he stated that the black population had performed those duties of responsible citizens, but it was also important for black people to display this to white Americans. Latimer did not believe all people were born citizens; one had to earn that right through proper action. He continued by contending: "2. Because, there is no separation of interests of the colored American from those of the white American, and it is our duty, to our country and to the world, that we are looking to the interest of the people at large, when we protest against the crime and injustice meted out to any class or condition of citizens." This second point came from his assimilationist stance. He did not want there to be a distinction between black and white. He also implied that the black population should not focus on the uplift of its own race, but people-at-large. He continued by invoking class in an effort to protect all classes. Once again he displayed his assimilationist leanings. Race was not the delineator of civilization, but class. The third and forth statements were similar in intent: "3. Because, the community which permits a crime against its humblest member to go unpunished, is nursing into life and strength a power which will ultimately threaten its own existence. 4. Because our history conclusively proves that the attempt to degrade any portion, class or race of our common [people], has always been fraught with more danger to the oppressor than to the oppressed." Latimer believed that some day the suppressor would have to reckon with the suppressed, and he concluded by advancing intellect over strength. "5. Because an even handed justice to all, under and through the law, is the only safe course to pursue; for strength will supersede intelligence in the control of our communities, and the asses heels [will] beat out the statesman's brains." His comments were very much in line with the black intellectual elite's vision of civilization: a raceless, but not classless society. Latimer was "heart and soul in the movement," but not in body. This sentiment is seen more precisely in his letter's conclusion, which he closed by passing on "hearty wishes for the successful termination of *your* movement" thereby distinguishing himself from the National Conference of Colored Men (emphasis added).[125]

From this point Latimer disappeared into the shadows of the corporate electrical culture and colored society—still very much involved, but not publicly visible. This disappearance can be explained by his world view, which paralleled that of Greener. They believed in uplift through individuality and independence, which dictated their efforts to avoid being seen at center stage. But this does not mean they were not on the stage. Black scholar William Ferris, who contended that Greener was the leading colored intellectual of the day, criticized Greener for his inaction on behalf of his race. In the wake of Booker T. Washington's "Atlanta Compromise" speech of 1895 and *Plessy* v. *Ferguson* in 1896, Greener's social standing, political prominence, and oratory skills had prepared him to step forward and restoke the waning fire ignited by Frederick Douglass, Alexander Crummell, J. C. Price, George T. Downing, John Mercer Langston, and others. But according to Ferris, Greener was not alone, and as "the industrial surrender, civil and political rights wave swept over the country . . . most of the educators, preachers, editors and politicians of the race lost their moorings and drifted with it."[126] Greener was not a willing inheritor of Negro leadership. To this end Greener wrote: "I have never aspired to be a leader . . . I am only ambitious to be a full fledged American citizen, demanding all my rights at all times and yielding none of them." He further commented, "as to being a producer of history, I take my hat off to such 'producers' and such 'History,' and prefer my seclusion among the quiet monks of the cloister, who preserve the sacred fire while noisy babblers and weak scribes rattle on."[127] Concerning racial agitation, he and Latimer did live the monk's life. They agreed that if all people performed their duties as "citizens," there would be no need to discuss the race question because all people would advance to civilization as each person who elevated himself or herself would concurrently elevate their race. They were living examples of their philosophy that every person could achieve civilization through the freedom to make one's own way.

Greener's actions were not always viewed as promoting racial uplift. Some attacked him, even more severely than Ferris, since his version of individualism often conflicted with the rising ideology of black nationalism. Calvin Chase, who edited a leading black newspaper, the *Washington Bee,* attacked both Greener and Robert Terrell for unsuccessfully attempting to gain membership to the Harvard Club. Chase "described them as typical examples of fair-complexioned, well-educated blacks who were always in search of means to abandon 'their own race' for 'white society.'"[128] Others also questioned Greener's commitment to the black community. When the American Negro Academy presented Greener's name for membership, strong opposition developed. The selection committee withdrew his name under pressure from outspoken opponents like Alexander Crummell. In 1898, Crummell wrote to journalist John E. Bruce, more commonly known as Bruce Grit, that Greener "has been for years a white man in New York and turned his back upon all his colored acquaintances."[129] Since Latimer and Greener were confidants, the impression that others had of Greener did not promise much for Latimer as a Negro activist and race champion. Both men made efforts to separate themselves from African American people at large and were not sympathetic to the struggles experienced by Negroes outside of their social class. It was not that they were naive about the difficulties of the common Negro; they simply believed that it was not their problem if others did not see the wisdom in their assimilationist leanings.

Latimer did not always remain a discreet actor. In 1902, he surfaced to defend a gentleman of his social, intellectual, and professional class, Samuel R. Scottron. Scottron was the only colored member of the School Board of Brooklyn. He served the board well for eight years, but at the end of the his eighth year New York City Mayor Seth Low did not renew his appointment. Apparently Scottron's predominantly white district pressured Mayor Low to withhold the position. Latimer was willing to be an advocate for Scottron. He facilitated the submission of a petition to Mayor Low requesting that Scottron be reappointed. This action was quite honorable, but Scottron's supporters did not expect that the petition was going to be a success. The petition closed by appealing to the mayor's sense of honor and proffered that "the appointment which his [Scottron's] good and faithful service . . . justly entitles him to receive, be supplemented by further action in placing him in a position equally honorable."[130] Thus, if Scottron could not regain his school board post, he would accept another position with an equal amount of prestige. Their efforts proved fruitless, but the petition signers did hold a tribute on May 9 to honor Scottron's service.[131]

Even though Latimer appeared to organize the protest, he was probably only partially involved. Latimer did not author the petition. He wrote to Scottron, "I herewith enclose a copy of a petition which several young men, occupying clerical positions down town, proposed to circulate for signatures." Regardless of the degree of Latimer's involvement, it is informative that this group of men chose him as the representative for Scottron's defense. Obviously these clerks considered Latimer a man of repute, and Latimer's signature appeared on the petition. He was willing to be the point man for this minor sedition because Scottron was "a colored man of means, influence and culture."[132] Latimer was not risking anything by stepping forward on Scottron's behalf.

Probably more endearing to Latimer was that Scottron was a resourceful inventor-entrepreneur. Scottron invented an adjustable mirror, window cornices, and other apparatuses.[133] He even went to the trouble of acquiring the mechanical skills to manufacture these devices himself. Scottron was a vocal proponent of the shop culture's emphasis on mechanical training. His seven years of technical training convinced him that "there is possibly no shop where one can serve and get a broader knowledge of applied mechanics than a well patronized patternmaking shop, bringing one as it does into a consideration of the various elements, substances; etc. used in manufacture."[134] This training provided him with the skills to avoid patenting unmarketable products. It should not be forgotten that Latimer was a product of the Follandsbee Machine Shop—a patternmaking shop—and these experiences forged a common bond between Latimer and Scottron. Without a respect for his technical creativity and "culture," Latimer might not have come to his aid.

Many of Latimer's actions display his conservative politics, but in two letters to Booker T. Washington he articulated his assimilationist views in writing in 1904. These letters addressed the July 30, 1903, uprising in Boston. Washington's scheduled appearance before the Boston arm of the National Negro Business League precipitated this skirmish. In preparation for the meeting members of Boston's anti-Washington faction, primarily William Monroe Trotter and those associated with his newspaper the *Guardian*, authored nine questions to be presented for Washington to address. The National Negro Business League meeting, held at the Columbus Avenue AME Zion Church, began with future Assistant Attorney General William H. Lewis introducing T. Thomas Fortune. During Lewis's introduction of Fortune, the Washington opposition in the audience hissed at the mention of Washington's name. As Fortune addressed the audience, Granville Martin attempted to force Fortune to answer an antagonistic question. Martin intended his outburst to begin the full-scale protest of Washington's appearance and disrupt the meeting to the point where it would not take place. Boston's National Negro Business League assumed, however, that Trotter and his allies would attempt to create a disturbance that evening and requested police protection. The police performed as expected and maintained order by removing Martin from the sanctuary of the church. Meanwhile, someone had scattered cayenne pepper close enough to Fortune that he had to pause to regain his composure. The tension was rising. As Lewis appealed for civilized discussion and began introducing Washington, the uproar began. Martin stormed back into the church and yelled another question. As Lewis commanded five police officers to arrest Martin, the crowd erupted into chaos. As small scuffles broke out in the audience, Trotter stood atop a chair and began to read from the list of questions. As a result, Trotter and his sister Maude were taken to jail. Boston's National Negro Business League did not allow this commotion to ruin their evening. After everything had returned to normal, Washington was introduced and delivered a standard speech on his political, economic, and social philosophy for the black community.[135]

The following February, Latimer corresponded with Washington. Latimer wrote Washington after having a conversation with a "young man from Boston"; to Latimer's disgust, this young man "attempted ineffectually to justify the Boston scandal." This unnamed individual sent Latimer a copy of the questions to which Trotter and his supporters wanted Washington's answers. One would assume that Washington had seen a copy of the questions, but just in case, Latimer forwarded the nine questions along with his letter. Latimer enclosed his own responses with the questions in order to show "how they would appeal to an entirely unbiased mind."[136] The first seven of the nine questions and then Latimer's answers demand being quoted in entirety because they precisely illustrate how he positioned himself in regard to the race question. Trotter's first question wanted Washington to address his position on Negro enfranchisement.

1. *In your letter to the Montgomery Advertiser, Nov. 27th, you said: "Every revised constitution through out [sic] the Southern States has put a premium on intelligence, ownership of property, thrift, and character." Did you not thereby endorse the disenfranchisement of our race[?]*

(1) To this the obvious answer is no. It is a statement of fact, and implies that if the states making such laws abide by them, the outcome will be beneficial to *all* the citizens of those states, and if they do not make those laws operative with regard to all citizens alike, they bring those laws and all others in to contempt, thereby encouraging lawlessness [and] all its attendant evils.

Latimer's answer was extremely naive. Latimer's comments about lawlessness imply that only an untrustworthy and antidemocratic state legislature would enact laws that were not beneficial for all of the state's citizens. He chose not see the constitutions of Southern states as a form of politics to maintain the racial balance in favor of white Southerners. Most Southern states abided by their laws, but the outcomes of these laws, like most laws, did not benefit all of the states' citizens alike. In his reply, Latimer ignores how "intelligence, ownership of property, thrift, and character" had been constructed and categorically used to oppress black people and strip them of any opportunity at equality.[137] He seemed to believe that Southern states were looking out for the good of all citizens and not just white citizens. The legislation satisfied property-owing Southerners, but African Americans, the people that these state's constitutions injured most, did not have the power to revolt, let alone judge these laws to be contemptible.

The second question posed to Washington concerned the power relations between black and white people.

> 2. *In your speech before the Century Club here in March you said: "Those are most truly free who have passed the most discipline." Are you not actually upholding oppression of our race as a good thing for us, advocating peonage?*
>
> (2) To this the answer is no. Like No. 1, it is a simple statement of fact; and puts in other words the well understood and accepted saying, that those only are fitted to command who have learned to obey. Freedom consists in proper use of privilege, and is an obligation of restraint as well as liberty to act.

For Latimer, freedom was not a God-given right, but an earned privilege. He also mistakenly associated command with prior compliance. According to this statement, black people should have been extremely ready for command after the tradition of forced obedience during slavery. The inherent flaw in his response was that he did not acknowledge the preexisting American system that barred African Americans from many of the privileges of freedom.

Trotter directed his third question at Washington's definition of freedom.

> 3. *Again you say: "Black men must distinguish between freedom that is forced and the freedom that is the result of struggle and self-sacrifice." Do you mean that the Negro should expect less from his freedom than the white man from his?*

(3) To this the answer is no, and the statement would have been none the less true if it had been asserted of all men.

The Emancipation Proclamation gave the Negro a freedom that was his [by] virtue of the power behind the proclamation to enforce it; but that freedom would have been of but little value to us had not public opinion (even in the South) acquiesced in a greater or less measure; and it is by the "struggle and sacrifice" of the last forty years, that we have gained the respect and sympathy of so many of [our] fellow countrymen, and made them our fellow allies in winning us a larger measure of freedom.

Latimer's life of freedom was grossly out of touch with the lives of most black people of the period. Perhaps his cordial relations with white men blinded him to all of the social and political injustices experienced by black citizens. Latimer appeared to have said that the growing white public acceptance of black freedom was responsible for the steadily improving race relations since Emancipation. This is astounding. Latimer lived through the end of Reconstruction as well as *Plessy* v. *Ferguson*, but in his life of relative wealth and freedom in the North, he did not encounter the decline in black freedoms and opportunities that resulted from Jim Crow policies. He believed that he was living a life of increased acceptance by his fellow Americans.

Trotter's questions continued to contest Washington's denigration of black people. In the fourth question, Trotter probed Washington's inference that black people were beasts.

4. *When you said: "It was not so important whether the Negro was in the inferior car as whether there was in that car a superior man not a beast," did you not minimize the outrage of the insulting Jim-crow car discrimination and justify the "bestiality" of the Negro?*

(4) Mr. Washington could answer "no" again and it needs no very wise man to discover his meaning to be, that if we devoted [our] attention to making the Negro a "superior man" we should soon cease to [have] occasion to condemn jim-crow cars.

No race is secure against injustice until its superior members are numerous [enough] to be always in evidence. Where these are the rare exceptions, discriminations can be justified.

Latimer wore his elitism and assimilationism proudly with his steady references to "superior men." His answer to the race problem is plainly seen in his rebuttal. Since he could not fathom that civilization was a socially constructed or a racially defined concept, the idea that black "superior men" or civilized men would alleviate all race problems was completely plausible. As for Jim Crow cars on railways, Latimer's statement implies that if black people could rise to the high level of American civilization, white people would no longer see the need to segregate themselves from a group of people considered grossly inferior. Latimer believed that the race's progression toward civilization was in the hands of the black community and had very little to do with the continued legal, social, and cultural oppression built into American society. He could not conceptualize that racism had little to do with being civilized. Moreover, he even went so far as to contend that in those certain instances when "superior members are always in evidence," discrimination against those perceived to be inferior is acceptable. It is unclear if Latimer understood that statements such as these could be used against him by those who would consider him to be inferior merely by the color of his skin.

Trotter, with his fifth question, challenged Washington's position on whether or not black people should possess political power.

> 5. *In an interview with the Washington Post, June 25, as to whether the Negro should insist on his ballot, you are quoted as saying: "As is well known, I hold that no people in the same economic condition as the masses of the black people of the south should make politics a matter of the first importance in connection with their development." Do you not know that the ballot is the only self-protection for any class of people in this country?*
>
> (5) The ballot is the only protection of the masses, but it is also true that no people who are situated as the Negro in this country, no people who are as ignorant and as easily misled to [their] own detriment, should make politics of the first importance in connection with their development; because, there is quite as much danger in the misuse of political right as there is in not availing one's self of it at all.
>
> The meat of this statement is: that we should modify our actions within our rights according to the conditions under which we must act, the principal thing to be kept in view being, a steady improvement in those qualities and acquirements necessary to the making of a good citizen.

Latimer's answer to this question sufficiently indicates where he had positioned himself on the Negro problem. He argued that for ignorant Negroes the effort required to cultivate the qualities of a good citizen were so arduous that franchise would only be an unnecessary burden. Political power, rather than enabling black people to control their own destinies within American society, could corrupt the ignorant Negro masses' development toward civilization. He viewed political power and franchise as distinctly disjointed from that which would allow black people to lift themselves out of their present conditions. It is ironic that the race uplift ideology to which Latimer subscribed helped to maintain a veiled slavery or a racial apartheid within post-Reconstruction America.

In terms of Negro rights, Trotter further attacked Washington's position as a Negro leader.

> 6. *In view of the fact that you are understood to be unwilling to insist upon the Negro having his every right (both civil and political), would it not be a calamity at this juncture to make you our leader?*
>
> (6) No man is responsible for what people are pleased to understand about [him] and in view of the fact that Mr. Washington is not a candidate for election to Negro leadership, this question is irrevelant, and wanting in sequence. I might add, that never within my knowledge have the colored people of this country elected a leader. We have many men called leaders, and Mr. Washington is one of them; but until we elected him as such, or he declares himself our leader, and asserts that he is authorized to speak for all of us, we cannot question his right to speak as he may see fit, or hail him into a court of impeachment.

Latimer did make a good point: the black population never voted for Washington to be their leader. But since a large segment of the black community could not cast any vote, black Americans could not elect a leader if they so desired. Furthermore, if Latimer thought that Washington had not been singled out as the most valued voice on the conditions of the Negro in America, he was most certainly deluded. Booker T. Washington wielded more political power that any other black leader of the time. Latimer was correct in stating the no one should question Washington's right to speak, but it was problematic when white America assumed that he was speaking for the homogeneous unit known as the Negro. In many ways, this was the problem; Washington was the dominant voice of a diverse and varied black community because he said what white America wanted to hear.

Finally, Trotter accused Washington of simply substituting one form of slavery for another.

7. *Don't you know you would help the race more by exposing the new form of slavery just outside the gates of Tuskegee than by preaching submission?*

(7) I cannot entertain a statement which bears no indication of the source from which it was taken but I will say, I should [require] very positive proof to convince me that Mr. Washington preached unqualified submission, as your question would imply.[138]

Latimer was ignoring the reality of the world in which he lived. His denial of Jim Crow, forced segregation, disenfranchisement, and the assault on black citizenship rights demonstrated his limited connection with the everyday existence of black people in America.

Latimer's responses to these seven questions tell us a great deal about his race philosophy. In each answer he distanced himself from the group of people he considered to be the Negro masses—the uneducated and uncivilized. Latimer did not see himself as having a connection to the Negro masses. He had already made the transformation to civilization—the transformation that Latimer believed was so utterly difficult for the common Negro. He was no longer a member of a backward race, but a member of civilization. He had assimilated into what he thought was to become a new raceless social, political, and cultural world. One cannot say that Latimer was fully a Bookerite. Some of his rhetoric about uplifting the race through its superior men strongly resembled that of Du Bois's ideology of the "Talented Tenth."[139] Yet, Latimer had become a vocal supporter of Washington, which was just as and maybe even more important than being an ideological supporter of Du Bois.

Washington liked what Latimer wrote and sent him a copy of *Up from Slavery*, to which Latimer commented that "it has been read by all the members of my family . . . months ago."[140] This correspondence was an opening for Latimer to build a stronger connection to the Washington machine. Sometime before May 31, Latimer wrote to Washington about the prospect of executing a drawing of Tuskegee. Washington wrote back that "a diagram of Tuskegee . . . will prove of infinite help to us and I shall be glad to have you undertake it."[141] Latimer's relation to the "Tuskegee Machine" can only be speculated. It is highly likely that he knew of Washington's activities through his relationship with T. Thomas Fortune. Latimer was on very friendly terms with Fortune. In 1899, Fortune wrote Latimer about purchasing some real estate that he controlled and the possibility of building on the land.[142] It is possible that Latimer, like Fortune, was trying to get involved with Washington for his own personal gain.[143]

Latimer also seems to have helped a younger associate secure a position at the Tuskegee Normal and Industrial Institute in 1908. This young gentleman, Henry Kraft, was the new electrical expert at Tuskegee. This was far from a menial position. His responsibilities included "superintending the dynamo room, the lighting plant, and giving instruction to the class in the simplest of electrical eng. theory."[144] Latimer may have been able to get Washington to extend him a favor, since Kraft graciously thanked Latimer for taking an interest in his situation. For a black man, Tuskegee was a very important place to be the superintendent of the electrical plant. In 1898, Tuskegee became the first black institution to teach courses on electrical technology. This coincided with the installation of an electrical plant and the retrofitting of the institute from gas to electric lighting. Tuskegee was not wired or prepared in any way for electric lighting; this was where the course in electrical engineering came into play. The course was a way to teach the students how to outfit the school with electrical power and run the system once fully installed. By the time the students finished their electrical education they were "first-class electricians."[145]

To associate Latimer's assimilationist views only with Washington would be an oversimplification. A variety of interactions shaped Latimer's position on the race question. Later in his life, Latimer began to move away from being a strong Washington supporter. The political decline of his close friend Greener probably reinforced his development of a slightly more liberal political stance. By 1908, "Greener finally realized that despite his being free born, educated, and socially prominent, he was still just another 'coon' in American society." Latimer was probably awakened by Greener's newly perceived racial consciousness.[146] Latimer's change in ideology was not radical by any means. The new direction he followed can be closely associated with the race philosophy of William Ferris. Latimer and Ferris began corresponding in the early 1910s and Ferris had a substantial impact on Latimer's American perspective.

Ferris, a product of both Yale and Harvard, was closely tied to the American Negro Academy.[147] An aspiring black leader who never quite broke through to develop a mass following, he was also an intellectual elitist. He believed the black race would have to be led to civilization by "an educated gentry." The black community had to produce more "thinkers, scholars, writers, orators, statesmen, and scientists," who would be celebrated throughout the world for their unfettered genius.

The development of a creative and productive race rather than an imitative one, would fracture the negative perception of black people. Ferris felt the common Negro did not see his vision. The Negro masses must unlearn the fatalistic belief in black inferiority and be taught "to respect his eminent men and refined women."[148] He partially held Booker T. Washington responsible for keeping this strain of thought alive by promoting racial subserviency as a means to uplift himself. Yet he admired Washington's ability to construct and organize the formidable "Tuskegee Machine."[149]

His program of race uplift combined the conflicting programs of Washington and Du Bois. He argued that the Negro needed both industrial and higher education. He argued that the Negro needed the ballot and wealth.[150] Once the black population had acquired all of the rights of citizenship, the Negro could progress toward civilization. Furthermore, Ferris maintained that the term Negro did not apply to the American black population. The word Negro conjured up images of savages of Africa, a people distinctly different from the American black man or woman. To solve this problem, Ferris coined the term "Negrosaxon." In his estimation, this new term accurately described the black population of the United States, who were hybrids between Negroes and Anglo-Saxons. The semantics of the new identification were most important. First and foremost it would not allow the American white population to continue to ignore the history of miscegenation in this country. The white population would have to address the systematic sexual abuse of black women. He went even further and fully advocated assimilation. On this point he emphatically stated that "[i]f the Negrosaxon expects to share in the political inheritance of the Anglo-Saxon, he must be made over in the likeness of the Anglo-Saxon. He cannot bleach out his complexion, or straighten his hair, or sharpen his nose, or thin his lips." He emphasized this point quite explicitly by arguing that the Negro must "in mind and character and disposition . . . become a black white man. Only after the Negrosaxon has been made over into the likeness of the white man can he hope to be made over into the image of God." In Ferris's ideology of progression toward civilization, Latimer is a fundamental exemplar. Ferris further attested that "our mission and destiny as a race is not to build up a Negro-ocracy or little Africa in America, but to appropriate Anglo-Saxon ideals and absorb and assimilate the Anglo-Saxon civilization." It was imperative that the Negro population strive to assimilate and not just emulate white civilization which according to Ferris was "the highest and best yet evolved in the history of the human race."[151] This was the state of assimilation that Latimer had achieved.

Latimer throughout his life endeavored to be an American. He had traded his credentials as a black man for those of a civilized man. Inventing was initially a way of expressing his technical interests. Latimer's technical proficiency was not the only reason he was able to become an integral member of the white male corporate electrical culture. Latimer became accepted by this culture because he bought into the racial ideology of this community and he knew his place within this culture. Latimer only moved in black circles with those who had achieved his level of assimilation. He was never a member of NAACP, National Negro Business League, or any prominent black political organization. Neither was he a member of any black fraternal or social organization. He was a Mason, but of the Guelph Lodge located in London. He was quite familiar with T. Thomas Fortune, John E. Bruce, Richard T. Greener, William Ferris, and many others who most certainly invited Latimer to participate in their varied activities. Yet, Latimer did not actively participate. His affiliation with these organizations would have preempted his assimilation into American culture.

By becoming an assimilated "Negrosaxon," of which Ferris wrote so forcefully, Latimer believed he would be able to shed the burden of the American slavery system, evade the socially, scientifically, and institutionally constructed perceptions of black inferiority, and elude the endless ways in which blackness was rearticulated as deviant, pathological, and, in general, undesirable. For Latimer to assimilate into this predominantly white world, he had to abandon or at least forfeit any hint of black cultural priorities or aesthetics, but this was not a problem for Latimer. He was not grappling with a type of Du Boisian double-consciousness; there was only one consciousness—that which white civilization exemplified. Yet, even if "blackness" was not a concern for Latimer, the dominant American culture rarely overlooked the historically constructed meanings of being black. But Latimer's assimilationist ideology directly contributed to his professional success and dictated his silence on race. He did not consider his racial heritage an issue to talk about, write about, or cultivate. Rather, it was something from which to escape. In his efforts to shed the negative representations associated with being a black man, he willingly let his race fade into the shadows. Latimer clearly understood what was required of him in order to become a civilized man acceptable to the dominant American culture and the electric lighting industry. To this end, Latimer partially used his technological skills to appropriate the privileges of whiteness. He had to evolve beyond the Booker T. Washington styled "good upstanding Negro" who always knew his proper place in society, to a Negrosaxon who was "in mind and character and disposition . . . a black white man."[152] And it was at this cultural station that Latimer thrived.

FIGURE 4.1. Shelby Jeames Davidson. 1916.
Moreland-Spingarn Research Center.

Chapter Four

Shelby J. Davidson: Adding Machines, Institutional Racism, and the Black Elite

The color line meets the colored man everywhere, and in a measure shuts him out from all respectable and profitable trades and calling . . . If he offers himself . . . to a Government Department as an agent, or an officer, he is sternly met on the color line, and his claim to consideration in some way is disputed on the ground of color.

—Frederick Douglass, 1886

Shelby Jeames Davidson's experiences were different from those characteristically associated with inventors of the late nineteenth and early twentieth centuries. First of all, Davidson's creative activities took place within the confining bureaucracy of the United States Treasury Department's Post Office Division—a location familiar with the use of new technologies, but unfamiliar with invention and development. In this unconventional environment, Davidson actively engaged in invention. Even though he worked within a nontraditional inventive space, Davidson began inventing for some of the traditional reasons associated with the inventive enterprise—the curiosity, excitement, intrigue, and potential financial gain of the new, novel, and unknown. For most inventors, environment has a strong influence on the projects they undertake. For Davidson, this was no different; he invented devices that would increase his division's efficiency and productivity by automating auditing procedures. Davidson envisioned an auditing environment in which the Post

Office Division performed all of its auditing tasks on adding machines. As he became more involved with adding machine technology, the meanings his inventions had for his personal and professional life began to change in a variety of ways. Professionally these meanings expanded from contributing to a government institution and becoming a valued federal employee, to creating an auditing environment of his technical design. This was crucial in order to craft himself as an indispensable and obligatory point of passage concerning adding machines, auditing practices, and technical knowledge within the Post Office Division. Personally these meanings changed from actualizing American civilization to increasing his social standing within the black community. By holding a government post, he maintained his social standing as the government's work space was segregated.

Davidson's patents contest the black inventor mythology tenet that a patent is the first and only of its kind. Davidson did create objects that were novel enough to receive patents, but other devices could perform the same tasks. Whether or not Davidson received a patent for his ideas, numerical computation would have been possible. The inventive career of Shelby Davidson is significant because it illustrates an additional way in which black people used invention. For Davidson used his inventive work to assist in temporarily gaining control of his professional environment, and this he parlayed into social and cultural advancement within the African American community. But it was much easier to hold onto his social and cultural status within the black community than to win a battle against the institutionalized racism inflicted by United States government officials and policies.

Howard University as a Learning Ground

Shelby J. Davidson was born on May 10, 1868, to Shelby Jeames and Amelia Scott Davidson in Lexington, Kentucky. Since Shelby was born after Emancipation, he was a member of the first generation of African American people to take advantage of the new educational opportunities available to the Negro population. He attended public school in his hometown of Lexington. After his years in Lexington, he ventured to Louisville to enroll in a course of normal school education at the state university. This program of education most likely concentrated on the standard course for black students, aiming to transform them into clean, productive, and upstanding citizens, eventually returning them to their communities to educate the Negro masses. This schooling did not provide the challenges or the career opportunities that a bright young man like Davidson desired. So in the fall of 1887, he enrolled in the premier institution for the education of people of African heritage, Howard University in Washington, D.C. It should be noted that Davidson entered Howard at nineteen, which indicates that as a youth he was primarily a student—another first among this generation of African Americans. The opportunity to study full time implies a level of family affluence. It is unclear how Davidson financed his Howard education, but it appears that he did not have the severe monetary problems encountered by many black students of his generation requiring them to enroll and reenroll regularly. Even if his family did not possess the financial wherewithal to send Shelby to Howard, the university would have endeavored to make it happen. His letter of acceptance stated that Howard would assist students financially "according to the peculiarities of the case." It was common for students to "earn their board by . . . waiting [tables] at boarding houses and hotels." The assistance that Howard offered did not come without strings attached. The letter closed by declaring that "if you proved worthy, in study and in conduct, we can beyond doubt put you . . . through college, by what you can earn and we can supplement."[1] As long as he did not cause trouble Howard would assist him, as it saw fit, to complete his college education.

Upon matriculation, Davidson's previous academic training was not up to the level that would have enabled him to enter Howard University's College Department. Davidson spent his first two years completing the preparatory program, after which he began his instruction within the College Department. Davidson's Howard University experience went smoothly until early 1893, at which point the university brought charges of rules violations against him and quickly expelled him along with several other students. The manner in which Davidson handled the situation is worthy of note. It shows that he was willing to challenge the domineering paternalism characteristic of the administration of black institutions of higher learning in the late nineteenth and early twentieth centuries. Davidson's tone bordered on the antagonistic, particularly for this period. This forthright delivery, in confronting a situation in which he was treated less than fairly, will be seen throughout his life. This type of confrontation foreshadowed the student revolts on many black campuses during the 1920s, from which Howard University did not escape.[2]

On February 4, 1893, Davidson received the following notice:

> Dear Sir: The President directs me to notify you to vacate your room in Clarke Hall on or before Tuesday, the 7th inst., and surrender the key to me. This is positive and must be observed.
> Yours truly, J. B. Johnson, Sec. and Treas.[3]

This notice completely caught Davidson by surprise. What disturbed him most was "that this demand was not based upon any allegation . . . or . . . disregard of any by-law or rule or announced examination."[4] He had no idea why he was being instructed to leave the dormitory. His situation became even more perplexing when, on February 6, he received the following communication:

> Dear Sir: The President has suspended his order, vacating your room, pending the action of the executive committee.
> Yours truly, J. B. Johnson, Sec. and Treas.[5]

Davidson was utterly confused at this juncture. First, the administration ordered him to remove his belongings as well as his person from Clarke Hall, then it temporarily postponed this demand. Davidson was still fuming because no official charges had been brought against him. In search of an explanation, Davidson made his way over to speak with Howard's president, Reverend J. E. Rankin, that same day. In their meeting, President Rankin intimated to Davidson that it was his inappropriate behavior that had placed him in this precarious situation. President Rankin informed Davidson that the university had initiated an investigation into "alleged wrong-doings against [him], in connection with a woman by the name of Mrs. Jennie Stewart."[6] This meeting afforded Rankin a convenient time to interrogate Davidson about his purported involvement with Mrs. Stewart. The allegation was very serious. Howard was investigating a violation of its strictly enforced ethics codes. Moreover, Jennie Stewart was a married woman. The implication was that Davidson had engaged in some sort of illicit affair with her. At a university that aimed to educate upstanding Negroes, this type of moral transgression was not taking lightly.

On February 8, Davidson received another message:

> Mr. S. J. Davidson,
> You are charged before the United Faculty with violation of Rule XI of Howard University regulations, to wit:

> "Students are strictly prohibited from receiving visits of the opposite sex at their rooms."
>
> For further consideration of the case the United Faculty will meet tomorrow . . . at 7 P.M. in the President's room, University Building. Please take notice.
>
> By order of the General Faculty:
> J. E. Rankin, President
> Geo. Wm. Cook, Secretary[7]

Davidson understood "please take notice" along with the indication of a date, time, and place, to mean that attendance was mandatory. However, this assumption was incorrect. When Davidson appeared at the President's room at seven that evening, President Rankin promptly denied him admission to this meeting concerning his academic fate. Davidson did not take this rebuff kindly. He returned to his room and penned President Rankin and Secretary Cook a scathing reply to the previous communications focusing on Howard University administration's blatantly mishandling of his situation. In his letter of February 9, he argued that "It will be manifestly UNFAIR and UNJUST to call upon me to answer so VAGUE and INDEFINITE a charge; this you should understand as well as I; nor am I informed WHO MY ACCUSERS ARE or the source from which the charges emanate. If charges in proper form shall be regularly presented against me I will be PREPARED TO MEET THEM. In the meantime it is only due to myself to say that THERE IS NOT THE SLIGHTEST FOUNDATION FOR THE VAGUE ACCUSATIONS AGAINST ME." He even invoked a touch of legality, insisting that the university had denied his "right to be heard by counsel." His caustic response concluded: "In every proper way I will be prepared, on ANY PROPER OCCASION OR TIME, to meet my accusers, if any, but I do not propose that there shall be any star chamber proceedings or that my character or reputation shall be assailed in any SECRET OR UNAUTHORIZED method."[8]

Davidson was correct in asserting that this case had been dealt with in a very unjust manner if this had been a civil suit; but it was not. His case was an internal Howard University matter. Thus, he was deluding himself if he expected this inquiry to have proceeded any differently. Davidson had been enrolled as a Howard student for nearly six years, and in that time he most certainly knew how the university handled infractions that interfered with the production of morally upstanding Negro students.

Davidson, of course, did not receive a response to his memorandum. The administration passed down the expected verdict on February 11. "S. J. Davidson of the College Department is hereby indefinitely suspended from Howard University for violation of Rule XI and gross falsehood respecting the same."[9] Davidson was not done fighting, however. He immediately disputed the authority of the board's actions because at no point during the entire proceedings did they grant him an opportunity to defend himself. He argued that since the entire proceedings had been falsely organized and performed, every statement made in reference to his suspension was null and void. The only response to this declaration was another communication stating again that he as well as four other students were "indefinitely suspended from Howard University."[10] This second notice specified that the executive committee, united faculty, and the president had full jurisdiction to handle his case however they saw fit. They deliberated on the case for three days and unanimously decided that suspension was the appropriate course of action. President Rankin indicated that he would gladly meet with any one of the suspended students, and if the case required further review, he would bring it to the attention of the members of the executive committee at their next annual meeting—which was not anytime soon. To add insult to injury, J. B. Johnson forcibly removed Davidson from the rooms for which he had paid rent through the end of the term.

Davidson was genuinely irate with this entire state of affairs. He was not willing to accept the verdict brought against him. He continued to fight back, partially out of disgust with his treatment, but more significantly because of what he had to lose: his Howard diploma. He enrolled at Howard approximately five and a half years prior to the incident, and he was not going to have this degree taken from him at the last hour. He was grappling for his future monetary security. He knew exactly what a degree from Howard University meant; it almost guaranteed social, if not financial, success. Between February and early May, Davidson spent a significant amount of his time preparing an appeal. On May 6, 1893, Davidson privately published his appeal, which emphatically proclaimed that his case had been handled illegally. He forwarded the twelve-page appeal to each of Howard University's trustees. The preliminary section of his appeal described the case up to his expulsion. The second half carefully dissected how, based on the university's charter, the administration had improperly handled his case. Davidson brought to light that the united faculty did not possess the authority to pass judgment in his case. The university's charter restricted the faculty's power to issues concerning the faculty. In addition, he brought forth the fact that the university was not "to 'enact bylaws . . . inconsistent with the laws of the United States.'"[11] It is upon this fact that he based his claim for a fair and honest trial. If the university was to enact bylaws that were consistent with federal laws, they could not dismiss the process of legal action granted to American citizens.

What made Davidson's case even stronger was that the charter incorporating Howard University made the Board of Trustees the incorporators of the university. This meant that all actions relating to degrees, suspensions, and expulsions had to pass the final vote of the Board of Trustees. The faculty could only recommend that the board take certain actions against students. Since the board had not convened a meeting after the administration passed judgment on Davidson's case, he had been illegally required to leave campus. Davidson argued that the united faculty betrayed "the letter and spirit of the Charter" by passing final judgment on his case.[12] Davidson's attack did not relent. He next dismantled the evidence assembled by the administration, the substance of which stemmed from three affidavits collected in private by one or more members of the faculty. The implication here was that university officials either intimidated or coerced students into making statements against Davidson. Moreover, Davidson reminded the Board of Trustees that William Bradley gave one of the three affidavits, the same Mr. Bradley who "was, shortly after his testimony was taken, suspended for misconduct involving disreputable proceedings in his examinations."[13] In Davidson's opinion, this fact reflected poorly on Bradley's integrity, and the entire body of testimony should be thrown out since its credibility was suspect at best. Even with this admirable attempt to regain his student status, Howard initially made no exceptions. But the university and Davidson did eventually come to terms, and he received a degree from Howard in 1896.

This case shows Davidson's character. He was willing to fight a system that most would not have challenged. The legal overtones in his responses to communications and in his appeal seem somewhat unusual at first. Davidson might have considered pursuing law after the completion of his Howard education, but his circumstances demanded that he commence studying the law immediately. The united faculty voted that he be expelled on February 13, and on February 15 he began to formally read law. By June 1896, he had completed readings in Blackstone's *Commentaries,* Kent's *Commentaries,* Parson's *On Contracts,* Stephen's *On Pleadings,* Byles's *On Bills,* Schouler's *Domestic Relations,* and Dunlap's *Book of*

Forms, standard texts for law students.[14] However, it was not until 1899 that the Kentucky state bar admitted Davidson. Another year passed before he became a member of the bar of the District of Columbia.[15] Davidson began studying law under the direction of William A. Cook, a member of one of the wealthiest and most powerful "first" black families of Washington.[16]

This connection at this young age strongly implies that Davidson's family was of equal social standing. This is based on two observations. First, he did not seem to have had any trouble paying his way through Howard University. When Howard expelled him, he had paid his rent until the end of the semester. In addition, he stated that he had more than one room, which indicates a level of financial security. Second, Davidson would not have been able to forge that high a level of social connections without a proper introduction. This introduction could have been provided by his family. Regardless, Davidson began to entrench himself within Washington's community of elite African Americans at an early age.

Considering the economic crisis of 1893 and his lack of a degree, Davidson was fortunate to find employment as a $600-a-year unclassified laborer for the Treasury Department. He secured this position through the help of William C. P. Breckenridge, a congressman from Kentucky's seventh district who apparently took Davidson under his wing.[17] During the late nineteenth and early twentieth centuries, government service was one of the most stable and respected occupations for African American people, making these jobs highly coveted.[18] After a few years Davidson began to rise through the government ranks. The Treasury Department transferred him to the office of the Auditor for the Post Office Department and promoted him first to an Assistant Messenger on February 4, 1897, then to a Money Order Assorter class C on May 1, 1898. The year 1899 commenced his rapid rise within the Treasury Department, and being admitted to the bars of Kentucky and the District of Columbia undoubtedly contributed to his advancement. Probably equally important, however, was that Howard University granted him an undergraduate degree.

Davidson's ascent within the federal government directly benefited from the aid of supporters, one of whom was House Representative Walter Evans. A letter addressed to Representative Evans of February 25, 1899, appears as follows: "Replying to your letter of the 20th instant, in which you call attention to the merits of Mr. Shelby J. Davidson, a clerk of the $840 class . . . requesting his promotion at the first opportunity to the thousand dollar grade, I beg to inform you that Mr. Davidson was appointed a laborer in this Department August 1, promoted to Assistant Messenger February 4, 1897, and to Money Order Assorter at $840 May 1, 1898. He will be further advanced whenever it can properly be done without injustice to or discrimination against others equally or more deserving."[19] Davidson was not the only recipient of preferential treatment to which the writer of the above excerpt alluded. It is well known that Booker T. Washington used his amicable relations with high-level government officials to obtain coveted appointments for his associates.[20] Connections to powerful people other than Booker T. Washington were equally important. It was not until 1909 that the State Department promoted the first Negro to a clerk from a messenger. This individual commented that his clerkship would not have been available if "his personal friend, the incoming Secretary of State, [had not] insisted the merit system recognize merit," or, more important, his "personal" friend's political power.[21] Davidson's next promotion, to the $900 grade, was equally swift. On August 16, 1899, a friend within the Treasury Department informed Davidson of this impending appointment. "Your name was sent up for promotion today and should there be no hitch at the Treasury it is quite likely that you may receive same this week. I write to suggest that it would be well to be in position to be sworn in at once should the Auditor's recommendation go through."[22] Thus, someone was looking out for Davidson. The depth to which he was connected to higher officials is unclear, but his series of swift promotions implies a judicious use of contacts. On September 18, the promotion went through, and by the second week of the new century, he had been promoted to the $1000 grade.[23]

The Post Office Division of the Treasury Department began testing the feasibility of using adding machines early in the twentieth century. It was at this time that Davidson became captivated by these highly complex devices. "[H]aving never seen an adding machine, the very sight of one being used was like a magnet, so fascinating that any spare moment . . . [was] spent looking at the mechanical wonder."[24] Understanding how these intriguing new machines worked consumed a considerable amount of Davidson's spare time. Luckily for Davidson, the Post Office Division had a great deal of success introducing mechanical computational devices. By 1901, the number of adding machines had risen to twelve. But performance slowed when the division encountered problems with their service provider. The unreliability reached a point of crisis when for a significant part of a week, approximately five of the machines were in serious need of repair. John B. Sleman, the head of the division, was desperately searching for a solution to their growing problem. Word made its way back to Sleman that Davidson seemed to have quite a command of the workings of adding machines. He asked, or more likely persuaded, Davidson to attempt to alleviate the situation by doing whatever he could to fix the machines. Davidson was understandably quite reticent about taking up this task, since Sleman notified him that "in the event of . . . damage he would be held responsible."[25] Davidson did not disappoint. Shortly thereafter, Sleman unofficially designated him the "Chief-clerk in charge of 'repairs, care and maintenance of adding machines.'"[26] He performed admirably enough to merit promotions in 1903, 1906, and finally in 1909 to an annual salary of $1600.[27] This income placed him among the uppermost economic level of black federal employees. As late as 1908, the federal government only employed approximately 1450 black workers. Of these workers, only three hundred held positions higher than that of a messenger or a common laborer; and of that three hundred not more than three or four colored men had advanced into supervisory positions.[28]

Davidson became the resident adding machine expert. This new responsibility was not necessarily a bonus for him. He commented that "[i]t required constant preparation for giving and advising the Office in all matters appertaining to every make of adding machine and its adaptability for . . . use." His daily work schedule was extremely busy because, in addition to "keeping machines in repair, testing all machines submitted for trial or purchase and looking after proper supplies [he] carried a regular section of auditing accounts."[29] The advent of this type of position is quite understandable. Instead of having to depend on outside support, the division filled that role internally, creating a job very similar to that of today's computer network engineers. This assignment enabled Davidson to begin creating a niche for himself in an increasingly competitive and racially constrictive environment. This niche was crucial to his social and professional advancement.

The Bethel Literary and Historical Association and the "Race Question"

Professionally, Davidson's career began to flourish. As his work for the Treasury Department blossomed, he also began scaling the all-important social ladders within Washington's colored community. This community of black elites was just as economically and socially stratified, if not more so, than whites at the turn of the century. Wealth, education, career, family history, culture, and, in many instances, color were the fundamental characteristics that the black elite used rhetorically and physically to delineate themselves from the black and white masses. This elite group of black individuals considered the white sentiment that all blacks were socially equal a complete falsehood. They were believers in a "talented tenth" before Du Bois articulated his position. Prior to the era of Jim Crow many black upper-class citizens, whose ancestors were freeman or slaves of interracial heritage, considered themselves the bridge between civilized white society and the unenlightened Negro masses.[30] This elite maintained a strict social distance between themselves and the large majority of so-called uncultured Negroes. This small group believed that if "they succeeded in convincing whites that they were in fact different from other blacks in education, refinement, manners, morals, wealth, and even complexion, they would be accorded the rights and privileges of first-class citizens."[31] But when this did not occur, they retreated even deeper into their exclusive social organizations. This attitude of superiority is quite interesting because most members of the black upper class were by no means as wealthy as their white counterparts. Very few came from "old" money or led the lives of the leisured rich. Most worked every day like the common black laborers to whom they were so indifferent, but the difference was that they were professionals. The black elite consisted of government workers, public school teachers, public school administrators, caterers, barbers, and to a lesser degree physicians, attorneys, congressmen, senators, university faculty, and administrators at black institutions.

Davidson was an integral member of the colored elite community in Washington—one of the major centers for the black upper class. Through the organization of exclusive clubs, the black elite easily controlled their social circles by separating themselves from the Negro masses. By the middle of the first decade of the twentieth century, Davidson had become a key member of Washington's most prestigious clubs. On March 4, 1905, the Pen and Pencil Club of Washington, "one of the best known elite black male organizations in black America," commissioned him as a Colonel. The Pen and Pencil Club initially formed as a literary society. But like many similar clubs, it was quickly transformed into a societal cloister. Davidson was also member of the more exclusive Mu-So-Lit Club, which catered exclusively to the finest of Washington's black male population. The group was financially solvent enough to own and maintain a lodge which "became a retreat for upper-class black men to find respite of a purely social variety from the strife of race and 'questions of the hour.'"[32]

In May 1905, the Bethel Literary and Historical Association (BLHA) elected Davidson president. The certificate of incorporation stated that the "particular business and object [of the BLHA] are the moral, educational, literary, musical, scientific, philosophic and historical improvements of its members."[33] This organization soon grew into one of the most important public forums for the discussion of race issues in the District. Their meetings were open to a more socially and economically diverse group than Davidson's other social organizations were. This did not mean, however, that people outside of his elite network had any meaningful input into whom the association invited to address their meetings, nor did nonelites substantially contribute to the discussions following the papers presented. The manner in which a select cohort of individuals were able to control the BLHA was by incorporating the organization into an association. The incorporation only permitted the "financial members" to vote on the appointment of officers. As of May 5, 1905, there where only thirty-nine financial members. Most of these members came from prominent families of the District. Names like Syphax, Fossett, Cook, and Tyson were on the books as financial members.[34] At the end of Davidson's term, the exclusion of nonfinancial members from voting in the BLHA's elections became a point of contention.[35]

There were two members of the BLHA, from an inventive standpoint, who are of special interest to the life of Shelby Davidson. The first is Robert Pelham. He was an inventor who moved from Detroit to Washington after receiving an appointment to the Census Bureau. He patented adding machine–related devices in 1905.[36] It is highly likely that Davidson spoke with Pelham about the development of adding machine augmentations. The second is Henry E. Baker. Baker attended the United States Naval Academy for a short period and completed his education at the Ben-Hyde Benton School of Technology in Washington from 1877 to 1879. He studied law in the 1880s and rose from the starting point of a Patent Office copyist in 1888 to a second examiner by the turn-of-the-century.[37] These two individuals are important because they show that not only were there black men in Washington involved in the development of new technological artifacts, but some of these people had definite connections with each other. In a sense, a loose and small community of African American inventors existed in Washington.[38]

From the prosperity of Davidson's social class, one might infer that the financial members of the BLHA would support the Du Boisian plan of moral, social, economic, and political development for the African American community rather than that of Booker T. Washington. Support for this assumption gains strength when one realizes that Lafayette Hershaw was a financial member of the BLHA. Du Bois's biographer, David Levering Lewis, asserts that Hershaw was "one of Du Bois' most valuable collaborators." Hershaw so firmly endorsed Du Bois's ideological goals that he placed his "professional [life] at [Du Bois's] service repeatedly and selflessly."[39] It would be naive to assume that every member of BLHA was an avid Du Bois supporter. One of the more active members of the BLHA was Kelly Miller. This well-known Howard University mathematics professor had a "propensity for standing on both sides of the [Washington–Du Bois] controversy."[40] Then there was John W. Cromwell, a Howard University law graduate, an influential editor, and school principal in the District, who viewed the debate slightly differently. He did not subscribe to the notion that the black elite should separate themselves from the common black citizen by ruling over them or bridging the various gaps between white and black society. On the contrary he adamantly believed that the black upper class should "become more actively involved in causes to uplift the masses culturally and materially."[41] The race question was an issue extensively debated by the BLHA during the year Davidson presided. The BLHA's topics of discussion clearly exemplify the questions that Davidson was thinking about after the turn-of-the-century. They also illustrate why invention and maintaining both his social status and his job were meaningful to him. Moreover, these discussions provide a backdrop from which to view Davidson's future experience within his division of the Treasury Department.

Two weeks before Christmas in 1905, the BLHA addressed the race question indirectly. This was a special night in which two of the best-known African American men of the period attended the meeting. That evening P. B. S. Pinchback, the former acting governor of Louisiana, graciously introduced the evening's speaker, Archibald Grimké. Grimké spoke on "The Secret of Success," focusing on the retention of employment. He said that success could only come through a consistent effort at the highest level. The recorder of minutes wrote that Grimké concluded by recounting "instances where occupations had fallen away from us, and urged us to do all in our power to retain our hold on positions now held."[42] The nature of this talk definitely points to a significant problem African Americans encountered with the entrenchment of Jim Crow into American society early in the twentieth century. It is telling that Grimké addressed the BLHA on this topic. It shows that the black elite were no longer exempt from race-based discrimination. It is intriguing that Grimké advised the assembled listeners that it was imperative to perform even better than before in order to maintain their present economic station. In a sense, Grimké accepted the discrimination against the black population, did not revolt against it, but only uttered timid advice.

On November 14, 1905, Colonel W. O. Crosby, of the Pension Bureau, and coincidentally the only white speaker for the series, lectured on the "Negro's Relation to Politics, and His Status as an American Citizen." Crosby began by declaring his sincerest concern for the American Negro population, whom his forefathers willfully oppressed through the bondage of slavery. After his kind opening comments, his talk took a significant turn in the opposite direction by insisting that the Fifteenth Amendment was a constitutional blunder. He argued that the vast majority of colored citizens did not possess the intellectual acumen or worldly preparation to participate in the governing process. He conceded that Negroes of Ohio and certain other enlightened enclaves possessed the intellectual capacity for full citizenship, but these communities were rare. He also commended colored newspapers and the formation of clubs, such as the BLHA, because they were the instruments to "stimulate free and independent thought" among Negroes. Yet, he denigrated black men and women by detailing ways in which their problems would have been less serious if the federal government had systematically established institutions to teach Negroes the art of government. Furthermore, he claimed Negroes had become overly attached to the Republican party and argued that they would be unable to reach their full potential in governmental participation if they continued to ally themselves strictly with one party. Crosby remarked that he and other "friends of the Negro disliked to see him bound to any political party so securely that he could not act independently."[43] If there were more free-thinking Negroes, the "open door" of legislative freedom would be a reality. His address clearly illustrated the paternalism ingrained in many white individuals who purported to be advocates for the colored population. It is not a surprise that a spirited discussion followed this paper. Everyone who commented on the essay for the most part agreed with the replies of John C. Dancy and Professor William A. Joiner, both of whom adamantly disagreed with Crosby's speculations on Negro franchise.[44] They stated that since Emancipation every man has the legal right to participate in the election of governing officials, and in many locations throughout the country Negroes had voted independently and had chosen to elect people of similar racial heritage. In response to this issue presented by a white government official, those in attendance showed a relatively unified front.

William S. Scarborough tackled the topic of "Racial Integrity" on January 2, 1906.[45] He began by declaring that the idea of racial integrity is quite absurd. Throughout the history of the world, migration by various racial and ethnic groups had completely eliminated the possibility of homogeneous races. He wanted to move toward what he defined as a more nationalistic definition of race. His rhetoric was laden with elitism. Societal differences should not be based on color, but rather the categories elite societies used to differentiate themselves from the remainder of the population. Two things should be noted about Scarborough and his speech. The first is that he was partially expressing his own agenda and possibly defending some of his actions. Scarborough married across the color line, going against the covenant of racial purity. This was a difficult question for the black elite, a considerable number of whom were quadroons or octoroons and not phenotypically recognizable as Negroes. By marrying across the color line, Scarborough placed himself in the middle of many discourses on race. Certain pockets in black elite communities did not have a problem with marrying across racial lines as long as one married within the same social class. Others would contend that by marrying a white woman Scarborough subscribed to the false belief that white was "better" than black. On this point he did not help his case by describing Africa as the home of the primitive races.[46] The statement showed that the racial ideology of the dominant American culture had colonized the minds of the best-educated colored citizens. It was a tactic, consciously and unconsciously, used by the black elite to separate themselves from what they and white society deemed the lower classes. With this maneuver, they could validate themselves as something better than the common Negro. This racial "positioning" is one of the numerous ways that the black community struggled internally with race questions.[47] The responses to Scarborough's paper were typical for members of his social circle: most felt that what he said was completely in order. Howard Professor Kelly Miller summed up the sentiment of the respondents when he stated "there is no race exclusiveness physically and no race culture . . . The difference between race factors disappear as we rise to the heights of learning and culture. Physical integrity is nothing compared with the psychic . . . moral, and spiritual excellence [that] will place the Negro on equal footing with all races."[48]

On November 21, 1905, the BLHA attacked one of the most volatile topics in the Negro community: the Washington–Du Bois debate. H. Rufus White, a Baltimore attorney, presented that evening's paper. White furnished the BLHA with a relatively unbiased account of each leader's ideological stance. He illustrated the ways both programs were beneficial for the black populace. He believed that higher education was best left to those capable of the requisite mental work. He asserted that since not every man could enter the lofty intellectual provinces inhabited by Du Bois, Washington's plan was ideal for those of lower intellectual abilities like the Negro masses. Once the discussion of White's paper began, the individuals in attendance disputed and soon dismissed his admirable attempt to show how the ideological concepts of both Washington and Du Bois could be used simultaneously to develop a politically, culturally, socially, economically, and morally strong black community.

A Mr. Matthews argued that "colored men had trades and applied them long before Mr. Washington was born." Matthews continued his assault on Washington by arguing that Washington was delusional if he believed that Negroes needed to be taught how to work. Matthews did not consider Washington worthy to be the leader of the Negro race. He found it despicable that Washington, during trips to the District, limited himself to the White House and did not spend any time with the people for whom the white-run government appointed him spokesman. A true leader should work to better the conditions of the Negro population instead of promoting a different version of subserviency. Professor T. J. Calloway, a classmate of Du Bois and friend of Washington, replied to the cutting response of Matthews, intimating that the criticism directed at these two great men was due to the ignorance of the accusers. The discussion continued with a Mr. Taylor from Maine, who had only praise for the work accomplished at Tuskegee; he contended that all Negroes should try to follow the principles espoused by both leaders. A calm came upon the meeting as several participants agreed that the best of Washington and Du Bois could be used for the advancement of the race. But Armond Scott, a local attorney, would not allow the onslaught against Washington to abate. He expressed his disappointment with those who thought Washington's work benefited the race. The record reports that "Mr. Scott thought [that] Mr. Washington [was] an enemy in disguise and characterized him as an apologist and cringer." The discussion appears to have continued to escalate until a Mr. Pincket concluded that in view of all the talk of independent thinking for Negroes, there should be more acceptance for each individual's own opinion on the manner in which the race should progress. Attorney L. G. Gregory, who wished that people could see something virtuous within Washington's and Du Bois's efforts, seconded the even-tempered comments of Pincket. Lafayette Hershaw, however, restoked the evening's argument. He lauded the scholarly works of Du Bois, which brought international acclaim to the intellectual abilities of the race, but he was at a loss when it came to explaining how Washington's ideology and actions helped advance the race. A response was forthcoming, but when "Mr. Lawson volunteered to answer . . . his reply was so tumultuous, that his words were lost."[49] The lively debate concluded when Rufus White commented that he hoped some day the race would benefit from the efforts of Washington at Tuskegee and Du Bois's Niagara Movement.

This debate shows that there was a variety of opinions on this disputed topic. A position acceptable to all did not exist. But one theme reccurred: the progress of the race. They may not have agreed on the best path for Negro progress, but consensus did exist on what the race was progressing toward. In most opinions, it was civilization. One of the main accoutrements of civilization was technology. To this end, Davidson understood what invention meant and could do for the race.

Inventing One's Place

As Davidson's social standing solidified, his inventive career began to emerge. In March 1906, Davidson filed his first patent application for an adding machine device. By this time, Davidson was solely in charge of his division's adding machines and witnessed the impact they were having on the work environment. In this position, he probably also witnessed the sharp adding machine sales upswing. The Treasury Department primarily purchased Burroughs machines and through his personal contact with this company, Davidson understood the great profitability a successful invention in the area of adding machines might have.[50] Between 1895 to 1900, Burroughs' sales grew nearly fivefold, from $63,700 to $322,934." By 1906 Burroughs' sales were $7.8 million and almost doubled to $14.8 million in 1907.[51] Because of Davidson's institutional setting, he no doubt saw inventing adding-machine augmentations as an excellent economic opportunity.

The turn-of-the-century's increased demand for labor-saving and information-handling technologies became partially embodied in scientific management.[52] The term *scientific management* is characteristically associated with the efforts to expand industrial production through bureaucratization and scientific studies to improve worker and mechanical efficiency. The ideologies that supported the scientific management rhetoric filtered their way from the industrial floor to the white-collar work environment. The large-scale scientific studies to improve industrial production had a symbiotic relationship with small-scale systemization of data processing. But enlarging corporate institutions and labor-saving devices produced more, not less work, and the increased commercial productivity resulted in more statistical data to be analyzed and used by an increasing number of corporate managers.[53] As the "managerial class" expanded, the importance and status of the "clerk" decreased. It can be argued that the use of the adding machine brought about the deskilling of certain workers. By mechanizing the art of computation, the skilled activity of numerical calculation was no longer necessary. The only skill one had to master was the rather simple one of operating an adding machine.

Davidson saw this happening; through the invention of artifacts and the environment for these devices, he could assure that he was not among those workers whose value and status decreased. He understood that adding machines would eventually replace many workers, and, at least for his division, he wanted to be the one controlling this transition. Davidson also recognized the decline in Negro appointments to federal positions and the increasing racial tension within government agencies. Thus, he had to find a way to make himself even more indispensable. His inventive activities were a solution to this dilemma. This was not the sole reason for Davidson's actions. He viewed himself as a promoter of civilization through the scientific and technological mechanization of the Treasury Department's calculating practices. The fact that his actions could exacerbate the crisis for colored government employees did not alter his inventive goals. It was important to help American society advance to a higher level of civilization through the production of technological artifacts—and a part of that ideology was to uplift himself in the process.

Davidson's invention of 1906, a paper-rewind mechanism, illustrates his desire to create practical enhancements to existing adding machines. The novelty of this device was that it provided a way to handle the roll of paper used by an adding machine. This apparatus would roll the paper strip compactly and "all danger of mutilation of the strip, the annoyance and delay . . . [of] gathering and winding up by hand the loose coils of paper at the end of the day's work [was] eliminated, and, if desired, the roll bearing of the rewound strip may be reversed, placed in the feed roll bearings, and the strip used again."[54] Davidson specifically created this invention to attach to the rear of a Burroughs-style adding machine, but it could be adapted to any other type of machine. This appliance consisted of two devices: a paper management system and an alarm for torn paper or the end of a paper roll. The paper-rewind apparatus consisted of two spools, a feeder and a rewinder, suspended behind the adding machine and attached to a support arm. The paper in the rewind roller was kept taut by a carefully devised ratchet mechanism. As the operator advanced the paper the pawl would disengage, a spring strip in contact with the ratchet teeth would turn the roll, and the pawl would reengage and pull the paper taut again (figs. 4.2, 4.3, and 4.4).

Davidson created three means, two electrical and one manual, to facilitate the movement of the arm controlling the ratchet mechanism. Of the electric designs, one used a solenoid while the other made use of an electro-magnet. Energizing the solenoid or the electro-magnet would force it to contract, moving the arm and concurrently disengaging the pawl. For either of these devices to work an electric circuit had to be completed. Davidson directly related the making and breaking of a circuit to the clutching action of an adding machine's motor. As an operator depressed the lever to clutch the motor, the clutch operating shaft would bring two contacts together to complete the circuit energizing the solenoid or the electro-magnet. The electric current for this device would come ideally from the adding machine's electric motor, but the devices were adaptable to use other sources such as wall or light plugs. The mechanical device worked similarly to the electrically driven units. The lever designed to advance the paper, when depressed, would force the movement of the pawl arm.

The other portion of this patent was an alarm system that would alert the operator that the paper strip broke or the paper spool was empty. Again, Davidson developed a manual as well as an electrical mechanism. The way these systems worked was that as the feeder spool supplied the adding machine with paper a spring loaded "feeler" arm rested on top of the paper. If the paper broke or reached the end of a roll, the feeler arm would fall down and in the electric device it would complete a circuit and ring a bell. The manual apparatus would also ring a bell, but it used a hammer connected to the feeler arm to hit a bell clapper.

This inventive effort illustrates Davidson's familiarity with electrical technology. It is not clear how Davidson, a formally trained attorney, acquired this technical ability, whether through his intimate interactions with adding machines, studying independently, enrolling in electrical courses at a technical institution, receiving instruction from a friend or colleague, or a combination of these, but this knowledge was vital in the development of the electrically powered devices. These material products of Davidson's technical creativity begin to show his inventive "personality." He was not attempting to be a large-scale Hughesian technological system-builder like Woods; but, Davidson and Woods do exhibit inventive similarities. Whereas Woods located reverse salients in systems of

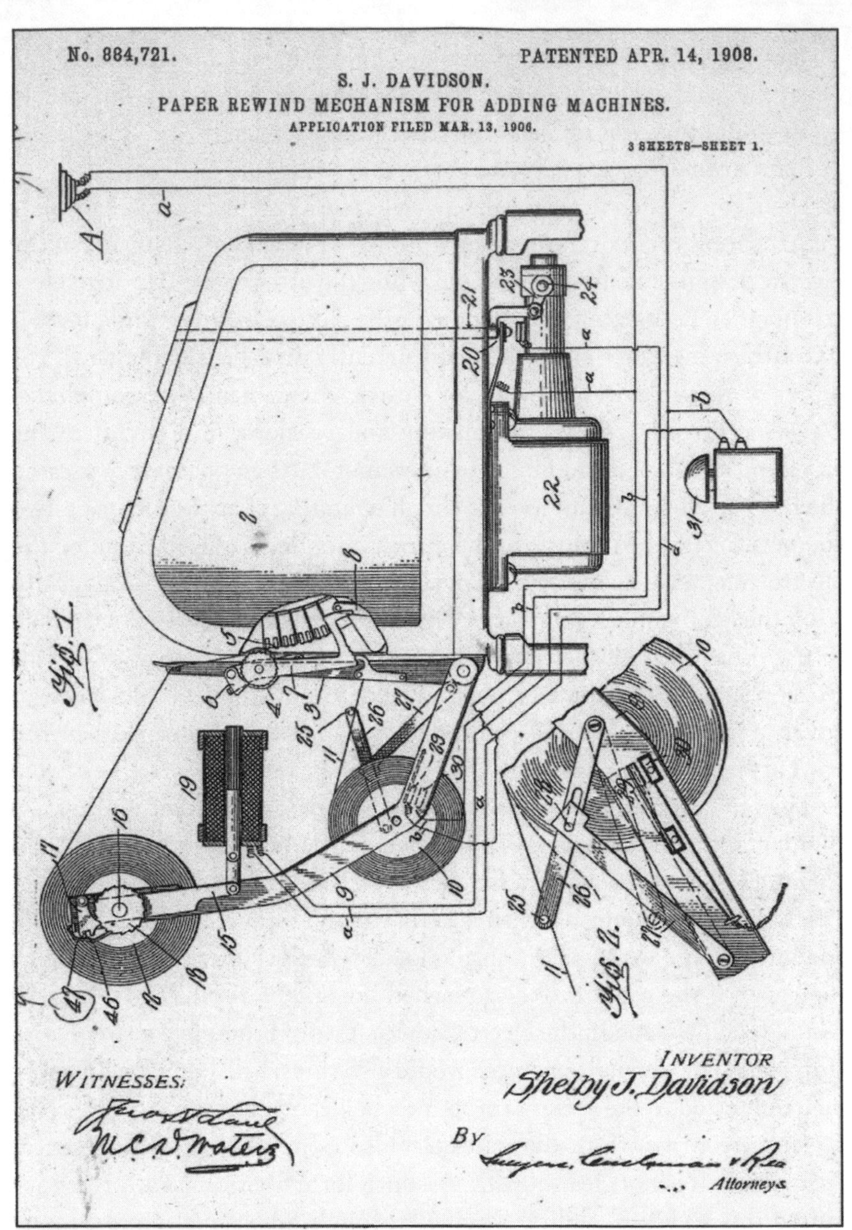

FIGURE 4.2. Davidson's adding machine paper management mechanism was intended to assist in the improvement of his adding machine environment. April 1908. National Archives.

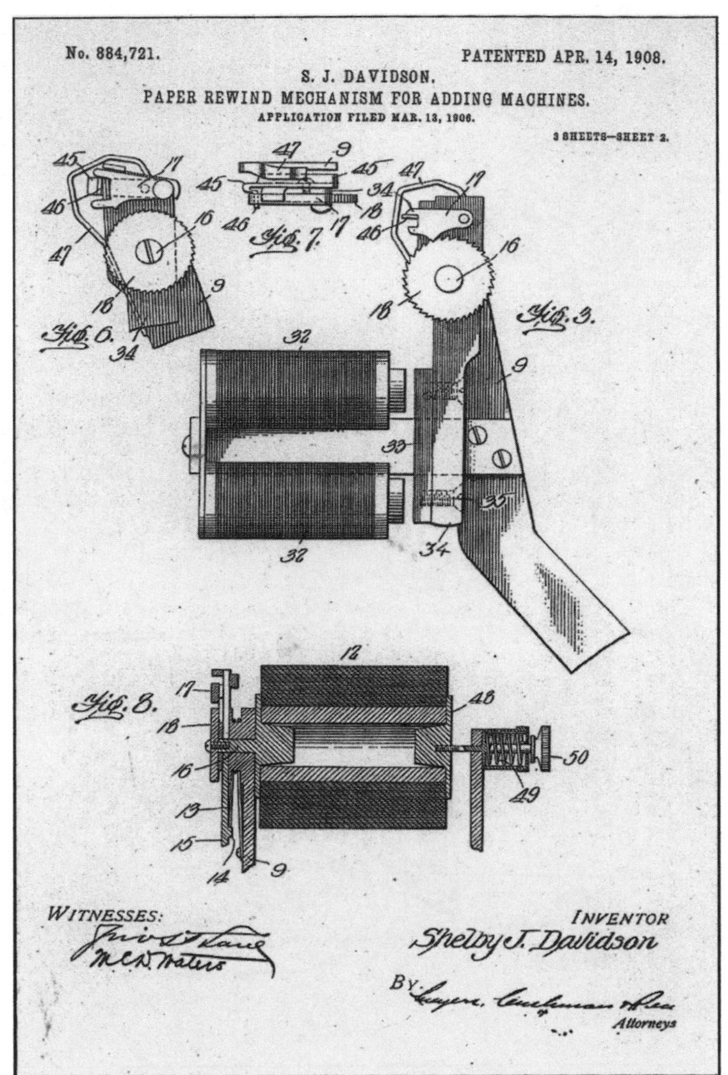

FIGURE 4.3. Rewind roller mechanism. National Archives.

communication and railway travel, Davidson detected smaller reverse salients in the small-scale system of an adding machine and focused on improving the functionality of this artifact. Davidson's talent for solving the technical problems that presented themselves within adding machines soon became greatly valuable to his career as a government employee.

As the Treasury Department began to implement his ingenious paper-

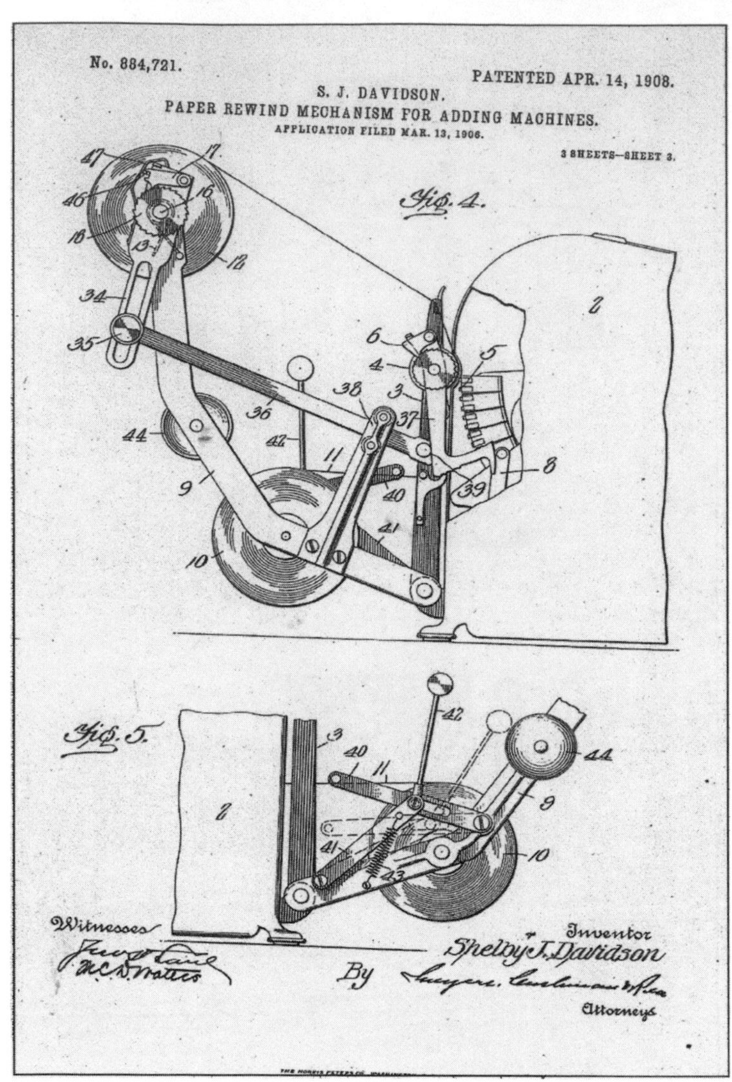

FIGURE 4.4. Rewind and alarm mechanism for adding machines. National Archives.

management device, his division's productivity increased—putting him in high favor. It was at this point that Davidson began to develop an entire adding machine environment for his division. If he could design this environment based on his vision and technical and material knowledge, he would make himself the obligatory point of passage for the knowledge of this adding machine environment and thereby secure for himself a significant amount of control over his employment situation. This would require some intricate maneuvering if he wanted to make his vision a reality. He wanted to be in control of the most important piece of this puzzle, which was the technical knowledge. There was one problem; he could not construct this work space entirely by himself, and that meant that he could not hoard his technical knowledge, skills, and practices. For his plan to work, he would have to disseminate his knowledge, skills, and practices to other individuals so that they could at least work the machines. More important, he had to make everyone come to the understanding that even if he shared his knowledge and skill with other workers he was the possessor of the highest order of knowledge and skill so as to not become obsolete and eventually dispensable.

In the spring of 1906, Davidson began to investigate ways to fully automate the division's computational procedures. The primary function of the Treasury Department's Post Office Division was to audit postal transactions. Some of the more complex and time-consuming transactions to audit were those having to do with money orders. At that time, the Post Office charged a different fee depending on the value of the money order. A sliding scale existed ranging from three cents to thirty cents based on the dollar value of the money order.[55] This auditing procedure had not been converted to adding machines because of its complexity. The complexity stemmed from the fact that two sets of numbers required tabulating. In Davidson's opinion, the auditing time of his division would significantly decrease if adding machines replaced the hand work. The current auditor, Ernest G. Timme, supported Davidson investigating this possibility further. Davidson's first idea was to have auditors use adding machines and have them write in the corresponding fees next to the printed money order values on the tabulating paper strip.[56] Yet, this just increased the time by mating the hand tabulation with the mechanical variation. Therefore, a way to fully automate this task was the logical next step.

To continue along this experimental path, Davidson needed to acquire four thirteen-bank machines. The standard machines of the day were eleven-bank, meaning that the largest number that could be added to was 999,999,999.99, or eleven vertical columns. He needed thirteen-bank machines so he could divide them into two sections, one of eleven banks and the other of two. One side would be used to print the money order value; on the other side, the fee for this money order would be printed. With this scheme it was possible to calculate a grand total for the money order amounts and the fees, but it was impossible to make the adding machine tabulate the money orders and their fees as two separate totals because the machine would view the two distinct printing actions as one computation. Consequently, since the division needed one total for the money order amounts and an additional total for the associated fees, each would have to be tabulated by hand. Regardless of this drawback, Davidson received a positive response from the Post Office Division about his idea of using thirteen-bank machines. The division was so enthusiastic about the potential of using adding machines that they quickly agreed to allow Davidson to order the four machines he required for his investigations.

In addition to being permitted to proceed with this research, Davidson received an extra bonus when he placed the order for the four Burroughs machines. Burroughs extended him an invitation to study adding machine repair at their factory in Detroit.[57] The Post Office Division encouraged Davidson to accept the invitation and granted him a leave of absence to study in Detroit from September 20, 1906 until mid October. Upon his return, Davidson was the most qualified member of his division to maintain and repair its adding machines. The skills Davidson acquired through his training and experience truly made him an obligatory point of passage for technical knowledge required for the Post Office Division's adding machines. In a sense he had learned, and was inventing, constructing, and developing the appropriate technical knowledge, practices, and artifacts that would be indispensable in the regular use and maintenance of the Post Office Division's adding machines.

While in Detroit, Davidson shared some of his ideas for new adding machines and augmentations with members of the Burroughs staff. This was not merely a friendly gesture; it was an intentional move to interest Burroughs in producing an adding machine that would solve his dilemma and eliminate the need for handwritten money order auditing. Evidently Davidson did not receive favorable responses to any of his suggestions because upon his return to Washington, he continued to research and develop an apparatus to automate money-order auditing. At this time he was still planning to build an adding machine that automatically printed the money order fee across from the amount of the purchased money order. But a solution to his major obstacle, a means to total the money order column and the fee column separately but simultaneously, had to be devised.

Davidson had to wait until January 1907 and the arrival of the new Burroughs machines before he could continue his research. Within that same month, Davidson organized a five-man research group—Mr. Nevins, L. H. Davis, J. G. Williams, and W. S. Bronsom, and himself—to help carry out his investigations. Initially, Davidson displayed a great deal of optimism about this program of inquiry. Unfortunately, as the group's experiments and tests proceeded, he soon realized that he was not going to be able to achieve the desired result. The primary problem was the inability to mate the mechanical action of the adding machine with the government's existing fee schedule, which bore such irregular proportions to the dollar values of the money orders that it seemed impracticable, if not impossible, to build an adding machine to handle both tabulations automatically. Moreover, Davidson's group did not possess the technical skills to develop a machine this mechanically complex. This failure directed Davidson to begin thinking about a new way to attack this problem that was within the limitation of his technical knowledge and skills. The temporary solution that Davidson settled on was a device that could be externally attached to an adding machine that would be able to print and tabulate the fees.[58] In his middle-management position, it made sense to construct an attachment that could be used on any adding machine. This device, in theory, would be considerably cheaper than buying an entirely new machine and its flexibility would be advantageous in an evolving office work space.

In December 1907, Davidson began to investigate the feasibility of producing an external attachment to record money order fees. He first began by studying the ways in which certain key depressions could facilitate the action of a separately attached device. In the spring of 1908, Davidson built and tested an overly complicated mechanical system of stops and plungers that were activated by various key depressions. Unfortunately, the tests did not prove successful. This design's major limitation hinged upon the fact that if the machine broke down during a regular work day, it would take a considerable amount of time to rectify the situation and return the machine to working order. The potential work delays and stoppages made this device unacceptable to the Treasury Department. Unfortunately, Davidson suffered an unknown sickness at this time that arrested his work and ended the project. While recovering from this ailment, Davidson was absent from work between July 9 and September 10, 1908. During this hiatus, Davidson began to reexamine carefully his fee recording apparatus, eventually devising a plan for an electromechanical device that he hoped would be a decided improvement over a purely mechanical design.[59]

Immediately upon his return, Davidson diligently proceeded to perfect his new idea. He was only able to work on inventing in the time outside of his scheduled Treasury Department hours, so he regularly came into the office early in the morning and departed late in the evening. This time was well spent. By December he had a working device, similar to his earlier creation, that married the electrical with the mechanical to produce an electro-mechanical system. Davidson again endeavored to obtain the formal institutional endorsement that he had lost when he was ill. This support manifested itself after a meeting in January 1909, with the recently appointed Post Office Auditor Merrit O. Chance. On January 14, Davidson submitted to Chance a proposal describing his goal of transferring the auditing of money order vouchers to adding machines. Auditor Chance was unaware that adding machine technology had advanced so much that the complex tabulations required for money-order auditing could be handled using adding machines. The prospect intrigued Chance enough that he gave Davidson the Post Office Division's blessing. He hoped that Davidson would succeed in producing his electro-magnetic fee add-on device and eventually increase the division's auditing speed.[60]

The apparatus that Davidson constructed at that stage of development was cumbersome at best. It straddled an adding machine like a yoke. It was basically a small adding machine, with a specific function, strapped to a larger adding machine. Davidson's device initially ran on battery power, but in actual use it would be shunted into the electric circuitry of the main adding machine. It had its own set of keys to record the money order fee amounts. When the operator depressed the specific fee key for the corresponding money order, the key—with a contact on the bottom—would touch a brass bar completing a circuit. The completion of this circuit would pull a lever away from a spring-loaded plunger which would strike the paper with the proper fee amount.[61] This contrivance was a solid first effort, but Davidson definitely needed to refine the electrical mechanisms before this device could be used in actual service. To this end, he enlisted the help of Edwin J. Dowling, the chief electrician of the Post Office Division, in late February 1909.[62] When Davidson went from a purely mechanical design to an electro-mechanical one, his new scheme required the skills of someone more familiar with electrical technology. Dowling added considerably to the effort and a portion of their combined work resulted in a joint patent application filed in 1911.[63]

When Davidson first began working with Dowling, one would have expected them to begin thinking about patenting, but they were not considering anything of the sort. The primary reason they did not move in this direction was that Davidson still had not solved the major technical problem of how to automatically print the correct fees and tabulate their total simultaneously with the money order amounts. In his quest for help, Davidson wrote to Alvan Macauley, the general manager of the Burroughs Adding Machine Company, on February 9, 1909. He asked if "it [was] possible to construct an adding machine so that in striking an amount of $1.00 to $2.50 it would automatically register $0.03 as fee and for amounts above $2.50 and to $5.00 automatically register a fee of $.05 and add and total?"[64] Davidson explicitly requested that Macauley forward this inquiry to the superintendent of inventions, Jesse G. Vincent—whose responsibilities included managing the invention of devices requested by customers.[65] Vincent let Davidson know that he had put an inventor on the project, although the inventor judged that the mechanism required to produce the desired results would be too complicated to make the device practical. Vincent did promise to look into the matter personally, but he was not particularly hopeful that he would devise a solution.[66]

Vincent's response was not the answer Davidson was searching for. He already knew the complexity of what he proposed. Since he was attempting to entice the Burroughs Corporation into taking up the construction of an automatic fee recording machine, he was hoping that his inquiry would have piqued its interest. To get Burroughs on board, Davidson attempted to give his letter to Macauley a bit more authority by stating that the Post Office Division had charged him with the task of finding a solution to this technical problem, whereas in actuality, Davidson was the one promoting the project to the Post Office Division. In this letter he also attempted to flatter Burroughs by claiming that he was fully confident that its wonderful machines could perform almost any assignment, and for those tasks that a standard Burroughs machine could not execute, the capable people at Burroughs could quickly produce an appliance to fill that void. If this adulation was not enough, Davidson supplied a financial reason for Burroughs to undertake this project. He wrote that if "such a machine [were] perfected, [it] would meet a long felt want and immediately become popular. Every office doing money-order business would be provided with one and absolute accuracy would be insured." A final bit of praise closed the letter. "I trust that your personal attention will bear fruits that will make the scheme practicable, of this I feel assured."[67] At first glance, these statements from a person who was conceivably still working on a device that he was "assured" Burroughs would produce are puzzling. Upon closer examination, this and other letters provide insight into what Davidson saw himself doing.

He was engaging in early scientific and technological management.[68] If he could persuade someone or some company to build a machine that would decrease auditing time, Davidson would be able to make an essential step forward in the organization and construction of the division's adding machine environment. Efficiency and productivity were his fundamental goals. The financial rewards of a patent did not specifically interest Davidson, but the political and social ramifications of creating a more productive auditing "plant" did command his interest. He was striving to improve his division's overall performance through technological means. This vision was at the crux of how Davidson conceptualized all of his activities for the Post Office Division. He labored to purchase or personally produce new technological appliances that would fit into his design of the most useful, productive, and efficient adding machine environment. Inventing was just one of the methods of achieving his goals. Davidson spent much of his time and effort thinking about how to design the most effective auditing atmosphere. In a passage of a letter Davidson wrote to Vincent on March 25, 1909, one can get a clearer sense of what Davidson was striving toward.

> We are very busy rearranging the rooms occupied by the adding machine plant, in order to accommodate more machines, and instead of attaching the machines to the drop light sockets, as heretofore, the room is being specially wired, after a scheme of my own, placing the connections in the base board and have the light attached to the machine by a perpendicular rod having a flexible arm adjustable to any angle. We have also provided for a table built after another design of my own, to do away with cumbersome desks. I think you will readily appreciate the advantage this will give us from a standpoint of display as well as for work. It is my purpose to have the most complete adding machine plant in the country and I am letting no opportunity escape me.[69]

This emphasis on efficiency through design is why Davidson so vigorously worked to stimulate Burroughs to become interested in creating a new adding machine applicable to the Post Office Division's auditing procedures. Davidson recognized that he and Dowling did not possess the technical skills to produce this new type of adding machine. If Burroughs would construct an automatic fee machine, Davidson would no longer need to continue plodding away at his research. It did not matter to Davidson who produced this contrivance, just as long as someone produced it and he would be able to supply his division. This new type of machine would be the perfect addition to the adding machine environment he was constructing. All of this work formed the heart of his plan which would be responsible for "reducing the working force, lessening the physical and mental labors for the employees and increasing efficiency, accuracy and absoluteness of the audit."[70] He viewed his work as crucial to the sustenance and advancement of the division.

Davidson may not have received a commitment from Burroughs to build the machine he desired, but it had not given up either. Vincent continued to look at the possibility of building a machine but wrote back to Davidson on April 13 concerning his doubts. In this reply, Vincent noted that after he had looked more closely into building a machine of the desired design, the prospect of manufacturing an automatic fee machine appeared to be even more daunting.[71] Since it appeared that Burroughs was not going to build the machine anytime soon, Davidson and Dowling continued their research which was progressing quite nicely. Davidson had no doubt that Burroughs would eventually surmount the technical difficulties and manufacture an automatic fee machine, but if he aimed to improve the Post Office Division's auditing performance during the interim, he would have to build the add-on device that he and Dowling had begun to develop.

Davidson and Dowling were very productive from the start of their collaboration in February. They settled on a design by the middle of March and soon thereafter began to execute a series of drawings exemplifying the invention. In April they disclosed this invention to others, started constructing a full-size example, and began reducing the apparatus to practice.[72] This device only partially fulfilled Davidson's requirements, since the operator had to depress a separate set of keys to print the fees. He envisioned that these two sets of action would eventually be integrated into one. Meanwhile, Davidson continued to correspond with Burroughs, even going so far as to send them sketches of this new appliance. Burroughs still did not take his prodding seriously. In reference to the design of April, Burroughs's Assistant General Manager A. J. Lauver wrote Davidson on June 16 and commented that "I am advised by Mr. Vincent that the fee registering device, which you suggest, is quite complicated, and that as yet he has not seen any way in which to simplify it so as to make the construction practicable."[73]

Davidson may not have developed a simple way to audit money orders automatically, but his other work was receiving recognition. On July 1, 1909, Auditor Chance promoted Davidson to a clerk, class 3. This promotion relieved him from his regular auditing duties. His new responsibilities were to concentrate on the perfection of "the new system of machine audit . . . work out the details . . . [and] instruct new clerks in the use of the adding machine."[74] Davidson would also handle any special situations that presented themselves. In this capacity, he was able to develop the adding machine environment based on his vision and design.

Davidson continued to pursue Burroughs into the fall. He even traveled to Detroit again to discuss the prospects of the creation of an automatic fee machine personally.[75] On this excursion he spoke with some of the same personnel from his previous trip and again attempted to convince them of the viability of such a product. Unfortunately their responses mirrored those of Vincent; it was not feasible. Davidson gave Burroughs one last try in late 1909, but to no avail. General Manager Macauley sent Davidson an emphatic rejection in December.

> We found it a practical possibility, but . . . [it] would cost so much to develop . . . that, in view of the comparatively limited call for it, we could not afford to do it at this time . . . It would doubtless cost $1000.00 or more to invent, design and build the first machine. You will readily understand that this would use up the profit on about as many machines as we could expect to sell to the Post Office Department. It would, moreover, take up the time of our inventors, and the facilities of our Experimental Departments, which are now on work on other machines which, when we are able to market them, can be sold by the hundreds if not thousands. These others are . . . the most important, and must have our time and attention.[76]

Davidson did not dwell on the Burroughs refusal. He moved on to another company that he hoped would be more receptive to constructing this machine.

Early in 1910, Davidson contacted the Connecticut Computing Machine Company about the likelihood that it would build an automatic fee machine. In March, Davidson met with the company's secretary, Edward Swift, in Washington. Swift's gracious letter of March 14 exuded confidence about a solution to the money order fee–auditing problem and promised that his company would soon be able to show Davidson "devices that will do [the] work better and quicker than anything . . . yet tried."[77] This was promising news for Davidson, whose obsession with an automatic fee machine was at its zenith. In replying to Swift, Davidson asserted that for this machine there was "a crying need and [it] will revolutionize the service so far as adding machines are concerned."[78]

It was also about this time that his efforts moved beyond the creation of an automatic fee machine to the construction of the perfect auditing environment. Federal positions were becoming harder to come by as the Taft administration instituted racially segregated work spaces. This situation was to get even worse under President Wilson, whose overt racism was encountered widely.[79] Davidson was probably beginning to feel this racially grounded pressure. An effective way to fight this discrimination was to make himself increasingly indispensable. He had designed much of the division's adding machine environment and had procured, invented, or was attempting to invent the material artifacts of this environment. But was that enough? Davidson wanted there to be no question of his value to the Treasury Department's Post Office Division. Thus, he planned to create a niche for himself by being the man responsible for revolutionizing the auditing procedures of the Post Office Division.

By May 1910, it looked like this was going to happen. Davidson and Dowling had a breakthrough back in December 1909.[80] What had previously caused the problems for Davidson and Burroughs was that adding machines turned their numbers on the 9 instead of the 0 that an automatic fee machine required. That is, in standard adding-machine action 9 turned to 10, but since the money order fees need to turn on the 0, it would be difficult to have this action work concurrently with existing adding machines. Separate mechanisms would be required for tabulating money orders and fees; and as Macauley stated, because of the very limited space within preexisting adding machines, it would have required too much money to design and manufacture a machine of this nature. But on May 30, 1910, after several months of "working out the circuits necessary to operate all the fees in the government schedule," the Davidson-Dowling attachment recorded a .05 cent fee for a money order of $2.51 for the first time.[81] Thus, they had figured out how to automate the fees with an external device. Davidson and Dowling, with the assistance of James Lucas, another worker in the division, continued the development of this device and by July it could handle all fees for money orders from one cent to one hundred dollars. They postponed working on their apparatus during much of August and September partially because of the summer heat, but mainly because Davidson was away from the District for a significant amount of this time.[82] They were not in a great hurry to proceed because they were not working toward a patent at that moment, and Davidson was still holding out hope that a large manufacturer would fabricate a single automatic fee machine. Yet Burroughs, the most capable adding machine company, had never shown much interest in the development of this specialized machine and the Connecticut Computing Machine Company had not informed Davidson that they had made any headway.

Davidson and Dowling resumed work on their apparatus in October.

They also began to make a concerted effort to patent their work. The reason for this change in approach is unclear. It is probable that Davidson spoke with government officials in other Treasury Department divisions and realized that there was a market for such a useful and flexible device. Furthermore, as a member of a very entrepreneurial segment of the African American community that had many inventors, Davidson may have seen this as a viable opportunity. Many members of the elite social organizations to which Davidson belonged invented, patented, and organized businesses around their marketable technologies. Thus, he was in regular contact with men who were quite knowledgeable about patenting and the business and financial aspects related to inventing. In an effort to secure a patent Davidson and Dowling began making drawings, constructing a wooden model, and investigating the optimal material out of which to build their latest automatic fee attachment. From mid January until mid March, they constructed and perfected an example of the actual artifact on which Davidson and Dowling jointly filed for a patent on March 9, 1911. On March 20, high-ranking officials issued their approval when Davidson gave them a demonstration of the device. On April 20, a bit of confusion was cleared up when Davidson filed a separate patent application for his intellectual property that had mistakenly been included in the joint Davidson-Dowling patent application.[83]

Davidson's life looked very promising in early 1911. He had risen to an important government position and created the environment for the Post Office Division's adding machines—almost single-handedly increasing the division's efficiency and productivity. He also held the vast majority of the pertinent technical knowledge, skills, and practices to be able to fully integrate artifacts into the division's auditing procedures by solving what he viewed as the most important technical problem. Socially he was an active member of the "best" circles of the colored community, but the next few years would bring great difficulties.

By January 9, 1912, the Patent Office suspended action on the automatic fee printing device patent applications filed by Davidson and by Davidson and Dowling because they had been brought into at least three interferences: #33,368 between Davidson-Dowling, Carroll, Vincent, and Dauber; #33,369 between Davidson, Carroll, and Dauber; and #34,174 between Davidson, Carroll, and Vincent. The interferences greatly irritated Davidson, since Vincent's company, Burroughs, had deemed his project to be impractical and Carroll's company, Connecticut Computing, did not inform him of its solution to the automatic fee problem. Now both had filed conflicting patent applications. Vincent and Carroll most certainly benefited from the open communication Davidson had with their specific organizations. Dauber did not contest the interference, but Connecticut Computing did stay involved in the cases and seemed to be slightly annoyed that Davidson had not notified them about his pending patent application. In this regard, Edward Swift of Connecticut Computing wrote Davidson. "You remember the night that I called at your house that I said to you. 'I cannot understand why you should try to get someone else to work up a post office fee machine, when you had already accomplished it,' referring of course to your getting us started. Your reply was, 'I had worked at it but had not succeeded and thought perhaps you could.' If I remember rightly this was before I had time to tell you that I had learned that we were going to be in interference. The same question keeps going through my mind and seems inexplicable."[84] Davidson did not see anything that was inexplicable. He viewed his work and subsequent invention as something completely different from what he requested that the Connecticut Computing Company do. He invented an automatic fee add-on which he considered something vastly different from an actual new machine even if the Patent Office did not see it that way.

Vincent and Burroughs had every intention of taking part in this interference battle. Shortly after Burroughs had dispatched to Davidson its final "no" about pursuing an automatic fee machine, the company also had a breakthrough. This development was not technological, however, but political. As stated before, the problem that existed was that the fees changed on the 0 instead of the 9, and the machines turned on the 9 instead of the 0. In the ensuing interference testimony, Vincent stated that he corresponded with E. S. Newman, Burroughs's Washington sales manager, about asking if the United States Post Office would consider changing the fee schedule to change on the 9 instead of the 0 to accommodate their machines. Vincent professed that authorities at the Post Office found his suggestion appealing. Yet, there was one important catch; the fee schedule could only be changed by an Act of Congress. According to Vincent, Newman indicated that if they could produce a machine that would perform admirably with the new fee schedule, an act could easily be passed. With Newman's supportive response, Vincent began making drawings for a machine where the fees changed on the 9 in late February 1910. Burroughs made quick work of getting a fully working machine together. They completed and tested a machine on March 17 and shipped it to Newman on April 18. Newman's intuition seems to have failed him, since he did not have much success promoting this new machine. In fact, by June 14, he had not receive a single order for the new device.[85]

This exchange is quite interesting in regard to Davidson because it is highly probable that he conferred a negative evaluation on the Burroughs machine.[86] From May 7 through May 14, 1910, the Treasury Department scheduled an exhibition of labor saving office devices. It extended invitations to several manufacturers and dealers to exhibit new and existing devices that could be useful to the Treasury Department. Newman most likely spoke with Vincent about this exhibition and wanted to show the new machine at the open house. If this was the case, the new Burroughs machine would have made it to Washington at the appropriate time and would account for Burroughs's expedient response. Merrit Chance, the exhibit organizer, wrote to all of the Treasury Department's divisions and required that each select a clerk knowledgeable about labor-saving devices to attend the exhibition.[87] As expected, the Post Office Division chose Davidson. Chance's letter indicated that this gathering was specifically for the internal appraisal of new and existing technology rather that an open house exhibition. C. A. McGonagle, the acting auditor of the Post Office Department, issued a letter to Davidson that contained the following instructions as to his duties: "You will carefully observe the various exhibits and witness the operations of the devices, and submit to the Auditor a report in writing as to the practicability for Departmental use of any of the machines or devices shown. You will also state whether or not it will, in your judgment, be advisable to make use of any such machines or devices in this office, giving the name and explaining in detail how such device or machine will facilitate or improve the efficiency of the work of this office."[88]

If the new Burroughs machine was part of the exhibit, it most certainly received a less than glowing rating from Davidson. The Burroughs machine did not provide a solution to his dilemma, it merely side-stepped it. This machine would only be of use in auditing money orders, whereas Davidson's interest lay in finding a device that could be used to audit and compound fees for any type of transaction within the Treasury Department. The Burroughs machine partially went against Davidson's agenda of creating the country's most efficient adding machine plant. His own work may have influenced his evaluation. In May 1910, Davidson was at the cusp of his research and of finally getting his device to perform the way he had planned. Now there was much more at stake inventively, and professionally as well. It was vital for Davidson's job security that he be known as the one who was personally responsible for the transformation of the Treasury Department's auditing procedures.

Unfortunately for Davidson, he lost the interference cases #33,369 and

#34,174 to Carroll and Vincent, respectively. The commissioner of interferences based his judgment on diligence and documentation. Davidson argued that he reduced his invention to practice in March 1909 and between December 1909 and July 1910, he completed the final drawings and design. From that point until the filing of the first patent application and the official demonstration in March 1911, he constructed and tested various prototypes. But the commissioner of interferences determined that Carroll had reduced his invention to practice before Davidson. Furthermore, Davidson was unable to produce any of the drawings that could coherently explicate his process of development to the final machine. He had not saved the material evidence to support his case. His inexperience in patent interference battles, reminiscent of Granville Woods's early in his career, was fundamentally responsible for his undoing. Conversely, Vincent, as the head of an industrial research laboratory, had signed and dated "Work Book" pages that detailed all of his inventive actions. Consequently, the evidence of Vincent won, even though he produced a machine that was not usable for money order auditing within the Treasury Department existing fee schedule.[89]

Fighting for Survival

Before Davidson's patenting efforts went sour, his professional situation was already veering in a less than positive direction. December 1910 saw a new auditor, Charles A. Kram, appointed. In March of the following year, Davidson had his first introductory meeting with Auditor Kram. Davidson was comfortable with this procedure. He had been through this process many times before and had become accustomed to the self-promotion required to familiarize an incoming official with one's skills and attributes. There always existed a degree of uncertainty in how a new official would treat the preexisting staff, so Davidson asked Auditor Kram about his status under the new administration up front. Kram responded very supportively to Davidson's query. Davidson wrote that Kram replied, "Mr. Davidson, your record is A1, and I am pleased with the energy and intelligence and especially the interest and enthusiasm you put into your work, you need have no question as to your status, you are doing a peculiar work for which you are peculiarly fitted and there is no one who can fill your place."[90] Davidson was not going to let the aura of this glowing response dissipate. He immediately pressed forward and asked about his chances of receiving an appointment to one of the four new positions being created at the next grade in July. At this point, Kram's endorsements derailed. Kram commented that based on Davidson's present work, he could not recommend him for a promotion. The only way that Davidson could be eligible to move up to the next higher grade was if he began a different line of work. Davidson was not taking no for an answer and proceeded to bombard Kram with this list of all of the creative work he had performed for the division, hoping to persuade Auditor Kram to change his mind. The list went as follows:

- Clamp-board for holding money orders, now in use on machines.
- Plan of voucher audit submitted to Auditor Timme (1906).
- Invented "Rewind Device" for saving paper, patented.
- Presented synopsis of plan resulting in present machine audit.
- Planned and secured the repair shop, in Bureau.
- Suggested and supervised test of placing transcripts on machine.
- Supervised the successful test of auditing certificates deposits.
- Standardized, through Board of Supplies, ribbons for machines.
- Suggested and planned style of table used for machines.
- Suggested and secured typewriter chairs for operators.
- Suggested and successfully tested placing all accounts on adding machine, large and small, which was doubted.
- Invented metal adjustable [money order] holder, saving eyes . . . offered to Bureau without cost.
- Invented "Automatic Fee Device," patent pending.[91]

Davidson's record of achievement did not sway Kram. Davidson was reasonably upset at Kram's lack of support. He had been a loyal and hardworking member of the Post Office Department and he believed that he deserved some form of material recognition and not merely Kram's kind words.

Davidson did not let Kram's denial ruffle him. If a promotion to one of the new positions was out of the question, Davidson wanted to know if at least he could be transferred to "one of the higher divisions where there would be no discrimination between me and my fellow clerks," which was becoming more overt in 1911.[92] Kram did not give an inch, stating "that he could not recommend it . . . for the good of the service."[93] These comments certainly had racial overtones to them. "The good of the service," deciphered meant that promoting Davidson would disrupt the white-male workers in the government's segregated work space. Kram's institutional policy was that a segregated environment would be beneficial to all employees because there would be less racial interaction, thereby decreasing racial conflict. Davidson was now directly confronted with the discrimination that was brought about by the Taft administration's efforts to segregate the government work setting.

Shortly after their first meeting, Auditor Kram began scheming to remove Davidson from his current position. Davidson never received any notice of this course of action. On July 1, they met again when Davidson, in a less than passive mood, caught Kram at lunch. Kram succeeded in mollifying Davidson. He told Davidson that "I hope you did not get discouraged at what I said to you at our last interview . . . I knew when you were settled you would see the justice of my claim . . . I am glad that you took it that way, I think I now have a plan which will suit you and . . . give you an opportunity for advancement."[94] A show of any more displeasure by Davidson would certainly have had a detrimental effect. Davidson had no other option but to play along since Kram controlled his future as a federal employee. But from his experiences of June, and his knowledge of being a black man in America, it is doubtful that he believed a word that Kram uttered.

On June 3, Davidson received an odd note attached to a memo from the chief of the division of money order auditing, W. H. Wanamaker. This attachment instructed him to submit a listing of the adding machine repair tools owned and loaned to the government. In hindsight, he thought that this survey was somewhat out of the ordinary. In particular the request for an inventory of the tools loaned to the government was odd, since all the tools were his property and had not been loaned. The inquiry was peculiar, but Davidson did not think much of it until shortly thereafter when a stranger spoke with him outside of the office. This anonymous man, who knew Kram personally, informed Davidson that soon he would no longer be the man "in charge" of the Post Office Department's adding machines. This unnamed individual further implied that it might be in Davidson's best interest to present his tools to Auditor Kram as a donation to the division. Davidson responded that he "did not think that the government could accept presents and that [he] could not make such a gift." If he cooperated, the unwelcome visitor told him, he may find himself the recipient of a promotion. Davidson mulled over the idea and after a few conversations with this individual, he "refused to consider anything of the kind."[95] Certain people, one of whom was Auditor Kram, were attempting to coerce Davidson into donating his tools to the office for an "eventual" promotion. Davidson was smart in not turning over his tools because a promotion for him was definitely not on anyone's agenda. It was also very shrewd to have someone unconnected to the Treasury

Department offer Davidson this. With this tactic, Davidson could not incriminate Kram or any other government officials who were privy to this plan. Yet he did say it required two or three conversations for him to refuse to play, so he probably did consider participating in this exchange. But, the manner in which the stranger approached Davidson was a clear signal that he was entering a no-win situation.

On July 24, 1911, the process of removing Davidson from his supervisory position began. He received the first of many short-term assignments, and as soon as he would complete each project someone else would come in and take command. Davidson was given the same explanation when pulled off each specific project: other activities needed his expertise. Dumbfounded, he continued to work diligently at the varied assignments, none of which had even the remotest relation to the maintenance of adding machines. Davidson now began to realize that the implications of the anonymous conversations were becoming a reality. He finally received some indication of his demotion on October 31. On that day, W. H. Wanamaker forwarded a communication stating: "Mr. Davidson, The Auditor has decided that the tools are your property and wants them removed at once."[96] Davidson boxed his tools that evening and removed them the next day. He tried unsuccessfully to have a meeting with Auditor Kram on October 31. After waiting three weeks before Kram would grant him an audience, the day before he was to go on leave until January 1, 1912, an irate Davidson sarcastically asked if the higher work Kram had mentioned in March was the miscellaneous piece work that had engaged his time for the past few months. He continued by asking why it was the case that in March he was indispensable for the proper performance of the division's adding machines, but he had hardly any connection to them since the end of July. Kram glibly retorted that he had not yet found the proper work for Davidson.

After Davidson began his vacation, the Post Office Division made certain personnel adjustments that infuriated him. The primary offense was the promotion of George B. Furman to the $1800 rank ahead of him. Davidson was upset because Furman entered government service many years after him. Furman had always followed him in promotions. They had eventually come to work for the same division; Furman was responsible for allocating auditing assignments to clerks, while Davidson maintained machines and assigned clerks to them. Furthermore, Davidson taught Furman how to perform his job.[97] In his opinion, Furman did not merit a promotion ahead of him. In Davidson's search for reparations, he communicated with Senator W. O. Bradley about this injustice. Senator Bradley wrote Assistant Treasury Secretary Andrews inquiring why Davidson had been dismissed from his post as superintendent of adding machines, why he had been relegated to miscellaneous work, and why when positions were available in July he had not received a promotion to the $1800 grade? Davidson's complaints soon made their way back to Auditor Kram, when Assistant Secretary Andrews wrote Kram about Senator Bradley's concerns. Kram's reply to Andrews completely contradicted the exemplary rating he bestowed upon Davidson in March. Kram began by claiming that previous administrations had looked too favorably upon Davidson's work and that Davidson received more than his fair share of promotions. He implied that Davidson's connections influenced previous administrators' decision about his advancement. Kram wrote to Andrew that "the correspondence on file in this office would seem to indicate that the importunity of his friends has perhaps unjustly expedited his advancement." While his friends may have tried to help him, there is no likelihood that he did not deserve his promotions. Kram also defended the promotion of Furman who, he contended, "was promoted solely on his record as a clerk," which certainly could not have been any more sterling than Davidson's record. He continued to denigrate Davidson by implying that others grossly exaggerated the significance of his work. Auditor Kram claimed that the position Davidson filled as superintendent of adding machines should have been occupied by a person paid at the $900 level. But since they did not have someone to fill the position, Davidson took over the responsibility because he had an "inclination for mechanical work." Davidson did have an inclination for working with adding machines, but his ability was much broader than merely repairing these technological artifacts. Kram did not credit Davidson with designing and constructing much of the auditing environment and inventing many of the devices that the division used. Davidson was vastly more important than Kram acknowledged. Kram's memorandum concluded by stating that "Mr. Davidson's abilities as a clerk have been overestimated. His work does not rise above the ordinary and is not such as to place him in line for promotion. There are in this office a large number of clerks of the $1600 class whose abilities are far superior to Mr. Davidson's. To promote him at this time would be to advance him arbitrarily over those who are entitled to first consideration."[98] This response was taken as the final word on Davidson's complaint.

When Davidson returned in January 1912, he entered a situation that was far from ideal. Formalized segregation had become a reality. Du Bois wrote about this new government policy in *The Crisis.* He stated that "in the Treasury and Postoffice [sic] Departments colored clerks have been herded to themselves as though they were not human beings." Du Bois also noted that others were in worse situations than Davidson. For instance, he mentioned "one colored clerk who could not actually be segregated on account of the nature of his work has consequently had a cage built around him to separate him from his white companions of many years."[99] Not only was Davidson disposed to one of the two dark and unsightly segregated rooms and required to perform menial work, but two weeks later officials transferred him to the poorest lit of the division's segregated rooms and placed him in the darkest corner. Auditor Kram planned to make Davidson pay for vocalizing his discontent. Davidson did actually meet with Kram to voice his displeasure with Furman's promotion and his working conditions. Kram responded that he based the promotion of Furman on his clerical record, and Davidson would have been considered if Kram had known he had performed clerical work—even though Kram had full knowledge of Davidson's clerical record. As for his dismal location, he was told, "this is the best we can do."[100]

This humiliation was the final straw for Davidson. He wrote to the highest-ranking black government official, U.S. Assistant Attorney General William H. Lewis, hoping he would be able to improve his situation. He detailed the events of the past year and indicated the positive recommendations that previous Auditors C. H. Keep, Henry A. Castle, Ernest G. Timme, and Merrit O. Chance had made. Davidson then proceeded to say why the Post Office Division of the Treasury Department had treated him so poorly recently. Davidson contended that it was

> because I am a colored man and this is the crux of the whole situation, I believe the whole situation of relieving me of the supervisory work on [adding] machines was for this reason and I, the only negro [sic] in this Bureau who had worked up from a laborer to such a place; why this shuffling this change from place to place and finally to the work where I began and made a record second to none and even outlined and helped to plan for the scheme? Every other man in a supervisory capacity on this division, except one has come on the work since I did and record to record have done no more than I by way of effort and the success of work assigned to me.

Davidson concluded this letter by proclaiming that his case was not an aberration.

> I submit this as a single instance of what the negro [sic] has to undergo in the classified service and there are many more, but fear that protestation will not be afforded, if disclosures are made, keeps them from being verified. Had I been white instead of colored I do not doubt at all that I would have been chief of one of the divisions instead of now being on trial, hounded, persecuted and expected to make another record in order to maintain my present rating and this under the most adverse and painful conditions . . . Bluntly put I have obeyed the mandate of the service . . . I have earned recognition, as long as I was quiet and content to so remain, all was well, as soon as I contended for what I had earned and had reason to expect, I am side-tracked and by shifting am expected to lose my rating, the whole situation is anomalous, unjust; it is just this that is enervating the service and causing reproach to government. [If] you will be able to do some good in this matter, your help will not be confined alone to me and mine, but there are others who will feel the benefits arising from this effort. I wish it understood that I do not contend that any place in government gives one a title thereto, but it has and is the practice where one has labored and wrought to let them have the fruit of their labors and not by displacement . . . to one who has done nothing to deserve it.[101]

In this last passage Davidson showed the contradictory nature of the life for the black middle class in the early twentieth century. Davidson had spent most of his life avoiding racial agitation because it often came at a price he was not willing to pay. He worked in a predominantly white world and lived in a culture whose members thought they related more closely to Victorian aristocrats than the "common" Negro. Davidson was fighting to hold onto the ideology that the black population could rise up to civilization by their hard work, education, and general civility. Yet, as the racial discrimination became legally institutionalized by the Plessy decision in 1896, equality for black citizens was a reality that could only be dreamed of. Davidson was reaching a point of transformation, his carefully prescribed silence was now of no benefit. He was no longer seen as a diligent, industrious, and conscientious valued employee; he was a colored man bound to the historical construction of black people as lazy, deviant, pathological, and undesirable. So he began to vocalize his discontent, in a frenetic effort to arrest his downward spiraling government career. In his effort to buoy his sinking career, he was banking on receiving a life-preserver from Assistant Attorney General Lewis. But Lewis would not have secured his lofty appointment unless he knew how to walk the racial tightrope. Moreover, Lewis who secured his appointment with the help of Booker T. Washington would not have been one to put his career in jeopardy for Davidson.[102] Davidson, a man who had been able to avoid the racial constraints of previous years, was now fully in their grasp. He seemed to be fighting for all exploited and undervalued black government workers. No matter how hard Davidson worked to invent an environment for the Treasury Department's Post Office Division, American racial discrimination would not allow him to succeed. Davidson resigned from government service in 1912.

Davidson had smartly positioned himself to leave the comfortable confines of government service. He would not have quit an unpleasant, but paying job, if he did not have an alternate plan. That alternative plan was to use his legal skills. The entire time Davidson worked for the Treasury Department's Post Office Division he was bolstering his legal credentials. In 1903, the District of Columbia Court of Appeals admitted him to practice law. Then in 1912, the United States Supreme Court admitted Davidson to practice law before the high court. So it seems that when he left government service he was in a good position to begin a legal career.[103] The law was not the only thing Davidson engaged himself with when he vacated his post. He had started a real estate business around 1909. "The House of Davidson" specialized in the management of "desirable properties for colored clients." By the mid 1920s he managed enough real estate to have a "corps of workmen" to maintain these properties.[104] It would appear that Davidson was doing well financially. Socially he continued to command a position of esteem in the elite black community. The General Alumni Association of Howard University elected him president in 1916 and 1917.[105] He also became more politically active and strengthened his relationship with the National Association for the Advancement of Colored People. In addition to being appointed a colonel in 1921, he was the executive secretary and chairman of the membership committee of the District of Columbia's branch of the NAACP in the early 1920s.[106] Davidson had built and lived a very comfortable life by the time he passed away in 1930.[107]

When Davidson left government service the automatic fee machine was not the only project on which he worked. He was also working on an early coin counting machine (fig. 4.5). A tabulation problem hindered the machine's usability. The device easily separated coins into their various denominations and would count them as they passed into their appropriate slots. A clocklike dial would indicate the number of coins. The problem was that the machine could not compound the total for all the coin denominations. That procedure had to be performed manually. So David-

FIGURE 4.5. One of the last devices Davidson would attempt to invent was a coin-counting machine. Moreland-Spingarn Research Center.

son was having familiar problems with a different machine. He eventually solved this problem and developed a working prototype all of which cost approximately one thousand dollars, most of which came from unknown financial supporters. It is unclear what resulted from this effort.[108] Davidson's ideas for this device and his adding machine patents did not revolutionize computation. The black inventor mythology would have one believe that accounting practices would be impossible if not for Shelby Davidson. Davidson's life illustrates the inherent problems in this belief. Considering the time in which he worked, Davidson patents are very important, but they do not carry the lofty meanings that the black inventor myth has constructed for inventions by African Americans.

During Davidson's tenure at the Post Office Division of the Treasury Department, he was unable to fully control the role his technical work played in his life. The black community accepted his technological work as an affirmation of his intelligence, but the American government culture did not see Davidson's work the same way. This culture, so intermeshed with racism, could not or did not want to see beyond this constraint. Davidson wanted his technological work to play the role of racial diminisher, but the culture refused to acknowledge his message.

Chapter Five

Back to the Future: Reassessing Black Inventors in the Twenty-first Century

In the final analysis, heroes exist in the legends from which they arise. Real life is made up of flesh and blood creatures who are eventful rather than event-making. The true heroes, then, are those with a hair more kindness, a mite more hope. They are those whose myopic enthusiasms and pedestrian virtues nurture the world.
—Wyn Wachhorst

In February 1997 the only black teacher in an overwhelmingly white suburban St. Louis elementary school invited me to speak to her class about black inventors. She did not specifically indicate what she wanted me to do, but from our brief discussions, it was abundantly clear that she wanted me to talk about the contributions that African Americans have made to America society through their inventions. I planned to accommodate her wishes, but in my zeal to develop new understandings of black inventors I also wanted to inject a bit of complexity into black inventors' lives, so as to not leave those students believing that black inventors were unadulterated heroes. Upon arriving at the school, this well-meaning teacher, to my dismay, had created an African American invention display case. Her cabinet was very thoughtfully put together. This teacher proudly placed a series of crisp white cards with the names of black inventors and their patent numbers in front of real and miniaturized representations of their inventions. Unfortunately, her case made the mythology associated with black inventors come alive and jump off the page more powerfully than any inventors' list ever could. She had made these inventions real for her students, but the inventors were still invisible. Nowhere could you find the human being behind the name, the patent number, or the artifact. Her display reinforced the understanding that inventions, not inventors, matter. Now, more than ever, I felt I had a responsibility to humanize black inventors by destabilizing their myth.

My quest to inform a small group of students about the lost history of black inventors took an abrupt turn when, to my surprise, between the time I agreed to come to the school and my actual arrival, a decision was made that I would be doing an all-school assembly! As I watched the rambling parade of more than four hundred students march past the black inventor case and fill the gymnasium, my agenda began to change. While being introduced, I looked out into a sea of whiteness to only notice a handful of brown faces. At that moment—a Black History Month assembly moment—I felt slightly uncomfortable about disrupting the black inventive myths that the only black teacher in this school had so dutifully reproduced. In probably one of the few assemblies focusing on African Americans, I could not point out some of the foibles of the very people they were there to celebrate, valorize, and perhaps emulate. I could not disturb the hero worship of Black History Month, so I gave them exactly what they expected to hear—that black inventors were great Americans and their inventions contributed to the development of the modern world. Reminiscent of works by William J. Simmons and D. W. Culp that attempted to prove that Negroes were capable of reaching civilization, I used black inventors as proof that people of African heritage contributed to the development of a technologically sophisticated American society. In my apprehension to problematize the myths of black inventors, I did little to advance the current understanding of black inventors during the late nineteenth and early twentieth centuries.

Nevertheless, the assembly pleased, everyone from students to teachers. My discussion reinforced what the teachers wanted the students to believe in—the American dream: that if they worked hard and persevered, they too could be remembered as important Americans. My presentation also substantiated the belief that racism does not inhibit the truly talented and those with the proper work ethic. I made it appear as if the racism of the late nineteenth and early twentieth centuries was not that bad if these black men succeeded. I had reproduced the representation of black inventors that this book argues against. Why? Initially I tried to intellectualize my behavior by telling myself that the complexity I wanted to infuse into black inventors' lives would have been difficult to present in a boisterous grade-school assembly setting. This attempt at rationalizing my role in the promulgation of the myths about black inventors was quite feeble. What made the assembly any different from that which I had planned for a smaller classroom group? Of course, the answer was, and still is, nothing. But, there was and still is a big difference: race. In the assembly, I felt uneasy about exposing some of the contradictions in the lives of black inventors unless there was someone besides the lone black teacher to do clean-up. I did not want the students or teachers to question whether or not African American inventors had contributed to American society and culture. As a black man in his late twenties in a fairly monoracial environment, I felt almost compelled to tow the racial line and maintain the heroism of black inventors. Again, why? At that moment—that Black History Month moment—I felt it was neither the time nor the place to present black inventors as problematic race champions and disturb the myths. It seemed disrespectful to perform criticism during the one month of the year when black cultural heroes and icons are publicly celebrated. Moreover, I did not want my criticism to be misinterpreted as a devaluation of their inventive work. As a result, I fell victim to retelling the myths.

My reaction signifies a problem. The problem is that within the study of African American life there is often little space for criticism. This problem is deeply historically rooted. African American communities have rightfully viewed criticism with suspicion since many critiques of black existence resemble the racial assumptions that historically have been used to denigrate African American people. My actions at the assembly partially responded to this historical legacy. This book speaks directly to the perils of performing criticism on African American heroes and addresses the need for change. As a result, the study of black inventors has to develop thoughtful, mature, appropriate, historically rooted forms of criticism. These forms of criticism will not only expose the failings and shortcomings of black inventors; they will enable us to embrace their achievement in a new and more human way. But developing this type of critical understanding of black inventors is far from easy. Currently, African American inventors are ennobled in the same ways that white inventors were celebrated during the early part of the twentieth century. Many white inventors have been critically examined, but three quarters of a century is too long to wait for this analytical gap to close before

African American inventors can be examined with a critical lens. It is time to develop a new critical consciousness about the lives of African American inventors.

Black History Month, with its solitary celebratory agenda, is one of the largest barriers for this reformation project. Black History Month, however, should not be considered a problem; the problem is how we study and use black inventors. Black History Month is tremendously important for the study of black inventors because those few weeks are primarily the only time when American society is interested in their work. It is one of the few moments when black inventors are discussed on a national level. Their patents and the meanings of their successes for African American people are put on display. Unfortunately, once Black History Month ends, black inventors are relegated to the deepest and darkest fringes of African American history. Moreover, when black inventors are placed alongside leaders like Martin Luther King, Jr., Malcolm X, and Rosa Parks, they take a free ride on the coattails of these black leaders and by a tenuous association are elevated to race champions. King, Malcolm, and Parks all have written histories, visibly familiar faces, and documented lived experiences that are markers of their race leadership, whereas these types of historical records do not yet exist for African American inventors. Accurate historical work on the lives of black inventors is needed before one can either assess whether black inventors were race champions or adequately engage in thoughtful criticism of them. In that regard, this book is a first step in detailing and reconstructing a historical record on which to examine black inventors. Moreover, since criticism is necessary to revise our understanding of black inventors, this book is also about critically infusing the essentialist black inventor with the complexities seen and experienced within African American life. For critical discussions of black inventors to emerge, forthcoming work must negotiate the narrow space existing between the binary opposites of myth making and sinister criticism. It is time to begin a critical reassessment about the uses and meanings of black inventors within American and African American society and culture.

This reassessment should begin with the black inventor myth and be critical of past portrayals of black inventors as race champion–heroes that have fundamentally contributed to American society. This study of Granville Woods, Lewis Latimer, and Shelby Davidson certainly calls the myth into question and illustrates that black inventors were not what we would like to think they were. As for being financially successful, none became wealthy from their inventive work. Woods passed away poor and anonymous. Davidson and Latimer were solidly middle class but not because of the successes of their inventions. Furthermore, none of their inventions can be considered a technological triumph. Both Davidson and Latimer received patents for devices that were obsolete fairly soon after the United States Patent Office granted them their legal monopolies. Woods received several patents, but their use and his financial compensation were minimal. From this evidence, I would argue that patents can no longer be considered the sole measure of success when examining black inventors. This study clearly illustrates that a large body of patents did not correlate with success. Of the three men studied, Latimer had the most "successful" professional life, but he did not patent much after he reached a secure position with the electrical community. As for being race champions, only Davidson had any regular social or political contact with the black community. Latimer's writings imply that he had a precarious relationship with the African American community, and Woods did not even consider himself an American Negro. Just because they were of African descent does not mean that they possessed a strong racial identification. Their identification was linked most strongly to individual accolades, personal social climbing, and financial aspirations. These inventors were just surviving, and much of their activity was self-serving. In this regard, they were no different from most white inventors of the period. As flawless African American cultural heroes, they fall short.

The most important thing, outside of the black inventor mythology, that binds these men together is race and the tragedy of racism in America, which is the defining characteristic of the black inventive experience before and after the twentieth century. American racism influenced their inventive lives in myriad ways. In the best situations, it only had a minor effect, but in the worst situations, it completely derailed their inventive ambitions. This is tragic because at some moment in their lives they all believed that their talents would shelter them from the racial realities of the day and would provide them access to all that America had to offer. Unfortunately, full access to this American dream was unavailable.

So where do we go from here? What happens when we disturb the black inventor myth? What are we left with? We are left with significantly more than what we began with—complex contradictory human beings. As we get a closer glimpse of the struggles they endured at a moment when American society was significantly more racist than it is today, their achievements become all the more astounding. We should commend their amazing ability to succeed in environments replete with racism. But we should not hide the fact that black inventors were not consistently fighting against racism or creating technological artifacts that revolutionized the modern world. To understand black inventors as full human beings, we must put their inventive work into proper historical, social, and cultural contexts. Granville Woods, Lewis Latimer, and Shelby Davidson are exemplars of black inventive life before and after the turn of the twentieth century and they should be treated as such. Their lives challenge us to reform the study of African Americans and technology. They push us to address how black people construct their cultural heroes. They prod us to be reflective and explore how African American history itself helps undermine the reclamation of black inventors' human complexity. They impel us to recognize that failure is just as informative as success. Black inventors also urge us to consider seriously the place of race within the construction of a modern technological nation. They provide a strong case for studying the effects of racism on this nation's technological production.

In studying black inventors we must develop our analytical lens to see past the material "stuff." The fact that black inventors patented is extremely important, but most of their inventions—like most inventions—should never be considered Promethean. Moreover, if we are going to use black inventors as African American cultural heroes, we must closely examine their commitments to black people in America. If we hope to reach the point of celebrating the triumphs of black inventors and looking upon their weaknesses with critical compassion, we must avoid the perils of overly focusing on the patented artifact and the construction of race champion–heroes. Black inventive life was as diverse and complicated as the communities to which these inventors belonged. There are certain things we should celebrate about these men, but certain things that have to be acknowledged as objectionable. Nevertheless, we must understand them and accept them as men of their times, and not what we would have hoped them to be.

Appendixes

Appendix A. The Patents of Granville T. Woods

U.S. Patent Number	*Description*	*Date Filed*	*Date Patented*
299,894	Steam boiler furnace	6/19/1883	6/3/1884
308,817	Telephone transmitter	6/18/1883	12/2/1884
315,368	Apparatus for transmission of messages by electricity	4/9/1884	4/7/1885
364,619	Relay instrument	9/17/1886	6/7/1887
366,192	Polarized relay	11/3/1886	7/5/1887
368,265	Electro mechanical brake	11/3/1886	8/16/1887
371,241	Telephone system and apparatus	6/1/1885	10/11/1887
371,655	Electro mechanical brake apparatus	10/2/1886	10/18/1887
373,383	Railway telegraphy	11/3/1886	11/15/1887
373,915	Induction telegraph system	5/21/1885	11/29/1887
383,844	Overhead conducting system for electric railway	5/2/1887	5/29/1888
385,034	Electro-motive railway system	8/23/1886	6/26/1888
386,282	Tunnel construction for electric railway	5/2/1887	7/17/1888
387,839	Galvanic battery	7/9/1887	8/14/1888
388,803	Railway telegraphy	7/14/1887	8/28/1888
395,533	Automatic safety cut-out for electric circuits	8/13/1887	1/1/1889
438,590	Automatic safety cut-out for electric circuits	4/8/1890	10/14/1890
463,020	Electric railway system	8/31/1891	11/10/1891
507,606	Electric-railway supply system.	3/2/1893	10/31/1893
509,065	Electric railway conduit	10/14/1892	11/21/1893
569,443	System of electrical distribution	2/5/1896	10/13/1896
630,280	System of electrical distribution	10/30/1896	8/1/1899
639,692	Amusement apparatus	9/27/1898	12/19/1899
656,760	Incubator	5/25/1900	8/28/1900
662,049	Automatic circuit-breaking apparatus	8/24/1898	11/20/1900
667,110	Electric railway	9/29/1897	1/29/1901
678,086	Electric railway system	7/24/1895	7/9/1901
681,768	Regulating and controlling electrical translating devices	1/14/1895	9/3/1901
687,098	Electrical railway	6/29/1900	11/19/1901
690,807	Method of controlling electric motors or other electrical translating devices	8/27/1892	1/7/1902
690,808	Method for controlling electric motors of other electrical translating devices	3/20/1895	1/7/1902
690,809	Apparatus for controlling electric motors of other electrical translating devices	8/27/1892	1/7/1902

690,810	Apparatus for controlling electric motors of other electrical translating devices	3/20/1895	1/7/1902
695,988	Electric railway	8/24/1900	3/25/1902
697,767	Electric railways	1/25/1898	4/15/1902
697,928	Electric railways	1/23/1898	4/15/1902
701,981	Automatic air brake	2/5/1901	6/10/1902
718,183	Electric railway system	10/30/1896	1/13/1903
729,481	Electric railway	11/24/1900	5/26/1903
755,825	Railway-brake apparatus	12/31/1902	3/29/1904
762,792	Electric-railway apparatus	10/12/1901	6/14/1904
795,243	Railway-brake apparatus	12/31/1902	7/18/1905
833,193	Safety apparatus for railways	2/19/1904	10/16/1906
837,022	Safety apparatus for railways	10/5/1904	11/27/1906
867,180	Vehicle-controlling apparatus	9/23/1899	9/24/1907

Source for all appendix graphs and tables: National Archives and Records Administration, Records of the Patent and Trademark Office, Record Group 241, Washington, D.C.

Appendix B. Granville T. Woods — Patents Filed Yearly

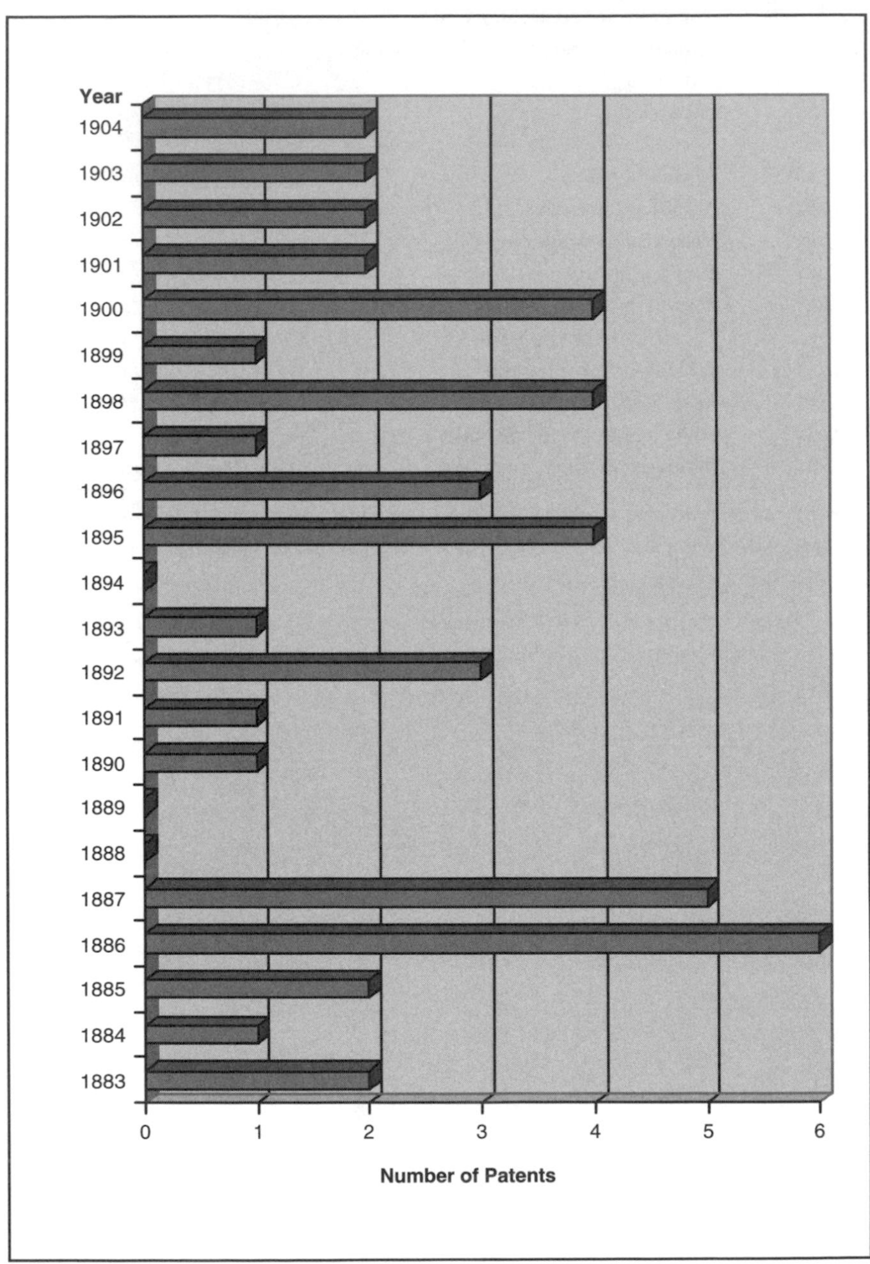

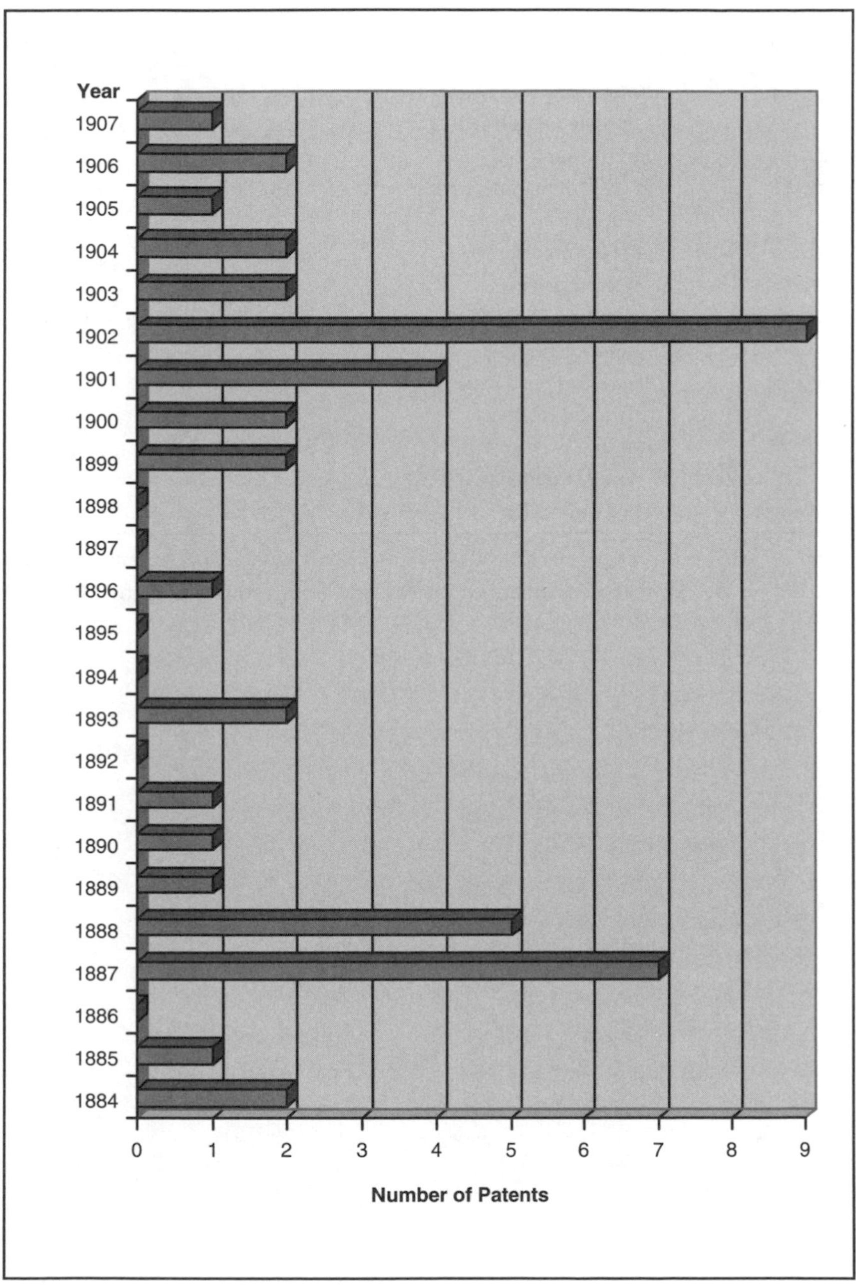
Year
1907
1906
1905
1904
1903
1902
1901
1900
1899
1898
1897
1896
1895
1894
1893
1892
1891
1890
1889
1888
1887
1886
1885
1884
0
1
2
3
4
5
6
7
8
9
Number of Patents

Appendix D. The Patents of Lewis H. Latimer

U.S. Patent Number	Description	Date Filed	Date Patented
147,363	Improvement in water-closets for railroad-cars	1/14/1874	2/10/1874
247,097	Electric lamp	4/18/1881	9/13/1881
252,386	Process of manufacturing carbons	2/19/1881	1/17/1882
255,212	Globe-supporter for electric lamps	9/7/1881	3/12/1882
334,078	Apparatus for cooling and disinfecting	9/3/1885	1/12/1886
367,651	Means for producing luminous effects	8/22/1890	10/10/1891
557,076	Locking-rack for hats, coats, umbrellas, &c.	8/26/1895	3/24/1896
781,890	Book-supporter	6/3/1904	2/7/1905

Source for all appendix graphs and tables: National Archives and Records Administration, Records of the Patent and Trademark Office, Record Group 241, Washington, D.C.

NOTES

ABBREVIATIONS

BTWC-MDLC	Booker T. Washington Collection, Manuscript Division, Library of Congress, Washington, D.C.
ENHS	Edison National Historic Site, East Orange, New Jersey
LHLC-SCSBC	Lewis Howard Latimer Collection, Schomburg Center for the Study of Black Culture, New York Public Library, New York, New York
LHLC-QBPL	Lewis Howard Collection, Queens Borough Public Library, Queens, New York
NARA	National Archives and Records Administration, Suitland, Maryland
WJHC-NMAH	William J. Hammer Collection, National Museum of American History Archives, Smithsonian Institution, Washington, D.C.
SJDC	Shelby J. Davidson Collection, Moreland-Spingarn Research Center, Howard University, Washington, D.C.

INTRODUCTION

1. Edwin T. Layton, "Conditions of Technological Development," in *Science, Technology, and Society: A Cross-Disciplinary Perspective,* ed. Ina S. Spiegel-Rösing and Derek de Solla Price (London: Sage, 1977), 198.

2. Merritt Roe Smith and Leo Marx, eds., *Does Technology Drive History? A Dilemma of Technological Determinism* (Cambridge, Mass.: MIT Press, 1994), xii.

3. Andrew Feenberg, "Subversive Rationalization: Technology, Power, and Democracy," in *Technology and the Politics of Knowledge,* ed. Andrew Feenberg and Alistar

Hannay (Bloomington: Indiana University Press, 1995); Langdon Winner, *The Whale and the Reactor: A Search for Limits in an Age of High Technology* (Chicago: University of Chicago Press, 1986).

4. Herman Gray, *Watching Race: Television and the Struggle for "Blackness"* (Minneapolis: University of Minnesota Press, 1995), 70–92; Marlon Riggs, *Color Adjustment* (San Francisco: California Newsreel, 1991).

5. Mary Tiles and Hans Oberdiek, *Living in a Technological Culture: Human Tools and Human Values* (New York: Routledge, 1995), 30.

6. Ronald Kline, "Construing 'Technology' as 'Applied Science': Public Rhetoric of Scientists and Engineers in the United States, 1880–1945," *Isis* 86 (June 1995): 197; Leo Marx, "The Idea of 'Technology' and Postmodern Pessimism," in *Technology, Pessimism, and Postmodernism*, ed. Yaron Ezrahi, Everett Mendelsohn, and Howard P. Segal (Amherst: University of Massachusetts Press, 1994), 14; and Judy Wajcman, *Feminism Confronts Technology* (College Station: Penn State University Press, 1991), 14–15.

7. William L. Van Deburg, *Black Camelot: African-American Cultural Heroes in Their Times, 1960–1980* (Chicago: University of Chicago Press, 1997), 4.

8. Leonard Steinhorn and Barbara Diggs-Brown, *By the Color of Our Skin: The Illusion of Integration and the Reality of Race* (New York: Dutton Books, 1999), 143–57.

CHAPTER 1: INVENTING THE MYTH OF RACIAL EQUALITY

Epigraph, Henry E. Baker, "The Negro as an Inventor," in *Twentieth Century Negro Literature*, ed. D. W. Culp (Naperville, Ill.: J. L. Nichols & Co., 1902), 399.

1. Thomas P. Hughes, *American Genesis* (New York: Penguin Books, 1989), 3.

2. Lewis Mumford, *Technics and Civilization* (New York: Harcourt Brace, 1934), 215–21.

3. Ruth Schwartz Cowan, *A Social History of American Technology* (New York: Oxford University Press, 1997), 123–24.

4. Ronald R. Kline, personal communication.

5. Wyn Wachhorst, *Thomas Alva Edison: An American Myth* (Cambridge, Mass.: MIT Press, 1981), 3.

6. Cowan, *A Social History of American Technology*, 124–30.

7. James D. Anderson, *The Education of Blacks in the South, 1860–1935* (Chapel Hill: University of North Carolina Press, 1988), 4–78; Eric Foner, *Reconstruction: America's Unfinished Revolution, 1863–1877* (New York: Harper & Row, 1988), 77–123; Rayford W. Logan, *The Betrayal of the Negro: From Rutherford B. Hayes to Woodrow Wilson* (New York: Collier Books, 1965), 125–62.

8. Foner, *Reconstruction*, 77–170; Logan, *Betrayal*, 165–74.

9. T. L. Stoddard, "Should the Negro Be Encouraged to Cultural Equality" (1929, typed manuscript, Du Bois Papers, Fisk University).

10. Steven Lubar, "The Transformation of Antebellum Patent Law," *Technology and Culture* 32 (October 1991): 932–59.

11. Attorney General Jeremiah S. Black to Joseph Holt, June 10, 1858, Office of the Secretary of the Interior, Records Concerning the Patent Office, 1849–1889, Letter Concerning the Patent Office, vol. 1 (1857–73), NARA; Norman O. Forness, "The

Master, the Slave, and the Patent Laws: A Vignette of the 1850s," *Prologue, 25th Anniversary* 26, no. 2 (1994): 48–54; Henry E. Baker, "The Negro as an Inventor," in *Twentieth Century Negro Literature*, ed. D. W. Culp (Naperville, Ill.: J. L. Nichols & Co., 1902), 400, Portia P. James, *The Real McCoy: African-American Invention and Innovation, 1616–1930* (Washington, D.C.: Smithsonian Institution Press, 1989), 48–52.

12. Woods' Testimony in Surrebuttal, Interference cases #18,207 & #18,210, 253, NARA, Record Group 241, taken from "A Colored Man's Invention," *New York Recorder*, February 13, 1892.

13. Monte Calvert, *The Mechanical Engineer in America, 1830–1910: Professional Cultures in Conflict* (Baltimore: Johns Hopkins University Press, 1967), 6–8, 277–81; Howard P. Segal, *Future Imperfect: The Mixed Blessings of Technology in America* (Amherst: University of Massachusetts Press, 1994), 51–61; Paul Israel, *From Machine Shop to Industrial Laboratory: Telegraphy and the Changing Context of American Invention, 1830–1920* (Baltimore: Johns Hopkins University Press, 1992), 5–23; Terry S. Reynolds, *The Engineer in America: A Historical Anthology from "Technology and Culture"* (Chicago: University of Chicago Press, 1991), 7–26.

14. Anderson, *The Education of Blacks*, 4–32, and Robert A. Margo, *Race and Schooling in the South, 1880–1950: An Economic History* (Chicago: University of Chicago Press, 1990), 6–32.

15. Alfred D. Chandler, Jr., *The Visible Hand: The Managerial Revolution in American Business* (Cambridge: Belknap Press of Harvard University Press, 1977), 188–206; Edwin T. Layton, *The Revolt of the Engineers: Social Responsibility and the American Engineering Profession* (Baltimore: Johns Hopkins University Press, 1986), 25–108; A. Michal McMahon, *The Making of a Profession: A Century of Electrical Engineering in America* (New York: IEEE Press, 1984), 31–98; David F. Noble, *America by Design: Science, Technology, and the Rise of Corporate Capitalism* (Oxford: Oxford University Press, 1977), 69–83; Leonard Reich, *The Making of American Industrial Research: Science and Business at GE and Bell, 1876–1926* (Cambridge: Cambridge University Press, 1985).

16. David E. Wharton, *A Struggle Worthy of Note: The Engineering and Technological Education of Black Americans* (Westport, Conn.: Greenwood Press, 1992), 57–64.

17. Charles W. Pierce, "How Electricity Is Taught at Tuskegee," *Colored American Magazine* 6 (May 1904): 666–73.

18. The first mention of the American Dream is attributed to James Truslow Adams, *The Epic of America* (Boston: Little, Brown, 1931); Merle Curti, "The American Exploration of Dreams and Dreamers," *Journal of the History of Ideas* 27 (April–June 1966): 391–416.

19. Jennifer L. Hochschild, *Facing Up to the American Dream: Race, Class, and the Soul of the Nation* (Princeton: Princeton University Press, 1995), 18.

20. Ibid., 55–88.

21. Louis R. Harlan, *Booker T. Washington: The Making of a Black Leader, 1856–1901* (New York: Oxford University Press, 1972), and *Booker T. Washington: The Wizard of Tuskegee, 1901–1915* (New York: Oxford University Press, 1983); Booker T. Washington, *The Future of the American Negro* (Boston: Small, Maynard & Co.,

1899); Booker T. Washington, *Up from Slavery: An Autobiography* (New York: Doubleday, Page & Co., 1901).

22. David Levering Lewis, *W. E. B. Du Bois: Biography of a Race, 1868–1919* (New York: Henry Holt & Co., 1993), and *W. E. B. Du Bois: The Fight for Equality and the American Century 1919–1963* (New York: Henry Holt & Co., 2000); W. E. B. Du Bois, *The Souls of Black Folk: Essays and Sketches* (Chicago: A. C. McClurg & Co., 1903).

23. Tony Martin, "Bibliophiles, Activists, and Race Men," in *Black Bibliophiles and Collectors: Preserving Black History*, ed. Elinor Des Verney Sinnette, W. Paul Coates, and Thomas C. Battle (Washington, D.C.: Howard University Press, 1990).

24. Michael Eric Dyson, *Reflecting Black: African American Cultural Criticism* (Minneapolis: University of Minnesota Press, 1993), xiv.

25. William J. Simmons, *Men of Mark: Eminent, Progressive, and Rising* (Chicago: Johnson Publishing Co., 1990 [1887]), 6.

26. Ibid., 7.

27. Gail Bederman, *Manliness and Civilization: A Cultural History of Gender and Race in the United States, 1880–1917* (Chicago: University of Chicago Press, 1995), 25.

28. D. W. Culp, ed., *Twentieth Century Negro Literature* (Naperville, Ill.: J. L. Nichols & Co., 1902), 5–6.

29. W. E. B. Du Bois, "Possibilities of the Negro: The Advance Guard of the Race," *Booklovers* 2, no. 1 (July 1903): 4.

30. Ruth M. Winton, "Negro Participation in Southern Expositions, 1881–1915," *Journal of Negro Education* 16, no. 1 (Winter 1947): 34–43.

31. Joel Williamson, *New People: Miscegenation and Mulattoes in the United States* (New York: New York University Press, 1980), 61–109.

32. W. E. B. Du Bois, "The Talented Tenth" in *W. E. B. Du Bois: Writings*, ed. Nathan I. Huggins, Library of America (New York: Viking Press, 1986) 847.

33. Nancy Leys Stepan, "Race and Gender: The Role of Analogy in Science," in *The "Racial" Economy of Science*, ed. Sandra Harding (Bloomington: Indiana University Press, 1993), 359–76; Nancy Leys Stepan and Sander L. Gilman, "Appropriating the Idioms of Science: The Rejection of Scientific Racism," in *The "Racial" Economy of Science*, ed. Sandra Harding, 170–93.

34. Bethel Literary and Historical Association 1905–6 Season Minutes, SJDC, 37. Scarborough imparted this opinion during a talk entitled "Race Integrity."

35. Zane L. Miller, "Race-ism and the City: The Young Du Bois and the Role of Place in Social Theory, 1893–1901," in *Technical Knowledge in American Culture: Science, Technology, and Medicine since the Early 1800s*, ed. Hamilton Cravens, Alan I. Marcus, and David M. Katzman (Tuscaloosa: University of Alabama Press, 1996), 112–24; Harlan, *Booker T. Washington: The Making of a Black Leader, 1856–1901* (1972), 3–108; Stephen R. Fox, *The Guardian of Boston: William Monroe Trotter* (New York: Athenaeum, 1970), 3–30; Judith Stein, *The World of Marcus Garvey: Race Class in Modern Society* (Baton Rouge: Louisiana State University Press, 1986), 24–37.

36. Cornel West, "The New Cultural Politics of Difference," in *Out There: Marginalization and Contemporary Cultures*, ed. Russell Ferguson et al. (Cambridge, Mass.: MIT Press, 1990), 28.

37. Stuart Hall, *Representation: Cultural Representations and Signifying Practices*

(London: Sage Publications, 1997), 239–56; Jan Nederveen Pieterse, *White on Black: Images of Africa and Blacks in Western Popular Culture* (New Haven: Yale University Press, 1992), 30–51.

38. James W. Loewen, *Lies My Teacher Told Me: Everything Your American History Textbook Got Wrong* (New York: Touchstone, 1995), 33.

39. Martin Luther King, Jr., *Where Do We Go from Here: Chaos or Community?* (Boston: Beacon Press, 1968), 43.

40. Ibid., 42.

41. Hochschild, *Facing up to the American Dream,* 30.

42. Ruth Schwartz Cowan, *More Work for Mother* (New York: Basic Books, 1983), 3–15.

43. bell hooks, "Marginality as a Site of Resistance," in *Out There: Marginalization and Contemporary Cultures,* ed. Russell Ferguson et al. (Cambridge, Mass.: MIT Press, 1990), 341.

44. Philip Scranton, "Determinism and Indeterminacy in the History of Technology," in *Does Technology Drive History?* ed. Merritt Roe Smith and Leo Marx (Cambridge, Mass.: MIT Press, 1994), 158.

45. Henry Louis Gates, Jr., and Cornel West, *The Future of the Race* (New York: Alfred A. Knopf, 1996), 84.

CHAPTER 2: LIARS AND THIEVES: GRANVILLE T. WOODS AND THE PROCESS OF INVENTION

Epigraph, "A Colored Man's Invention," *New York Recorder,* February, 13, 1892, and Woods' Testimony in Surrebuttal, Interference cases #18,207 & #18,210, 252.

1. Granville Woods—Certificate and Record of Death, State of New York, Department of Health, Bureau of Record and Statistics, No. 3757, 1910.

2. Michael C. Christopher, "Granville T. Woods: The Plight of the Black Inventor," *Journal of Black Studies* 11 (March 1981): 271; David E. Wharton, *A Struggle Worthy of Note: The Engineering and Technological Education of Black Americans* (Westport, Conn.: Greenwood Press, 1992), 5; Louis Haber, *Black Pioneers of Science and Invention* (New York: Harcourt, Brace, & World, 1970), 60; W. J. Simmons, *Men of Mark* (Chicago: Johnson Publishing Co., 1970 [1887]), p. 51.

3. United States Census, 1910, vol. 148, ed. 449, sheet 9, line 96. Yet, it does indicate that he was born in October 1863.

4. Granville Woods—Certificate and Record of Death, State of New York, Department of Health, Bureau of Record and Statistics, No. 3757, 1910.

5. For biographical sketches, see the *Cleveland Gazette,* August 7, 1886; *New York Recorder,* February 13, 1892; *New York Herald,* February 14, 1892; *New York Times,* February 14, 1892; *New York Tribune,* February 15, 1892; *Brooklyn Eagle,* February 14, 1892; *Brooklyn Times,* February 15, 1892; *Brooklyn Citizen,* February 14, 1892; *Street Railway News,* April 2, 1892.

6. S. W. Balch, "Electric Motor Regulation," *Cosmopolitan Magazine,* April 1895, 761.

7. William J. Simmons, *Men of Mark: Eminent, Progressive, and Rising* (Chicago: Johnson Publishing Co., 1990 [1887]), 107. I focus on Simmons's account since all the other secondary literature has used this work to some degree or other.

8. Ibid., 107–8. Woods stated that after 1872 he was a "drill engineer . . . handling locomotives in the yards and immediate vicinity of the particular yards to which [he] was assigned." He does not say where this is, but it had to have been in Ohio or he would have made that distinction. Woods' Testimony in Surrebuttal, Interference cases #18,207 & #18,210, 282.

9. *New York Recorder*, February 13, 1892. Woods stated that Simmons supplied the information for the article. Woods' Testimony in Surrebuttal, Interference cases #18,207 & #18,210, 253.

10. "The Motor of General Slocum's Road: Arrest of the Negro Who Perfected Its Invention," *Brooklyn Daily Eagle*, March 7, 1892.

11. *Street Railway News*, April 2, 1892.

12. Simmons, *Men of Mark*, 51.

13. Woods' Testimony in Surrebuttal, Interference cases #18,207 & #18,210, 282, and Woods' Testimony, Interference Case #10,580, 7. Washington Court House is a city located about 70 miles northeast of Cincinnati.

14. David A. Gerber, *Black Ohio and the Color Line, 1869–1915* (Urbana: University of Illinois Press, 1976), 10–12; Wendell P. Dabney, *Cincinnati's Colored Citizens* (Cincinnati: Dabney Publishing Co., 1926), 33; Kenneth L. Kusmer, *A Ghetto Takes Shape: Black Cleveland, 1870–1930* (Urbana: University of Illinois Press, 1980), 3–31.

15. Schammel was a machinist friend of Woods's who had seen most of his drawings and experiments. Barnett was acquainted with Woods because "he was corresponding . . . with [Barnett's] cousin." See Woods' Testimony, Interference Case #10,580, 59.

16. Aaron Klein, *The Hidden Contributors: Black Scientists and Inventors in America* (New York: Doubleday, 1971), 67.

17. He showed both the drawings and the model to James Barnett and Charles Hesser.

18. The smallpox was probably contracted through interaction with Thomas J. Schammel. See Woods' Testimony, Interference Case #10,580, 46–47.

19. This account does not correspond with what he said later in his testimony. He stated that "I left Boston November 18, 1884, and I stopped only one day in New York, and have not been there since. Mr. Humphreys furnished me with a ticket when I went to New York"; Interference Case #10,580, 84. It could have been the case that Humphreys paid for his ticket to New York, but the time he spent in the city does not correspond. But if he only stayed in New York for one day, how did he know that Beckwith left for Europe a week later?

20. Woods patented an "Electro-Magnetic Brake Apparatus" on October 18, 1887, United States Letters Patent #371,655, Record Group 241, NARA.

21. Granville T. Woods, "Steam-Boiler Furnace," United States Letters Patent #299,894, filed June 19, 1883, issued May 12, 1884, Record Group 241, NARA.

22. Granville T. Woods, "Telephone-Transmitter," United States Letters Patent #308,817, filed June 18, 1883, issued December 2, 1884, Record Group 241, NARA.

23. Granville T. Woods, "Apparatus for Transmission of Messages by Electricity," United States Letters Patent #315,368, filed April 9, 1884, issued April 7, 1885, Record Group 241, NARA.

24. Lewis Montgomery Hosea was a well respected Cincinnatian. He came from a

well-to-do Cincinnati family and was also a judge and state senator. He was a very active member of Cincinnati's scientific community as a member of the Cincinnati Society of Natural History and the Ohio Mechanics Institute. He was the chairman of the department of science and arts for several years, and a fellow of the American Association for the Advancement of Science. In addition he along with S. A. Miller published the *Cincinnati Quarterly Journal of Science*, the *Scientific Proceedings of the Ohio Mechanics' Institute*, and *Cincinnati: The Queen City, 1788–1912* (Cincinnati: S. J. Clarke Publishing Co., 1912), CHS.

25. Klein, *The Hidden Contributors*, 68–69.

26. Claude Fischer, "Touch Someone: The Telephone Industry Discovers Sociability," *Technology and Culture* 29 (1988), 34.

27. Klein, *The Hidden Contributors*, 70.

28. "Recent Progress in Electricity: The Phelps System of Telegraphing from a Railway Train While in Motion," *Scientific American* 52 (February 21, 1885), 118–19.

29. Ibid., 118

30. Neither Phelps or Woods were the first to patent in this area. One of the first patents of this ilk was granted to Ezra T. Gilliland. "Car-Telegraph," United States Letters Patent #247,127, issued September 13, 1881. This system was similar to the Woods's device that used roof contacts.

31. They were two of many who knew of Woods's work on a first-hand basis. At this point in his career he does not seem very protective of his ideas almost to the point of seeming very naive.

32. Granville T. Woods, "Induction Telegraph System," United States Letters Patent #373,915 Wrapper Ledger, Record Group 241, NARA.

33. "Phelps' Case," *Granville T. Woods* v. *Lucius Phelps*, Railway Telegraph Interference, Interference Case #10,580, 1.

34. "Argument in Behalf of Phelps," Woods vs. Phelps, Induction Railway Telegraph Interference, 36, 38–39; "Argument in Behalf of Woods," Granville T. Woods vs. Lucius J. Phelps, Railway Induction Telegraph Interference, 1–3, 12; "Decision," Woods v. Phelps, Induction Telegraph System, 10, 12, all Interference Case #10,580, Record Group 241, NARA.

35. "Before the Examiners-in-Chief, on Appeal," Woods vs. Phelps, Improvement in Induction Telegraph Systems, Interference Case #10,580, 3. Phelps's attack on Woods's diligence broke down in the appeal. The examiner wrote: "Phelps in his able and exhaustive argument, in which he attempts to show that Woods had at best . . . a very loose and imperfect idea or conception of the matter at issue, and that all he did was experimental and abandoned, concludes by holding that he had forfeited and lost all that he had accomplished and all right to a patent. This presupposes that he had invented something to *abandon* and *forfeit*." (emphasis added), 3.

36. *Catholic Tribune*, January 14, 1886.

37. *American Catholic Tribune*, April 1, 1887.

38. Testimony in Chief on Behalf of Woods, Interference cases #18,207 & #18,210, 33.

39. Esmond's Testimony in Rebuttal of Woods, Interference case #18,207 & #18,210, 24–25.

40. "John A. Gano Dead," miscellaneous newspaper clipping, 1898, CHS.

41. The belief that the Woods Electric Company was completely self-organized is a common misperception in all previous work studying Woods. These types of organizations were rather normal at the time, particularly for promising inventors who did not have the money or wherewithal to financially support inventions by themselves. Thomas P. Hughes, *Elmer Sperry: Inventor and Engineer* (Baltimore: Johns Hopkins University Press, 1971), 24–26, 37–42.

42. Woods' Testimony in Surrebuttal, Interference cases #18,207 & #18,210, 27–29, 30, 32; Digest of Assignment of Property Rights in Patents, volume 16, November 8, 1889–May 25, 1891, 128, 181 (a,b,c); Liber Books—T 41: 478–79, V 42: 296–99, 300–302, 303, NARA.

43. This may not have been Woods's and Zerbe's first meeting because Zerbe had stated that "I knew Woods in Cincinnati."

44. Testimony on Behalf of Enholm, Interference case #15,666, 13, and Oscar A. Enholm, "Supply System for Electric Railways," United States Letters Patent #540,653, filed November 3, 1891, patented June 11, 1895, Record Group 241, NARA.

45. Testimony on Behalf of Enholm, Interference case #15,666, 132–33, Woods Brief-Interference case #18,207 & 18,210, 36–37, Esmond's Testimony in Rebuttal of Woods, Interference case #18,207 & #18,210, 128–29. In the original contract these changes are made in Zerbe's hand, which he did not deny. He attempted to absolve himself from the wrongdoing by stating that these changes were initialed by Woods who had full knowledge of them, which was untrue.

46. Digest of Assignment of Property Rights in Patents, volume 17, May 26, 1891–January 28, 1893; and Liber Book I46, 265, NARA.

47. Granville Woods, "Electric-Railway Conduit," United States Letters Patent #509,065 Wrapper Cover, Record Group 241, NARA.

48. Woods' Testimony in Surrebuttal, Interference cases #18,207 & #18,210, 144–46, 149, 192–93; Testimony on Behalf of Enholm, Interference case #15,666, 146–55; Testimony in Chief on Behalf of Woods, Interference cases #18,207 & #18,210, 76–77, and Woods brief, Interference cases #18,207 & #18,210, 26–28, and Esmond's Testimony in Rebuttal of Woods, Interference case #18,207 & #18,210, 17–19.

49. Woods' Testimony in Surrebuttal, Interference cases #18,207 & #18,210, 32–33. See also Testimony in Chief on Behalf of Woods, Interference cases #18,207 & #18,210, 77, and Esmond's Testimony in Rebuttal of Woods, Interference case #18,207 & #18,210, 145–46, 286–87.

50. Woods' Testimony in Surrebuttal, Interference cases #18,207 & #18,210, 35. Arthur Zerbe did comment that the damage was superficial. See Esmond's Testimony in Rebuttal of Woods, Interference case #18,207 & #18,210, 303.

51. Woods' Testimony in Surrebuttal, Interference cases #18,207 & #18,210, 72–73, 181, 186–87, 190–91, 196, 210, 213–14, and Esmond's Testimony in Rebuttal of Woods, Interference case #18,207 & #18,210, 34–37.

52. "Judgment of Interference," Enholm v. Woods, Electric Railways, Interference case #15,666, Record Group 241, NARA. See also Esmond's Testimony in Rebuttal of Woods, Interference case #18,207 & #18,210, 31.

53. For the Coney Island System see also Testimony in Chief on Behalf of Woods,

Interference cases #18,207 & #18,210, 10, 11, 78, 79, 99–100; and Woods' Testimony in Surrebuttal, Interference cases #18,207 & #18,210, 150, 249–56.

54. This invention assigned to Chandler and never assigned to the Universal Electric Company. This is quite interesting because the Universal Electric Company, for whom he was working at that time, did not allow him to contact other companies. Thus, it was evident that Woods did not uphold his end of his contract.

55. Ronald R. Kline, *Steinmetz: Engineer and Socialist* (Baltimore: Johns Hopkins University Press, 1992), 73.

56. Arthur Kennelly to F. W. Hastings, January 28, 1892, Thomas Edison Papers, Reel 109: Frame 965, ENHS.

57. Arthur Kennelly to F. W. Hastings, February 7, 1892, Thomas Edison Papers, Reel 109: Frame 973, ENHS.

58. Arthur Kennelly to F. W. Hastings, February 15, 1892, Thomas Edison Papers, Reel 109: Frame 978, ENHS.

59. "Warning!!" *Electrical Age* 2: 31, and "Warning," *Street Railway News* 7: 9. See also Esmond's Testimony in Rebuttal of Woods, Interference case #18,207 & #18,210, 174–75.

60. "The Motor of General Slocum's Road: Arrest of the Negro Who Perfected Its Invention," *Brooklyn Daily Eagle*, March 7, 1892.

61. Woods called him Judge McKenna and Zerbe called him Judge Kenna, I believe the latter is correct since Woods's attorney made specific references to him during Zerbe's cross-examination. See Esmond's Testimony in Rebuttal of Woods, Interference case #18,207 & #18,210, 193.

62. C. H. Lawton to Hon. W. E. Simmonds, Dec. 2, 1891, Interference cases #18,207 & #18,210, Wrapper, Record Group 241, NARA.

63. As an aside, Woods also received a Canadian patent #41,803 for this invention on February 4, 1893. See "Affidavit of Granville T. Woods," United States Letters Patent #509,065, Record Group 241, NARA.

64. Woods' Testimony in Surrebuttal, Interference cases #18,207 & #18,210, 31–32, 193–95, and Testimony in Chief on Behalf of Woods, Interference cases #18,207 & #18,210, 45, 46, 102, 125, 127.

65. Commissioner of Patents to Granville T. Woods, July 14, 1896, United States Letters Patent #678,086 Wrapper, Record Group 241, NARA.

66. United States Letters Patent #678,086 Wrapper Ledger, Record Group 241, NARA.

67. Testimony in Chief on Behalf of Esmond, Interference Cases #18,207 & #18,210, 28; and "Decision," Interference Case #18,210, 4-6, Interference Case #18,210 Wrapper, Record Group 241, NARA.

68. "Decision," Interference Case #18,207, 3-6; "Decision," Interference Case #18,210, 11; "Appeal," Interference Cases #18,207 & #18,210, 3-4. United States Patent Office Interference Cases #18,207 & #18,210 Wrapper, Record Group 241, NARA.

69. Commissioner of Patents Allen to Granville Woods, May 8, 1901, and Commissioner of Patents Allen to Granville Woods, May 17, 1901, United States Patent Office Interference Cases #18,207 & #18,210 Wrapper, Record Group 241, NARA.

70. Stuart Bennett, *A History of Control Engineering: 1800–1930* (London: Peter Peregrinus, 1979), 172.

71. Digest of Assignment of Property Rights in Patents, volume 23, August 15, 1901–August 13, 1902, 4(a). NARA.

72. Kline, *Steinmetz*, 96.

73. Digest of Assignment of Property Rights in Patents, NARA.

74. Thomas P. Hughes, *Networks of Power: Electrification in Western Society, 1880–1930* (Baltimore: Johns Hopkins University Press, 1983), 79–105.

75. Hughes, *Elmer Sperry*, 27–102; Matthew Josephson, *Edison: A Biography* (New York: McGraw-Hill, 1959), 59-130.

76. Woods' Testimony in Surrebuttal, Interference cases #18,207 & #18,210, 252; and "A Colored Man's Invention," *New York Recorder*, February 13.

77. Hughes, *Networks of Power*, 5–17.

78. Patent correspondence in patent wrappers of Woods's patents, Record Group 241, NARA.

CHAPTER 3: LEWIS H. LATIMER AND THE POLITICS OF TECHNOLOGICAL ASSIMILATIONISM

Epigraph, William Ferris, *The African Abroad, or, His Evolution in Western Civilization*, vol. 1 (New Haven, Conn.: Tuttle, Morehouse & Taylor, 1913), 400–401.

1. Kevin K. Gaines, *Uplifting the Race: Black Leadership, Politics, and Culture in the Twentieth Century* (Chapel Hill: University of North Carolina Press, 1996), 1–46.

2. *The Latimer Journal, and North Star*, November 1842, in Asa J. Davis, "The George Latimer Case: A Benchmark in the Struggle for Freedom," in *Blueprints for Change: The Life and Times of Lewis H. Latimer*, ed. Janet M. Schneider and Bayla Singer (New York: Queens Borough Public Library, 1995), 13–15.

3. Ibid., 15.

4. George Latimer and James Gray must have had a decent relationship because he was able to earn money and visit his wife at night, but Gray still considered him very much his property. The money he saved help secure passage northward. Davis, "The George Latimer Case: A Benchmark in the Struggle for Freedom," in *Blueprints for Change*, 15; and Winifred Latimer Norman and Lily Patterson, *Lewis Latimer* (New York: Chelsea House Publishers, 1994), 20.

5. Davis, "The George Latimer Case," in *Blueprints for Change*, 8, 15; for a detailed discussion of George Latimer, see 8–19, and Norman and Patterson, *Lewis Latimer*, 19–27.

6. Davis, "The George Latimer Case," in *Blueprints for Change*, 7.

7. Norman and Patterson, *Lewis Latimer*, 29–30.

8. Frederick Douglass to Lewis Latimer, September 16, 1894, LHLC-SCSBC.

9. Lewis H. Latimer, "1911 Logbook," Sunday Mar 12, LHLC-QBPL. (The pages from the Logbook are from the dates printed on the top of the pages since the Logbook was not paginaged.)

10. By this time the Latimer family had expanded to four children: George, Jr., Margaret, William, and Lewis; Norman and Patterson, *Lewis Latimer*, 30.

11. Latimer, "1911 Logbook," Monday Mar 13, Wednesday Mar 15; Norman and Patterson, *Lewis Latimer*, 32. Latimer wrote, "my father went out of my life." This

phrase is vague and probably purposely so. George Latimer left his family, but he may not have left the area. A letter from Frederick Douglass of September 16, 1894, to Lewis Latimer stated, "I saw your father for [a] moment in Boston, last Spring. He seemed in good health," indicating that he was in the area at some point. Yet Gerald Norman, George Latimer's grandson, conjectured that his grandfather left for England, where he published his autobiography under a pseudonym; see miscellaneous correspondence, LHLC-SCSBC. Norman may have thought this because of a letter describing a slave's escape from slavery and subsequent trip to England, France, Germany, and Russia. Letter written on the opposite side of W. J. Jenks stationary, LHLC-QBPL.

12. Lewis stated that because of their financial situation "his two brothers were sent to a state institution . . . the Farm School from here they were bound out." George worked for a farmer, William for a hotel keeper, Margaret was "taken by a friend," probably as a house girl, and Lewis remained at home because he was too young to go to the Farm School. See Latimer, "1911 Logbook," Tuesday Mar 14.

13. Norman and Patterson, *Lewis Latimer*, 34; Latimer, "1911 Logbook," Thursday Mar 16.

14. Norman and Patterson, *Lewis Latimer*, 40. Upon enlistment Latimer was assigned to the *USS Ohio* serving only until September 29, and was discharged from the *USS Massasoit* as a cabin steward. Letter to Hon. Commissioner of Pensions, September 1, 1894, LHLC-SCSBC. Latimer, however, calls himself a cabin boy. See Latimer, "1911 Logbook," Friday Mar 17.

15. Latimer, "1911 Logbook," Friday Mar 17 and Thursday Mar 16.

16. *The Boston Directory, Embracing the City Record, a General Directory of the Citizens, and a Business Directory* (Boston: Davenport, 1870), 1056. The firm dropped Halsted, becoming Crosby & Gould in the 1870s, and finally reorganized into Crosby & Gregory before the 1880s.

17 Latimer, "1911 Logbook," Friday, Mar 17 and Saturday Mar 18.

18. Monte Calvert, *The Mechanical Engineer in America, 1830–1910: Professional Cultures in Conflict* (Baltimore: Johns Hopkins University Press, 1967), 41–86, 123.

19. Latimer, "1911 Logbook," Sunday Mar 19. The pay was impressive considering that renowned electrical engineer, Charles Steinmetz, started as an assistant draftsman at $12.00 a week in 1889. Kline, *Steinmetz*, 28.

20. Anonymous sketch prepared for the Edison Pioneers—possibly written by Latimer because his handwriting and initialling are at the top of the page; LHLC-SCSBC.

21. Paul Israel, *From Machine Shop to Industrial Laboratory: Telegraphy and the Changing Context of American Invention, 1830–1920* (Baltimore: Johns Hopkins University Press, 1992), 5–23.

22. Letter from Edwin W. Hammer, 1, LHLC-QBPL.

23. Lewis H. Latimer and Charles W. Brown, "Improvement in Water-Closet for Railroad-Cars," United States Letters Patent #147,363, filed January 14, 1874, patented Feb. 10 1874, Record Group 241, NARA.

24. Ibid., Wrapper, Letter dated January 21, 1874, Record Group 241, NARA.

25. Kenneth R. Manning, "The Culture of Invention in Boston," in *Blueprints for Change*, 21–31.

26. It is unclear what Latimer was referring to because Bell called many devices related to telephony "telephone patents"; Bayla Singer, "Inventing a Better Life: Lewis H. Latimer's Technical Career, 1880–1928," in *Blueprints for Change*, 34.

27. Bell was the professor of vocal physiology and elocution at the School of Oratory at Boston University. See Robert V. Bruce, *Alexander Graham Bell and the Conquest of Solitude* (Boston: Little, Brown & Co., 1973), 98.

28. Latimer, "1911 Logbook," Saturday Nov 18, Friday Nov 17; Singer, "Inventing a Better Life," in *Blueprints for Change*, 34.

29. John Henrik Clarke, "Lewis Latimer: The Bringer of the Light," in *Blacks in Science Ancient and Modern*, ed. Ivan Van Sertima (New York: Transaction, 1994), 233; "Lewis Howard Latimer," in *The Dictionary of American Negro Biography*, ed. R. W. Logan and M. R. Winston (New York: W. W. Norton, 1982), 386.

30. As suggested in Phil Petrie, "Lewis Latimer Helped Light the Way," *Encore American and Worldwide News*, October 18, 1976, 2.

31. Latimer, "1911 Logbook," Sunday Mar 19.

32. Letter from Edwin W. Hammer, 1, LHLC-QBPL.

33. Latimer, "1911 Logbook," Monday Mar 20. His sister Margaret married Augustus Hawley.

34. Latimer, "1911 Logbook," Monday Mar 20. See also Latimer, "Testimony on behalf of Charles G. Perkins," 1, LHLC-QBPL.

35. Latimer, "1911 Logbook," Monday Mar 20. Latimer writes that "he said he used to work for the same people."

36. Lewis H. Latimer, "The Progress of Invention," taken from an unknown Bridgeport newspaper dated February 15, 1880, LHLC-QBPL.

37. "Lewis Latimer Affidavit," complete set of Complainant's Affidavits, Edison Electrical Light Co. et al. vs. Columbia Incandescent Lamp Co., 91, 69, series 2, box 35, folder 2, WJHC-NMAH.

38. Miscellaneous article, from an unknown Bridgeport newspaper, dated winter of 1879–80, LHLC-QBPL.

39. Miscellaneous article, from an unknown Bridgeport newspaper, date unknown, LHLC-QBPL.

40. Latimer, "The Progress of Invention."

41. Schuyler was an electrical engineer who started his own self-named company after he left the United States Electric Lighting Company in 1881, which Thomson-Houston eventually bought in 1889. Harold Passer, *The Electrical Manufacturers, 1875–1900: A Study in Competition, Entrepreneurship, Technical Change, and Economic Growth* (Cambridge: Harvard University Press, 1953), 52–54.

42. Sawyer evidently had a falling out with Maxim, stating that "in his last attempt at electric lighting he [Maxim] has made wholesale appropriation of people's property," some of which was Sawyer's. Furthermore, Sawyer was appalled that Maxim publicly claimed others' inventions as his own. Norman and Patterson, *Lewis Latimer*, 56.

43. Passer, *The Electrical Manufacturers, 1875–1900*, 88, 147.

44. "Lewis Latimer Affidavit," complete set of Complainant's Affidavits, Edison Electrical Light Co. et al. v. Columbia Incandescent Lamp Co., 93, series 2, box 35, folder 2, WJHC-NMAH. The factory was completed in late November or early De-

cember, 1880. Lewis Latimer, "Testimony on Behalf of Charles G. Perkins," 2, LHLC-QBPL.

45. "The Columbia," *Scientific American* 42 (May 22, 1880), 326.

46. Latimer, "1911 Logbook," Wednesday Nov 15.

47. The Edison Companies were the Edison Electric Light Company, Edison Lamp Works, Edison Machine Works, Edison Tube Company, and others. When reference is made to the Edison Company it is to the Edison Electric Light Company, which was the parent company, unless otherwise stated. Thomas P. Hughes, *Networks of Power: Electrification in Western Society, 1880–1930* (Baltimore: Johns Hopkins University Press, 1983), 41.

48. Passer, *The Electrical Manufacturers, 1875–1900,* 148.

49. Latimer, "1911 Logbook," Wednesday Nov 15.

50. Passer, *The Electrical Manufacturers, 1875–1900,* 89, 96.

51. Paul Israel, *Edison: A Life of Invention* (New York; John Wiley & Sons, 1998), 86–87, 191–207.

52. Thomas P. Hughes, "Edison and Electric Light," in *The Social Shaping of Technology,* ed. Donald MacKenzie and Judy Wajcman (Philadelphia: Open University Press, 1985), 39–52; Hughes, *Networks of Power,* 18–46.

53. Lewis Latimer, "Testimony on Behalf of Charles G. Perkins," 6, LHLC-QBPL.

54. Ibid., 8, 9.

55. Ibid., 9–10. The comments on Maxim's negative impact on the inventive environment are probably very accurate, but one has to consider the timing. Latimer gave this testimony in 1889, the year the infringement court case began between the Edison Electric Light Company and United States Electric Lighting. So this could have been testimony to place the Edison Company, for whom Latimer worked in 1889, in a dominant position in this case.

56. Israel, *Edison,* 195. Israel also notes that many key assistants were handsomely compensated for their work, 195, 199, 211.

57. See "Lewis Latimer Affidavit," complete set of Complainant's Affidavits, Edison Electrical Light Co. et al. v. Columbia Incandescent Lamp Co., 91, series 2, box 35, folder 2, WJHC-NMAH.

58. Hughes, *Networks of Power,* 113.

59. Latimer, "1911 Logbook," Wednesday Nov 15 and Tuesday Nov 14.

60. Arthur Bright, *The Electric-Lamp Industry: Technological Change and Economic Development from 1800 to 1947* (New York: Macmillan & Co., 1949), 48.

61. Lewis H. Latimer, "Process of Manufacturing Carbons," United States Letters Patent #252,386, filed February 12, 1881, issue January 17, 1882, Record Group 241, NARA.

62. Lewis H. Latimer Affidavit, "Process of Manufacturing Carbons," United States Letters Patent #252,386 Wrapper Ledger, dated April 4, 1881, Record Group 241, NARA. Latimer assigned the patent to the United States Electric Lighting Company.

63. Joseph Nichols and Lewis Latimer, "Electric Lamp," United States Letters Patent #247,097, filed April 18, 1881, issued September 13, 1881, Record Group 241, NARA.

64. John Tregoing and Lewis H. Latimer, "Globe-Supporter for Electric Lamps,"

United States Letters Patent #255,212, filed September 7, 1881, issued March 21, 1882, Record Group 241, NARA.

65. Lewis Latimer Affidavit, complete set of Complainant's Affidavits, Edison Electrical Light Co. et al. v. Columbia Incandescent Lamp Co., 91, 69, series 2, box 35, folder 2, WJHC-NMAH; Lewis Latimer, "Testimony on Behalf of Charles G. Perkins," 2, LHLC-QBPL.

66. Edison Pioneers Sketch, labeled LHL, LHLC-SCSBC; letter from Edwin W. Hammer, 1, LHLC-QBPL.

67. Latimer, "1911 Logbook," Monday Nov 13.

68. Bright, *The Electric-Lamp Industry*, 72.

69. Passer, *The Electrical Manufacturers, 1875–1900*, 32.

70. Lewis Latimer Affidavit, complete set of Complainant's Affidavits, Edison Electrical Light Co. et al. v. Columbia Incandescent Lamp Co., 92, 69, series 2, box 35, folder 2, WJHC-NMAH; Mary Latimer, "Diary," Friday, 8 January 1882, LHLC-QBPL.

71. Latimer, "1991 Logbook," Sunday Nov 12.

72. Aaron Klein, *The Hidden Contributors: Black Scientists and Inventors in America* (New York: Doubleday, 1971), 102.

73. Latimer, "1911 Logbook," Saturday Nov 11.

74. Rayford Logan, *The Betrayal of the Negro: From Rutherford B. Hayes to Woodrow Wilson* (New York: Collier Books, 1965), 23–47.

75. Latimer, "1911 Logbook," Saturday Nov 11.

76. Edison Pioneers Sketch, labeled LHL, LHLC-SCSBC.

77. Letter from Edwin W. Hammer, 2, and "Biographical Sketch," both LHLC-QBPL.

78. Norman and Patterson, *Lewis Latimer*, 63.

79. Letter from Edwin W. Hammer, 2, LHLC-QBPL.

80. Lewis Latimer, "Testimony on Behalf of Charles G. Perkins," 12–13, LHLC-QBPL.

81. Ibid., 1. Perkins was also the electrical engineer of the Perkins Electric Lamp Company. It remained in existence after he left.

82. Passer, *The Electrical Manufacturers, 1875–1900*, 151.

83. Ibid., 152.

84. Letter from Edwin W. Hammer, 2, LHLC-QBPL. Sometime after 1885 or in 1886 Latimer officially became associated with the engineering department; Edison Pioneers Sketch, labeled LHL, both LHLC-SCSBC.

85. Edison Pioneers Sketch, labeled LHL, LHLC-SCSBC.

86. Latimer, "1911 Logbook," Saturday Nov 11.

87. Bright, *The Electric-Lamp Industry*, 39–40; Robert Friedel and Paul Israel, with Bernard S. Finn, *Edison's Electric Light: Biography of an Invention* (New Brunswick, N.J.: Rutgers University Press, 1986), 115–17.

88. Passer, *The Electrical Manufacturers, 1875–1900*, 152–53.

89. Bright, *The Electric-Lamp Industry*, 88.

90. Letter from Edwin W. Hammer, 2, LHLC-QBPL.

91. Letter from J. H. Vail, "To Whom it May Concern," June 7, 1889, LHLC-QBPL.

92. Letter from John F. Randolph of July 29, 1889, whose heading begins "L. H. Latimer Esq.," LHLC-QBPL.

93. Letter from Edwin W. Hammer, 2,.

94. Passer, *The Electrical Manufacturers, 1875–1900,* 157; Bright, *The Electric-Lamp Industry,* 89.

95. Lewis H. Latimer to Thomas A. Edison, June 16, 1888, Thomas Edison Papers Reel 124: Frame 156, ENHS.

96. Alfred Tate to Lewis H. Latimer, June 20, 1888, Thomas Edison Papers Reel 122: Frame 372, ENHS.

97. John F. Randolph to Lewis Latimer, July 29, 1889, LHLC-SCSBC.

98. Bright, *The Electric-Lamp Industry,* 85.

99. Thomas P. Hughes, *Elmer Sperry: Inventor and Engineer* (Baltimore: Johns Hopkins University Press, 1971), 61, 71.

100. "Mr. Easton's Mem. for Meeting of Patent Litigation Committee, March, 1891," Thomas Edison Papers Reel 131: Frame 652, ENHS.

101. Passer, *The Electrical Manufacturers, 1875–1900,* 100–104, 321–29. Regardless of the economic maneuverings, the court decided the suit in Western Electric's favor in 1895. Bright, *The Electric-Lamp Industry,* 86–87.

102. William Edward Sawyer, *Electric Lighting by Incandescence, and Its Application to Interior Illumination: A Practical Treatise* (New York: D. Van Nostrand Co., 1881). For further elaboration see Singer, "Inventing a Better Life," in *Blueprints for Change,* 42. A Mr. Kennelly, possibly Arthur Kennelly, a consulting electrician and a well-known expert, also had a part in the printing of Latimer's book. A letter from the Van Nostrand Company stated that Kennelly "has made numerous corrections, and he suggests the omission of his paper on the Meter." Therefore, this was not an undertaking by Latimer alone. See D. Van Nostrand Company to L. H. Latimer, July 23, 18–, LHLC-QBPL.

103. Lewis H. Latimer, *Incandescent Electric Lighting: A Practical Description of the Edison System* (New York: D. Van Nostrand Co., 1890), 74.

104. Ibid., 75.

105. Francis R. Upton to S. D. Greene, October 17, 1892, LHLC-SCSBC. In this letter Upton mentions a "Rotating Wheels" patent that is at present unidentified. Nevertheless, Upton stated that "if the Latimer patents are considered to have any claims broad enough to cover our present wheel in any way, or to cover electric wheels in any way . . . [it] should be procured." At that time Greene was the general manager of the Lighting Department for General Electric and Upton was the manager of the Harrison Works. This appears to be a version of Latimer's patent for a "Means of Producing Luminous Effects," Letter Patent #367,651, patented October 10, 1891.

106. Mary Latimer, "Diary," 8 March 1882, LHLC-QBPL.

107. Frederick P. Fish to L. H. Latimer, Esq., May 19, 1898, LHLC-SCSBC. Fish was one of Thomson-Houston's negotiators in the organization of General Electric; see Passer, *The Electrical Manufacturers, 1875–1900,* 322–24.

108. Lewis H. Latimer, "Apparatus for Cooling and Disinfecting," United States Letters Patent #334,078, filed September 3, 1885, issued January 12, 1886, Record Group 241, NARA.

109. Passer, *The Electrical Manufacturers, 1875–1900*, 329–34; Leonard Reich, *The Making of American Industrial Research: Science and Business at GE and Bell, 1876–1926* (Cambridge: Cambridge University Press, 1985), 56.

110. Bernard W. Carlson, *Innovation as a Social Process: Elihu Thomson and the Rise of General Electric, 1870–1900* (New York: Cambridge University Press, 1991), 294–301; Reich, *The Making of American Industrial Research*, 51–53.

111. Passer, *The Electrical Manufacturers, 1875–1900*, 322–25.

112. Ibid., 321–22.

113. Ibid., 328.

114. Ibid., 329–34; Reich, *The Making of American Industrial Research*, 56.

115. Bright, *The Electric-Lamp Industry*, 4, 37, 89–90; "Columbia Company Wins" *Western Electrician* 69 (April 22, 1893); "Lewis Latimer Affidavit," complete set of Complainant's Affidavits, *Edison Electrical Light Co. et al.* v. *Columbia Incandescent Lamp Co.*, 91, 69, series 2, box 35, folder 2, WJHC-NMAH.

116. "Memo.—Mr. Latimer's Theory on the Goebel Lamp Case," LHLC-SCSBC.

117. Ibid.

118. "My Situation as It Looked to Me in 1912," sketch, LHLC-QBPL.

119. Wesley T. Hammer to Winifred L. Norman, September 12, 1973, LHLC-QBPL.

120. Copy of letter located in the Edison Pioneers Annual Meeting and Luncheon Program, February 11, 1925, 69, series 2, Box 41, folder 2, WJHC-NMAH. The other founding members were: Arthur S. Beves, Chas. A Benton, Chas. S. Bradley, Wm. M. Brock, H. A. Campbell, Wm. Carman, Philip S. Dyer, Geo. G. Grower, Edwin W. Hammer, Wm. J. Hammer, Wilson S. Howell, Alfred W. Kiddle, Robt. T. Lozier, H. A. MacLean, T. C. Martin, Samuel Z. Mitchell, Samuel D. Mott, Sidney Paine, F. D. Potter, Christian Rach, Fredk. A. Scheffler, F. S. Smithers, Francis R. Upton, Frank A. Wardlaw, Peter Weber, Schuyler S. Wheeler, Fremont Wilson.

121. Constitution and By-Laws of the Edison Pioneers, 1921, 69, series 2, Box 40, WJHC-NMAH.

122. Greener's credentials are exemplary. He graduated from Andover Academy, Oberlin, and, in 1870, Harvard. He taught metaphysics and logic at the University of South Carolina from 1873 to 1877, was an instructor of Law at Howard University from 1877 to 1880, served as dean of the Law School from January 1879 to July 1880, and was an American consul in Bombay, India, in January 1898 and in Vladivostok, Russia, from July 1898 to 1905. Latimer probably met Greener shortly after he received the appointment as the chief examiner of the Municipal Civil-Service Board for New York City in 1895. See Logan, *Betrayal of the Negro*, 329; J. L. Nichols and William H. Crogman, *Progress of a Race* (Naperville, Ill.: J. L. Nichols & Co., 1920), 379–80; and Allison Blakely, "Richard T. Greener and the Dilemma of the 'Talented Tenth,'" *Journal of Negro History* 59, no. 4 (October 1974): 305–21.

123. "Call for a National Conference," September 10, 1895, LHLC-SCSBC.

124. Richard T. Greener to Lewis H. Latimer, December 6, 1895, 2, LHLC-SCSBC.

125. Copy of printed letter from the Detroit Republican, December 21, 1895, LHLC-SCSBC.

126. William Ferris, *The African Abroad, or, His Evolution in Western Civilization* 2 (New Haven, Conn.: Tuttle, Morehouse, & Taylor Press, 1913): 774.

127. Richard T. Greener, "Reply to Stewart," *The Freeman*, January 25, 1896, in Blakely, "Richard T. Greener and the Dilemma of the 'Talented Tenth,'" 311.

128. Willard B. Gatewood, *Aristocrats of Color: The Black Elite, 1880–1920* (Bloomington: Indiana University Press, 1990), 163–64.

129. Alfred A. Moss, Jr., *The American Negro Academy: Voice of the Talented Tenth* (Baton Rouge: Louisiana State University Press, 1981), 32.

130. Petition "To the Honorable Seth Low," LHLC-SCSBC.

131. "Testimonial to Mr. Samuel R. Scottron in recognition of his faithful service as a member of the Board of Education, May 9th, 1902," LHL-QBPL.

132. Lewis Latimer to S. R. Scottron Esq., Jan. 22, 1902, LHLC-QBPL.

133. Portia P. James, *The Real McCoy: African-American Invention and Innovation, 1619–1930* (Washington, D.C.: Smithsonian Institution Press, 1989), 89–90.

134. Samuel Scottron, "Manufacturing Household Articles," *Colored American Magazine* 6 (October, 1904): 621.

135. Louis Harlan, *Booker T. Washington: The Wizard of Tuskegee, 1901–1915* (New York: Oxford University Press, 1983), 49–58; Stephen R. Fox, *The Guardian of Boston: William Monroe Trotter* (New York: Athenaeum, 1970), 44–47.

136. L. H. Latimer to Booker T. Washington, letter 1, February 6, 1904, reel 244, BTWC-MDLC.

137. George M. Fredrickson, *The Black Image in the White Mind: The Debate on Afro-American Character and Destiny, 1817–1914* (New York: Harper & Row, 1971).

138. L. H. Latimer to Booker T. Washington, letter 2, February 6, 1904, reel 244, BTWC-MDLC. Latimer's answers came from letter 2 and the questions from letter 1.

139. W. E. B. Du Bois, "The Talented Tenth," in *The Negro Problem: A Series of Articles by Representative American Negroes of To-day*, ed. Booker T. Washington et al. (New York: James Pott & Co., 1903), 33–75.

140. L. H. Latimer to Booker T. Washington, February 24, 1904, reel 244, BTWC-MDLC.

141. Booker T. Washington to L. H. Latimer, May 31, 1904, LHLC-SCSBC.

142. T. Thomas Fortune to L. H. Latimer, January 30, 1899, LHLC-QBPL. "I control these lots. If I can get you and Webster to go into the scheme I desire that we should build out there and get into there May 1. Will you meet me at Webster's house at 11 o'clock Sunday next and go out and look at the situation? Yours truly, T. Thomas Fortune." The letter discusses real estate in Richmond Hills on Staten Island.

143. Emma Lou Thornbrough, *T. Thomas Fortune: Militant Journalist* (Chicago: University of Chicago Press, 1972), 126–45.

144. Henry Kraft to Lewis Latimer, August 29, 1908, LHLC-QBPL.

145. Charles W. Pierce, "How Electricity Is Taught at Tuskegee," *Colored American Magazine* 6 (May 1904): 666–73.

146. Blakely, "Richard T. Greener and the Dilemma of the 'Talented Tenth,'" 319.

147. Moss, *The American Negro Academy*; Wilson Jeremiah Moses, *The Golden Age of Black Nationalism, 1850–1925* (New York: Oxford University Press, 1978), 211–17; Gaines, *Uplifting the Race*, 100–127.

148. Ferris, *The African Abroad*, 2:401, 404, 409.

149. Ibid., 340, 397.

150. Ibid., 329.

151. Ibid., 304, 307, 308.

152. Ibid., 304.

CHAPTER 4: SHELBY J. DAVIDSON: ADDING MACHINES, INSTITUTIONAL RACISM, AND THE BLACK ELITE

Epigraph, Frederick Douglass, *Three Addresses on the Relations Subsisting between the White and Colored People of the United States* (Washington, D.C.: Gibson Brothers, Printers and Book Binders, 1886), 8–9.

1. Letter from Rev. William W. Patton, D.D., to Shelby J. Davidson, SJDC.

2. Raymond R. Wolters, *The New Negro on Campus: Black College Rebellions of the 1920s* (Princeton: Princeton University Press, 1975).

3. Statement of Facts and Appeals from the Decision and Action of the United Faculty of Howard University Against Shelby Jeames Davidson, 3, SJDC.

4. Ibid.

5. Ibid., 4.

6. Ibid.

7. Ibid.

8. Ibid., 5.

9. Ibid., 6.

10. Statement of Facts and Appeals from the Decision and Action of the United Faculty of Howard University Against Shelby Jeames Davidson, 6, SJDC. The other students were I. H. Hudgins, P. W. Frisby, J. T. Greene, J. J. G. Weaver.

11. Ibid., 8–9.

12. Ibid., 9.

13. Ibid., 10.

14. William A. Cook, Letter of reference June 11, 1896, SJDC.

15. Biographical sketch headed "Shelby J. Davidson," 1, SJDC.

16. Willard B. Gatewood, *Aristocrats of Color: The Black Elite, 1880–1920* (Bloomington: Indiana University Press, 1990), 39–40, 44.

17. "Clerk Becomes Inventor," *New York Age* 25 (March 30, 1911): 3.

18. Laurence J. W. Hayes, *The Negro Federal Government Worker: A Study of His Classification Status in the District of Columbia, 1883–1938* (Washington, D.C.: Howard University, 1941), 19–35; Samuel Krislov, *The Negro in Federal Employment: The Quest for Equal Opportunity* (Minneapolis: University of Minnesota Press, 1967), 7–22.

19. Treasury Department, Office of the Secretary, to Hon. Walter Evans, February 25, 1899, SJDC.

20. Louis R. Harlan, *Booker T. Washington: The Wizard of Tuskegee, 1901–1915* (New York: Oxford University Press, 1983), 3–31.

21. Constance McLaughlin Green, *The Secret City: A History of Race Relations in the Nation's Capital* (Princeton: Princeton University Press, 1967), 159.

22. Treasury Department, Office of the Auditor for the Post-Office Department, to Mr. S. J. Davidson, August 16, 1899, SJDC.

23. This promotion took place on January 12, 1900.

24. "Clerk Becomes Inventor," *New York Age* 25 (March 30, 1911): 3.

25. Ibid.

26. Shelby J. Davidson to Hon. William H. Lewis, Assistant Attorney General United States, letter 1, January 27, 1912, SJDC.

27. July 1, 1903 at $1200, September 18, 1906 at $1400, and July 1, 1909 at $1600.

28. Green, *The Secret City*, 159.

29. Shelby J. Davidson to Hon. William H. Lewis, Assistant Attorney General United States, letter 1, January 27, 1912, SJDC.

30. Joel Williamson, *New People: Miscegenation and Mulattoes in the United States* (New York: Free Press, 1980), 61–109.

31. Gatewood, *Aristocrats of Color*, 24.

32. Ibid., 214.

33. Certificate of Incorporation of the Bethel Literary and Historical Association, SJDC. This group was founded in 1881 by Bishop Daniel Payne of the AME church; Green, *The Secret City*, 123.

34. The financial members were Dr. and Mrs. H. L. Bailey, Henry E. Baker, Dr. H. L. Baker, Dr. W. L. Board, Ella M. Boston, Mattie R. Bowen, George F. Collins, John H. Cook, J. R. Coombs, Prof. John W. Cromwell, Shelby J. Davidson, B. F. Davis, Thos. M. Dent, R. J. Dickey, W. H. Fossett, L. G. Gregory, John P. Green, W. J. Hall, Prof. Lafayette M. Hershaw, George W. Jackson, M. L. Jordan, Millie G. Lewis, John L. Love, M. Grant Lucas, G. S. Mabrey, Prof. Kelly Miller, Dr. W. P. Napper, L. H. Neill, Robert Pelham, Dr. W. K. Price, O. M. Randolph, Prof. W. H. Richards, Dr. George H. Richardson, Rev. Oscar J. W. Scott, John A. Simms Sr., A. A. Syphax, Louis Thompson, H. C. Tyson, Dr. J. B. Williams.

35. Minutes of the Bethel Literary and Historical Association, May 15, 1906, and "The Bethel Literary in a New Role," SJDC.

36. Portia P. James, *The Real McCoy: African-American Invention and Innovation 1619–1930* (Washington, D.C.: Smithsonian Institution Press, 1989), 86.

37. Andrew Hilyer, *Twentieth Century Union League Directory* (1901 reprint: Alexandria, Va.: Chadwyck-Healy, 1987), 32; Laurence J. W. Hayes, *The Negro Federal Government Worker: A Study of His Classification Status in the District of Columbia, 1883–1938* (Washington, D.C.: Howard University, 1941), 23.

38. For the black inventors of Washington, D.C., see James, *The Real McCoy*, and Hilyer, *Twentieth Century Union League Directory*.

39. David Levering Lewis, *W. E. B. Du Bois: Biography of Race, 1868–1919* (New York: Henry Holt & Co., 1993), 219, 319.

40. Ibid., 289.

41. Gatewood, *Aristocrats of Color*, 56.

42. Minutes of the Bethel Literary and Historical Association, 34, SJDC. The page numbers are taken from the typed transcript of the minutes.

43. Ibid., 20.

44. Dancy was appointed the Recorder of Deeds by President T. Roosevelt apparently with the help of Booker T. Washington; Gatewood, *Aristocrats of Color*, 304. Joiner was director of the Teachers' Training School at Howard University; William A. Joiner, *A Half Century of Freedom of the Negro in Ohio* (Xenia, Ohio: Smith Adv. Co., 1915), 51.

45. At the time of his talk, Scarborough was the vice-president of Wilberforce Uni-

versity, soon to be president in 1908, and was one of the more respected Negro scholars of the period; D. W. Culp, ed., *Twentieth Century Negro Literature* (Naperville, Ill.: J. L. Nichols & Co., 1902), 414.

46. Ibid., 37.

47. Gatewood, *Aristocrats of Color*, 149–81.

48. Minutes of the Bethel Literary and Historical Association, SJDC, 38–39.

49. Ibid., 24, 25, 27.

50. The Patent Office granted William S. Burroughs the first patent (#388,116), for an adding machine. Burroughs with Thomas Metcalfe, R. M. Scruggs, and William Pye formed the American Arithmometer Company in St. Louis the same year. The company's name was changed to the Burroughs Adding Machine Company in 1905 and the company moved its facilities to Detroit. G. Harry Stine, *The Untold Story of the Computer Revolution: Bits, Bytes, Bauds, and Brains* (New York: Arbor House, 1985), 51, 53.

51. James W. Cortada, *Before the Computer: IBM, NCR, Burroughs, and Remington Rand and the Industry They Created* (Princeton: Princeton University Press, 1993), 33, 35, and table 2.4.

52. Edwin T. Layton, *The Revolt of the Engineers: Social Responsibility and the American Engineering Profession* (Baltimore: Johns Hopkins University Press, 1971), 134–53; Frederick W. Taylor, *The Principles of Scientific Management* (New York: Harper, 1911), 9–29; Samuel Haber, *Efficiency and Uplift: Scientific Management in the Progressive Era, 1890–1920* (Chicago: University of Chicago Press, 1964), 18–30.

53. James R. Beniger, *The Control Revolution: Technological and Economic Origins of the Information Society* (Cambridge: Harvard University Press, 1986), 390–425; Cortada, *Before the Computer*, 29.

54. Shelby J. Davidson, "Paper-Rewind Mechanism for Adding-Machines," United States Patent #884,721, filed March 1, 1906, patented April 14, 1908.

55. Brief on Behalf of Davidson, Interference Cases #33,369 & #34,174, 1, SJDC.

56. Handwritten Statement, SJDC, 1.

57. Ibid., 2.

58. Ibid., 3.

59. Ibid., 4.

60. Ibid., 7.

61. Behalf of Davidson, Interference Cases #33,369 & #34,174, 4–6; handwritten statement, 6, both SJDC.

62. Preliminary Statement of Dowling and Davidson, Interference Case #33,368, 1, SJDC.

63. Brief on Behalf of Davidson, Interference Cases #33,369 & #34,174, 3, 5, SJDC. Davidson, however, stated that he "was the nucleus of the joint invention, in fact, was the means of inducing Mr. Dowling to seriously consider the plan presented"; Handwritten Statement, 7, SJDC.

64. Shelby J. Davidson to Mr. Alvan Macauley, February 3, 1909, SJDC.

65. Vincent Record, Interference Cases #34,174, 15, SJDC.

66. J. G. Vincent to Shelby J. Davidson, February 23, 1909, SJDC.

67. Shelby J. Davidson to J. G. Vincent, March 25, 1909, SJDC.

68. Daniel Nelson, ed., *A Mental Revolution: Scientific Management since Taylor* (Columbus: Ohio State University Press, 1992), 5–39.

69. Shelby J. Davidson to J. G. Vincent, March 25, 1909, SJDC.

70. "Clerk Becomes Inventor," *New York Age* 25 (March 30, 1911): 3.

71. J. G. Vincent to Shelby J. Davidson, April 13, 1909, SJDC.

72. Preliminary Statement of Dowling and Davidson, Interference #33,368 and Preliminary Statement of Shelby J. Davidson, Interference #33, 369, SJDC.

73. A. J. Lauver to Shelby J. Davidson, June 16, 1909, SJDC.

74. Shelby J. Davidson to Hon. William H. Lewis, Assistant Attorney General United States, letter 1, January 27, 1912, SJDC.

75. Handwritten statement, 8, SJDC.

76. Alvan Macauley to Shelby J. Davidson, December 9, 1909, SJDC.

77. Edward S. Swift to Shelby J. Davidson, March 14, 1910, SJDC.

78. Shelby J. Davidson to Edward S. Swift, March 19, 1910, SJDC.

79. Logan, *The Betrayal of the Negro*, 359–64, and Hayes, *The Negro Federal Government Worker*, 37–72; James W. Loewen, *Lies My Teacher Told Me: Everything Your American History Textbook Got Wrong* (New York: Touchstone, 1995), 26–29.

80. (Appeal) Brief on Behalf of Davidson, Interference Cases #33,369 & #34,174 , 8–9, SJDC.

81. The fees were .03 cents for money orders from $0.00 to $2.50 and .05 cents for $2.51 to $5.00, and so on. Brief on Behalf of Davidson, Interference Cases #33,369 & #34,174, 6, and a page headed "Initial arrangements for automatic fee attachment," SJDC.

82. Page headed "Initial arrangements for automatic fee attachment," SJDC.

83. Brief on Behalf of Davidson, Interference Cases #33,369 & #34,174 , 3, SJDC.

84. Edward S. Swift to Shelby J. Davidson, July 6, 1911, SJDC.

85. Vincent's Record, Interference Case #34,174, 16–18.

86. In the Brief on Behalf of Davidson 8, he stated that "[t]here is nothing in the record to indicate that the authorities ever saw this machine after it was shipped to the Washington agent or that any official notice was taken of it, or of the suggestion to have the fee system changed. In fact, such a suggestion could not have been considered other than in the light of a joke." This is difficult to believe in light of the exhibit of labor-saving devices. Newman would certainly have been invited and if he had the machine in his possession he would certainly have brought it with him.

87. M. O. Chance to Honorable C. A. McGonagle, May 2, 1910, SJDC.

88. C. A. McGonagle to Shelby J. Davidson, May 3, 1910, SJDC.

89. (Appeal) Brief on behalf of Davidson, Interference Cases #33,369 & #34,174, 1–11. See also Vincent's Record, Interference Case #34,174, 20–24.

90. Shelby J. Davidson to Honorable William H. Lewis, Assistant Attorney General United States, letter 2, 2, SJDC. It is important to note that Lewis was a black man which is definitely one of the reasons Davidson was writing to him. Lewis, an Amherst and Harvard Law graduate, was the first African American to hold a subcabinet rank. Logan, The Betrayal of the Negro, 328, 360, 425.

91. Shelby J. Davidson to Hon. William H. Lewis, Assistant Attorney General United States, letter 1, January 27, 1912, SJDC.

92. Shelby J. Davidson to Honorable William H. Lewis, Assistant Attorney General United States, letter 2, 2, SJDC.

93. Ibid., 3.

94. Ibid., 3.

95. Ibid., 4

96. Ibid., 5.

97. Ibid., 6.

98. Auditor Chas. A. Kram to Assistant Secretary Andrews, December 9, 1911, SJDC.

99. W. E. B. Du Bois, "Another Open Letter to Woodrow Wilson," *Crisis,* September 1913, in David Levering Lewis, *W. E. B. Du Bois: A Reader* (New York: Henry Holt & Co., 1995), 445–47.

100. Shelby J. Davidson to Honorable William H. Lewis, Assistant Attorney General United States, 6, SJDC.

101. Ibid., 7–8.

102. Louis Harlan, *Booker T. Washington: The Wizard of Tuskegee, 1901–1915,* 348; Stephen R. Fox, *The Guardian of Boston: William Monroe Trotter* (New York: Athenaeum, 1970), 44–45.

103. J. L. Nichols and William H. Crogman, *Progress of a Race* (Naperville, Ill.: J. L. Nichols & Co., 1920), 360.

104. "House of Davidson" inquiry letters, SJDC.

105. *Howard University Record: Alumni Number,* April 1916 (Washington, D.C.: Howard University), SJDC.

106. NAACP documents, SJDC.

107. As for his personal life, he married Leonora Coates on February 1, 1894. Leonora was quite an enterprising person herself. She was a beauty culturist and chiropodist. She taught these subjects at the National Institute for Women and Girls. For a short period she even marketed her own lineaments. Furthermore, she owned and managed a cafeteria business. Obituary, Leonora C. Davidson, SJDC.

108. Untitled biographical sketch, SJDC.

CHAPTER 5: BACK TO THE FUTURE: REASSESSING BLACK INVENTORS IN THE TWENTY-FIRST CENTURY

Epigraph, Wyn Wachhorst, *Thomas Alva Edison: An American Myth* (Cambridge, Mass.: MIT Press, 1981), 223.

Essay on Sources

Historical information and documentation about black inventors is quite limited. In writing this book, I used the following manuscript collections: the Booker T. Washington Collection, Manuscript Division, Library of Congress, Washington, D.C.; Cincinnati Historical Society; the Papers of Thomas A. Edison, Edison National Historic Site, East Orange, New Jersey; Granville T. Woods Collection, Ohio Historical Society Archives, Columbus; Lewis Howard Latimer Collection, Schomburg Center for the Study of Black Culture, New York Public Library; Lewis Howard Latimer Collection, Queens Borough Public Library, Queens, N.Y.; Patent and Interference Case Files: 1838–1900, Record Group 241, National Archives and Records Administration, Suitland, Maryland, and Washington, D.C.; William J. Hammer Collection, National Museum of American History Archives, Smithsonian Institution, Washington, D.C.; Shelby J. Davidson Collection, Moreland-Spingarn Research Center, Howard University, Washington, D.C. The best, not to mention relatively untapped, source of information is located within the Patent and Interference Case Files: 1838–1900 in the Records of the Patent and Trademark Office at the National Archives and Records Administration, Washington, D.C.

The main source for the historical documentation on Granville T. Woods comes from interference case testimony—case numbers 10,580, 13,286, 13,733, 15,666, 18,207, and 18,210—during the 1890s. The Cincinnati Historical Society and the Granville T. Woods Collection at the Ohio Historical Society Archives in Columbus house documents relating to his experiences in Ohio. Biographical sketches of Woods can be located in the *American Catholic Tribune*, April 1, 1887; *Cleveland Gazette*, August 7, 1886; *New York Recorder*, February 13, 1892; *New York Herald*, February 14, 1892; *New York Times*, February 14, 1892; *New York Tribune*, February 15, 1892; *Brooklyn Eagle*, February 14 and March 7, 1892; *Brooklyn Times*, February 15, 1892; *Brooklyn Citizen*, February 14, 1892; *Catholic Tribune*, January 14, 1886; *Street Railway News*, April 2, 1892; S. W. Balch, "Electric Motor Regulation," *Cosmopolitan Magazine*, April 1895, p. 761.

Other authors have written about Granville Woods, including Michael C. Christopher, "Granville T. Woods: The Plight of the Black Inventor," *Journal of Black Studies* 11 (March 1981); Wendell P. Dabney, *Cincinnati's Colored Citizens* (Cincinnati: Dabney Publishing Co., 1926); "Granville Woods—Ohio's Forgotten Inventor," *Ohio Historical Society Echoes,* April 1975; Harry A. Ploski and Ernest Kaiser, eds., *Afro USA* (Bronxville, N.Y.: Bellwether Publishers, 1971); Gilbert A. Williams, "Granville T. Woods: Inventor of the Telephone Transmitter," *Western Journal of Black Studies* 19 (1995). For the conditions for African Americans in Ohio, see Wendell P. Dabney, *Cincinnati's Colored Citizens* (Cincinnati: Dabney Publishing Co., 1926); David A. Gerber, *Black Ohio and the Color Line, 1869–1915* (Urbana: University of Illinois Press, 1976); Kenneth L. Kusmer, *A Ghetto Takes Shape: Black Cleveland, 1870–1930* (Urbana: University of Illinois Press, 1980).

The Woods family's history and his early years are a mystery. The family arrived in the United States, probably around 1860, and settled in Columbus, Ohio, sometime afterward. His death certificate shows that he lived in the United States 50 out of his 54 years. The article by S. W. Balch, "Electric Motor Regulation," stated that Woods and his parents came to the United States when he was sixteen, but the few sources that exist do not support this late arrival. Moreover, it is still necessary not to rule out completely the possibility that he intentionally created his Australian birth. His parents, Martha and Tailer Woods, had four children, Granville, Lyates, Rachel, and Henrietta. Woods's mother's name is considered to have been Martha, because on his death certificate indicated that her maiden name was Martha; this may have been a recording error, however. Woods's father's name was always thought to be Tailer, but Granville's great-nephew called his great-grandfather William in typed letter dated April 15, 1977, which is a short family history, at Granville T. Woods Collection, Ohio Historical Society Archives, Columbus.

I contend that Woods was not an American Negro, although others have treated him as black. If others had not considered Woods a Negro, he would not have been included the contemporary literature that spoke of black progress, for example, D. W. Culp, ed., *Twentieth Century Negro Literature* (Naperville, Ill.: J. L. Nichols & Co., 1902), 403, 412–13; Wendell P. Dabney, *Cincinnati's Colored Citizens* (Cincinnati: Dabney Publishing Co., 1926), 72; W. E. B. Du Bois, "Possibilities of the Negro: The Advance Guard of Race," *Booklovers* 2, no. 1 (July 1903): 4; Paul Laurence Dunbar, "Representative American Negroes," in *The Negro Problem: A Series of Articles by Representative American Negroes of To-day,* ed. Booker T. Washington et al. (New York: James Pott & Co., 1903), 206; William H. Ferris, *The African Abroad,* vol. 2 (New Haven, Conn.: Tuttle, Morehouse & Taylor, 1913), 791; Kelly Miller, *Race Adjustment: Essays on the Negro in America* (New York: Neale Publishing Co., 1908), 197; Giles B. Jackson and D. Webster Davis, *The Industrial History of the Negro Race of the United States* (1908, reprint: Freeport, N.Y.: Books for Libraries Press, 1971), 100; G. F. Richings, *Evidences of Progress among Colored People* (Philadelphia: G. S. Ferguson Co., 1905); William J. Simmons, *Men of Mark: Eminent, Progressive, and Rising* (Cleveland: George M. Rewell & Co., 1887; Chicago: Johnson Publishing Co., 1990), 107–12. Some of his inventions were included in the Negro Building of the Atlanta Cotton States and International Exposition of 1895; see New York at the Cotton States and International Exposition, *Report of the Board of Commissioners Representing the State of New York at the Cotton States and International Exposition held at Atlanta, Georgia, 1895* (New York: Wynkoop, Hallenbeck, Crawford, & Co., 1895).

The two primary archival resources for Lewis Latimer are the Lewis Howard Latimer Collection at the Schomburg Center for the Study of Black Culture, New York Public Library and the Lewis Howard Latimer Collection at the Queens Borough Public Library, Queens, New York. Documents connected to his experiences with the Edison companies are located at the Edison National Historic Site, East Orange, New Jersey. The Booker T. Washington Collection within the Manuscript Division of Library of Congress contains Latimer's correspondence with Washington. The William J. Hammer Collection within the National Museum of American History Archives at the Smithsonian Institution has documents related to the Edison Pioneers.

The main secondary literature on Latimer are "Lewis Latimer," *The African-American Encyclopedia*, ed. Michael W. Williams (New York: Marshall Cavendish, 1993), 947; John Henrik Clarke, "Lewis Latimer: The Bringer of the Light," in *Blacks in Science Ancient and Modern*, ed. Ivan Van Sertima (New York: Transaction, 1994): Lewis H. Latimer, *Incandescent Electric Lighting: A Practical Description of the Edison System* (New York: D. Van Nostrand Co., 1890); "Lewis Howard Latimer," in *The Dictionary of American Negro Biography*, ed. R. W. Logan and M. R. Winston (New York: W. W. Norton, 1982); Phil Petrie, "Lewis Latimer Helped Light the Way," *Encore American and Worldwide News*, October 18, 1976, p. 2; Janet M. Schneider and Bayla Singer, eds., *Blueprints for Change: The Life and Times of Lewis H. Latimer* (New York: Queens Borough Public Library, 1995); Winifred Latimer Norman and Lily Patterson, *Lewis Latimer* (New York: Chelsea House Publishers, 1994).

The question of whether or not Woods and Latimer knew each other persists. One would suspect that the two most prominent black electrical men in the United States during the late nineteenth century would have known each other. Moreover, they lived in relatively close proximity to each other—both living in and around New York City. Currently, the evidence that exists does not confirm or refute the likelihood that they knew each other. No correspondence between the two has as yet been uncovered and I have already shown they did not move in the same social circles. But I am confident that at the very least, they knew of each other. Woods might have discovered Latimer through his efforts to find support for his inventive work. The electrical community in New York City was substantial, but not all that large. Woods, although on the fringe, had to know many of the people at the center of the electrical industry. Latimer could have known about Woods from a variety of different sources. One way might have been through his interviewing for the Edison legal department. It is highly likely that he ran across Woods in his investigations. Chances are fairly good that Latimer had heard of Woods through the newspaper reporting of his legal battles with James Zerbe. These events were also published in some of the local electrical journals, which Latimer may have read at one time or another. The most probable way that Latimer learned of Woods in a business setting is through his work for the Board of Patent Control. As chief draftsman he probably saw most of the patent drawings that made their way through that division and could have acquired knowledge of Woods in that manner. The most convincing piece of information indicating that Woods and Latimer knew of each other was that George Stockbridge, an attorney who defended Woods in an interference case, was Latimer's friend. In the existing group of Latimer papers there is a humorous drawing done for Stockbridge. It would have been unusual for Stockbridge not to mention one to the other. It can even be speculated further that, if they knew each other, Latimer may have facilitated Woods's obtaining the support of General Electric and Westinghouse, and the reason that no correspondence or acknowledgment of this connection exists is that they did not want to arouse any negative resentment if people found out that they were connected in anyway. Regardless, it is highly likely that Latimer and Woods were cognizant of the other's existence.

The main source of documents for Shelby J. Davidson are within the Shelby J. Davidson Collection of the Manuscript Department of the Moorland-Spingarn Research Center at Howard University. For Davidson's experiences in Washington, D.C., see "Clerk Becomes Inventor," *New York Age* (March 30, 1911); Laurence J. W. Hayes, *The Negro Federal Government Worker: A Study of His Classification Status in the District of Columbia, 1883–1938* (Washington, D.C.: Howard University, 1941); Andrew Hilyer, *Twentieth Century Union League Directory* (1901 reprint: Alexandria, Va.: Chadwyck-Healy, 1987); Samuel Krislov, *The Negro in Federal Employment: The Quest for Equal Opportunity* (Minneapolis: University of Minnesota Press, 1967); Constance McLaughlin Green, *The Secret City: A History of Race Relations in the Nation's Capital* (Princeton: Princeton University Press, 1967).

Most of the general information about black inventors has come from Henry E. Baker, *The Colored Inventor: A Record of Fifty Years* (New York: Crisis Publishing Co., 1913) and "The Negro as an Inventor," in *Twentieth Century Negro Literature*, ed. D. W. Culp (Naperville, Ill.: J. L. Nichols & Co., 1902), 399–413; McKinley Burt, Jr., *Black Inventors of America* (Portland, Ore.: National Book Co., 1969); Patricia Carter-Ives, *Creativity and Invention: The Genius of Afro-Americans and Women in the US and Their Patents* (Arlington, Va.: Research Unlimited, 1988); Lewis Haber, *Black Pioneers of Science and Invention* (New York: Harcourt, Brace, & World, 1970); Robert Hayden, *Eight Black American Inventors* (New York, Addison-Wesley, 1973); Portia P. James, *The Real McCoy: African-American Invention and Innovation, 1619–1930* (Washington, D.C.: Smithsonian Institution Press, 1989); Aaron Klein, *The Hidden Contributors: Black Scientists and Inventors in America* (New York: Doubleday, 1971); Charles W. Pierce. "How Electricity Is Taught at Tuskegee," *Colored American Magazine* 6 (May 1904): 666–673; Vivian Sammons, *Blacks in Science and Medicine* (New York: Hemisphere Publishing Co., 1990); William J. Simmons, *Men of Mark: Eminent, Progressive, and Rising* (Cleveland: George M. Rewell & Co., 1887); David E. Wharton, *A Struggle Worthy of Note: The Engineering and Technological Education of Black Americans* (Westport, Conn.: Greenwood Press, 1992).

This work is greatly indebted to the vast literature of African American studies and history. The African American history and education sources I have used are James D. Anderson, *The Education of Blacks in the South, 1860–1935* (Chapel Hill: University of North Carolina Press, 1988); W. E. B. Du Bois, *The Souls of Black Folks: Essays and Sketches* (Chicago: A. C. McClurg & Co., 1903); William Ferris, *The African Abroad*, vols. 1 and 2 (New Haven, Conn.: Tuttle, Morehouse & Taylor, 1913); Eric Foner, *Reconstruction: America's Unfinished Revolution, 1863–1877* (New York: Harper & Row, Publishers, 1988); George M. Fredrickson, *The Black Image in the White Mind: The Debate on Afro-American Character and Destiny, 1817–1914* (New York: Harper & Row, 1971); Henry Louis Gates, Jr., and Cornel West, *The Future of the Race* (New York: Alfred A. Knopf, 1996); Willard B. Gatewood, *Aristocrats of Color: The Black Elite, 1880–1920* (Bloomington: Indiana University Press, 1990); William

A. Joiner, *A Half Century of Freedom of the Negro in Ohio* (Xenia, Ohio: Smith Adv. Co., 1915); Rayford W. Logan, *The Betrayal of the Negro: From Rutherford B. Hayes to Woodrow Wilson* (New York: Collier Books, 1965); Robert A. Margo, *Race and Schooling in the South, 1880–1950: An Economic History* (Chicago: University of Chicago Press, 1990); Alfred A. Moss, Jr., *The American Negro Academy: Voice of the Talented Tenth* (Baton Rouge: Louisiana State University Press, 1981); Ruth M. Winton, "Negro Participation in Southern Expositions, 1881–1915," *Journal of Negro Education* 16, no. 1 (Winter 1947): 34–43; Raymond R. Wolters, *The New Negro on Campus: Black College Rebellions of the 1920s* (Princeton: Princeton University Press, 1975).

In writing about African American leaders and leadership, I relied upon Allison Blakely, "Richard T. Greener and the Dilemma of the 'Talented Tenth,'" *Journal of Negro History* 59, no. 4 (October 1974), 305–21; W. E. B. Du Bois, "Possibilities of the Negro: The Advance Guard of the Race," *Booklovers* 2, no. 1 (July 1903); W. E. B. Du Bois. "The Talented Tenth," in *The Negro Problem: A Series of Articles by Representative American Negroes of To-day*, ed. Booker T. Washington et al. (New York: James Pott & Co., 1903), 33–75; Kevin K. Gaines, *Uplifting the Race: Black Leadership, Politics, and Culture in the Twentieth Century* (Chapel Hill: University of North Carolina Press, 1996); Stephen R. Fox, *The Guardian of Boston: William Monroe Trotter* (New York: Athenaeum, 1970); Louis R. Harlan, *Booker T. Washington: The Making of a Black Leader, 1856–1901* (New York: Oxford University Press, 1975) and *Booker T. Washington: The Wizard of Tuskegee, 1901–1915* (New York: Oxford University Press, 1986); Martin Luther King, Jr., *Where Do We Go from Here: Chaos or Community?* (Boston: Beacon Press, 1968); David Levering Lewis, *W. E. B. Du Bois: Biography of a Race, 1868–1919* (New York: Henry Holt & Co., 1993) and *W. E. B. Du Bois: The Fight for Equality and the American Century, 1919–1963* (New York: Henry Holt & Co., 2000); Tony Martin, "Bibliophiles, Activists, and Race Men," in *Black Bibliophiles and Collectors: Preserving Black History*, ed. Elinor Des Verney Sinnette, W. Paul Coates, and Thomas C. Battle (Washington, D.C.: Howard University Press, 1990); Zane L. Miller, "Race-ism and the City: The Young Du Bois and the Role of Place in Social Theory, 1893–1901," in *Technical Knowledge in American Culture: Science, Technology, and Medicine since the Early 1800s*, ed. Hamilton Cravens, Alan I. Marcus, and David M. Katzman (Tuscaloosa: University of Alabama Press, 1996); 112–24, Wilson Jeremiah Moses, *The Golden Age of Black Nationalism, 1850–1925* (New York: Oxford University Press, 1978); J. L. Nichols and William H. Crogman, *Progress of a Race* (Naperville, Ill.: J. L. Nichols & Co., 1920); Judith Stein, *The World of Marcus Garvey: Race Class in Modern Society* (Baton Rouge: Louisiana State University Press, 1986); Emma Lou Thornbrough, *T. Thomas Fortune: Militant Journalist* (Chicago: University of Chicago Press, 1972); Booker T. Washington, *The Future of the American Negro* (Boston: Small, Maynard & Co., 1899); Booker T. Washington, *Up From Slavery: An Autobiography* (New York: Doubleday, Page & Co., 1901).

Resources that I used in discussing the American dream and the representation of African Americans are James Truslow Adams, *The Epic of America* (Boston: Little, Brown, 1931); Gail Bederman, *Manliness and Civilization: A Cultural History of Gender and Race in the United States, 1880–1917* (Chicago: University of Chicago Press, 1995); Merle Curti, "The American Exploration of Dreams and Dreamers," *Journal of the History of Ideas* 27 (April–June 1966): 391–416; Michael Eric Dyson, *Reflecting*

Black: African American Cultural Criticism (Minneapolis: University of Minnesota Press, 1993); Herman Gray, *Watching Race: Television and the Struggle for "Blackness"* (Minneapolis: University of Minnesota Press, 1995); Stuart Hall, *Representation: Cultural Representations and Signifying Practices* (London: Sage Publications, 1997); Jennifer L. Hochschild, *Facing Up to the American Dream: Race, Class, and the Soul of the Nation* (Princeton: Princeton University Press, 1995); bell hooks, "Marginality as a Site of Resistance," in *Out There: Marginalization and Contemporary Cultures,* ed. Russell Ferguson et al. (Cambridge, Mass.: MIT Press, 1990); James W. Loewen, *Lies My Teacher Told Me: Everything Your American History Textbook Got Wrong* (New York: Touchstone, 1995); Jan Nederveen Pieterse, *White on Black: Images of Africa and Blacks in Western Popular Culture* (New Haven: Yale University Press, 1992); Marlon Riggs, *Color Adjustment* (San Francisco: California Newsreel, 1991); Leonard Steinhorn and Barbara Diggs-Brown, *By the Color of Our Skin: The Illusion of Integration and the Reality of Race* (New York: Dutton Books, 1999); William L. Van Deburg, *Black Camelot: African-American Cultural Heroes in Their Times, 1960–1980* (Chicago: University of Chicago Press, 1997); Cornel West, "The New Cultural Politics of Difference," in *Out There: Marginalization and Contemporary Cultures,* ed. Russell Ferguson et al. (Cambridge, Mass.: MIT Press, 1990); Joel Williamson, *New People: Miscegenation and Mulattoes in the United States* (New York: New York University Press, 1980).

I am equally indebted to the literature of the history of technology. In thinking about the place of technology within American life, I relied on Ruth Schwartz Cowan, *More Work for Mother* (New York: Basic Books, 1983) and *A Social History of American Technology* (New York: Oxford University Press, 1997); Andrew Feenberg. "Subversive Rationalization: Technology, Power, and Democracy," in *Technology and the Politics of Knowledge,* ed. Andrew Feenberg and Alistar Hannay (Bloomington: Indiana University Press, 1995); Claude Fischer, "Touch Someone: The Telephone Industry Discovers Sociability," *Technology and Culture* 29 (1988): 32–61; Robert Friedel and Paul Israel, with Bernard S. Finn, *Edison's Electric Light: Biography of an Invention* (New Brunswick, N.J.: Rutgers University Press, 1986); Thomas P. Hughes, "Edison and Electric Light" in *The Social Shaping of Technology,* ed. Donald MacKenzie and Judy Wajcman (Philadelphia: Open University Press, 1985); Ronald Kline, "Construing 'Technology' as 'Applied Science': Public Rhetoric of Scientists and Engineers in the United States, 1880–1945," *Isis* 86 (June 1995): 197; Edwin T. Layton, "Conditions of Technological Development," in *Science, Technology, and Society: A Cross-Disciplinary Perspective,* ed. Ina S. Spiegel-Rösing and Derek de Solla Price (London: Sage, 1977); Steven Lubar, "The Transformation of Antebellum Patent Law," *Technology and Culture,* 32 (October 1991): 932–59; Leo Marx, "The Idea of 'Technology' and Postmodern Pessimism," in *Technology, Pessimism, and Postmodernism,* ed. Yaron Ezrahi, Everett Mendelsohn, and Howard P. Segal (Amherst: University of Massachusetts Press, 1994); Lewis Mumford, *Technics and Civilization* (New York: Harcourt Brace, 1934); Philip Scranton, "Determinism and Indeterminacy in the History of Technology," in *Does Technology Drive History?* ed. Merritt Roe Smith and Leo Marx (Cambridge, Mass.: MIT Press, 1994); Howard P. Segal, *Future Imperfect: The Mixed Blessings of Technology in America* (Amherst: University of Massachusetts Press, 1994); Merritt Roe Smith and Leo Marx, eds., *Does Technology Drive History:*

A Dilemma of Technological Determinism (Cambridge, Mass.: MIT Press, 1994); Mary Tiles and Hans Oberdiek, *Living in a Technological Culture: Human Tools and Human Values* (New York: Routledge, 1995); Judy Wajcman, *Feminism Confronts Technology* (College Station: Penn State University Press, 1991); Langdon Winner, *The Whale and the Reactor: A Search for Limits in an Age of High Technology* (Chicago: University of Chicago Press, 1986).

To conceptualize corporate engineering practice, I referred to Stuart Bennett, *A History of Control Engineering, 1800–1930* (London: Peter Peregrinus, 1979); Arthur Bright, *The Electric-Lamp Industry: Technological Change and Economic Development from 1800 to 1947* (New York: Macmillan & Co., 1949); Robert V. Bruce, *Alexander Graham Bell and the Conquest of Solitude* (Boston: Little, Brown &Co., 1973); Monte Calvert, *The Mechanical Engineer in America, 1830–1910: Professional Cultures in Conflict* (Baltimore: Johns Hopkins University Press, 1967); Bernard W. Carlson, *Innovation as a Social Process: Elihu Thomson and the Rise of General Electric, 1870–1900* (New York: Cambridge University Press, 1991); Thomas P. Hughes, *Elmer Sperry: Inventor and Engineer* (Baltimore: Johns Hopkins University Press, 1971), and *Networks of Power: Electrification in Western Society, 1880–1930* (Baltimore: Johns Hopkins University Press, 1983); Paul Israel, *From Machine Shop to Industrial Laboratory: Telegraphy and the Changing Context of American Invention, 1830–1920* (Baltimore: Johns Hopkins University Press, 1992) and *Edison: A Life of Invention* (New York; John Wiley & Sons, 1998); Matthew Josephson, *Edison: A Biography* (New York: McGraw-Hill, 1959); Ronald R. Kline, "The Myth of Electrical Wizards in a Corporate Age: Edison, Steinmetz, and Tesla" (personal communication, 1990) and *Steinmetz: Engineer and Socialist* (Baltimore: Johns Hopkins University Press, 1992); Edwin T. Layton, *The Revolt of the Engineers: Social Responsibility and the American Engineering Profession* (Baltimore: Johns Hopkins University Press, 1971); A. Michal McMahon, *The Making of a Profession: A Century of Electrical Engineering in America* (New York: IEEE Press, 1984); Harold Passer, *The Electrical Manufacturers, 1875–1900: A Study in Competition, Entrepreneurship, Technical Change, and Economic Growth* (Cambridge: Harvard University Press, 1953); Leonard Reich, *The Making of American Industrial Research: Science and Business at GE and Bell, 1876–1926* (Cambridge: Cambridge University Press, 1985); Terry S. Reynolds, *The Engineer in America: A Historical Anthology from "Technology and Culture"* (Chicago: University of Chicago Press, 1991); William Edward Sawyer, *Electric Lighting by Incandescence, and Its Application to Interior Illumination: A Practical Treatise* (New York: D. Van Nostrand Co., 1881); Wyn Wachhorst, *Thomas Alva Edison: An American Myth* (Cambridge, Mass.: MIT Press, 1981).

Managerial studies used in this work are James R. Beniger, *The Control Revolution: Technological and Economic Origins of the Information Society* (Cambridge: Harvard University Press, 1986); Alfred D. Chandler, Jr., *The Visible Hand: The Managerial Revolution in American Business* (Cambridge: Belknap Press of Harvard University Press, 1977); James W. Cortada, *Before the Computer: IBM, NCR, Burroughs, and Remington Rand and the Industry They Created* (Princeton: Princeton University Press, 1993); Samuel Haber, *Efficiency and Uplift: Scientific Management in the Progressive Era, 1890–1920* (Chicago: University of Chicago Press, 1964); Thomas P. Hughes, *American Genesis* (New York: Penguin Books, 1989); Daniel Nelson, ed., *A Mental*

Revolution: Scientific Management since Taylor (Columbus: Ohio State University Press, 1992); David F. Noble, *America by Design: Science, Technology, and the Rise of Corporate Capitalism* (Oxford: Oxford University Press, 1977); Frederick W. Taylor, *The Principles of Scientific Management* (New York: Harper, 1911) 9–29.

Index